The 1848 Revolutions in German-Speaking Europe

THEMES IN MODERN GERMAN HISTORY SERIES

Already published in this series:

Social Democracy and the Working Class in Nineteenth and
Twentieth Century Germany
STEFAN BERGER

Ethnic Minorities in Nineteenth and Twentieth Century Germany:
Jews, Gypsies, Poles, Turks and Others
PANIKOS PANAYI

The 1848 Revolutions in German-Speaking Europe

Hans Joachim Hahn

Routledge
Taylor & Francis Group

LONDON AND NEW YORK

First published 2001 by Pearson Education Limited

Published 2013 by Routledge
2 Park Square, Milton Park, Abingdon, Oxon OX14 4RN
711 Third Avenue, New York, NY 10017, USA

Routledge is an imprint of the Taylor & Francis Group, an informa business

ISBN 13: 978-0-582-35765-5 (pbk)

British Library Cataloguing in Publication Data
A CIP catalogue record for this book can be obtained from the British Library

Typeset by Graphicraft Limited, Hong Kong in 10/13pt Sabon

Contents

Preface

Yet another attempt to write a book on the German revolutions of 1848/9 could surely be seen at best as ambitious, at worst as a foolhardy or superfluous undertaking. A decade ago, at the beginning of his brilliant and comprehensive survey of research on the German revolutions, Dieter Langewiesche observed that 'a flood of publications' had rendered a discriminating understanding quite unfeasible.[1] Even earlier, in 1931, Veit Valentin, one of the great specialists on this subject, had conceded that he could not bring new insights to bear on the revolution's 'central core of events', and hoped to do little more than extend the borders of this central core.[2] With the 150th anniversary of the revolutions just behind us, the prospect of introducing new insights or presenting fresh perspectives has therefore become even more problematic.

In my own case the situation is exacerbated by the fact that I am an intruder into the discipline of history. Aware of the ferocity with which the historical establishment treats such 'interlopers', my chance of achieving credibility must be minimal. And yet, a century and a half ago, scholars with a broadly literary background would have been regarded with a certain respect by historians, since most members of any arts faculty would have involved themselves with historical studies. Maybe the much-employed concept of 'interdisciplinarity' will provide me with an authorized entry?

Approaches to the German revolutions of 1848/9

It will have become clear by now that this book has not been written for specialists in the field of nineteenth-century German history, but rather is intended for undergraduates and students with a general interest in German social and cultural issues. It often strikes me as a sad reflection of our times that too many German studies programmes and even some German history courses tend to concentrate almost exclusively on contemporary issues, often limited to the last fifty years or focusing solely on Nazi Germany. I firmly believe that such a truncated approach can do little to help students gain a deeper insight into the true character of their 'target country' and, denied a means of comparison, students are often less capable of appreciating their own historical legacy. I have considered it one of my chief tasks to assume the role of interpreter in familiarizing an English-speaking readership with the complexities of social, political and cultural life in Germany during the period of the revolutions. For this reason, I have drawn mainly on publications in German, many of which have never been translated into English. Furthermore, I have tried to indicate how, and to what extent, the events of 1848/9 had a significant impact on the shaping of modern Germany so that, even today, certain arguments continue to occupy the political agenda.

My own approach, interdisciplinary by choice as well as by necessity, allows me to discuss a number of essentially German issues which still preoccupy the public debate. While a majority of historians now accept that the theory of a German *Sonderweg* (special development) is outdated and that each nation has its own 'peculiarities'[3] determining its identity over generations, the concept of Germany as a *verspätete Nation*,[4] a late-developer among European nation states, still has its advocates. This theory has much to recommend itself when Germany is compared with her Western European neighbours, but an analysis of her internal development could stand this on its head, suggesting that the objective of nationality came too early in her development and well before the crucial, democratic concepts of the Enlightenment could shape the German public mind. This metaphor of inversion suggests Karl Marx, with his proclaimed aim of turning Hegel upside down and standing him on his feet rather than his head[5] in order to give priority to economic and material issues over philosophical and ideological ones. As a result of Marx's influence, studies of the German revolutions have too often given an exaggerated role to workers and peasants, at best supported by craftsmen and the petit bourgeoisie, as the prime movers of the revolution. While nobody would deny these groups their important role within the course of the revolutions, especially in Vienna and Berlin and in the more industrialized regions of the Rhine province and of Silesia, it must be recognized that the revolutionary inspiration and leadership came from within the ranks of Germany's academic community, from its many advocates, writers, historians and teachers. For this reason prominence has been given in this study to the Pre-March movement, with its protests and struggles against the oppressive and reactionary Metternich system and with its efforts to encourage the still rather hesitant development of a German public mind. The Napoleonic period has also been included, in so far as the seismic impact of the French Revolution can hardly be overstated as a catalyst for the earliest example of an indigenous German reform movement, as manifested in the Stein–Hardenberg reforms in Prussia. In both cases, developments seemingly on the fringes of the European stage deserve some attention. Switzerland, for instance, which has so often been neglected, confirmed its importance as a country which not only adopted democratic ideas from France, but also facilitated their passage into central Europe, initially to southwestern Germany, but eventually across the whole of the 'Third Germany'.

A further issue which seemed to have been affected by Marx's inversion of Hegel concerns the ideological sequence of events. Specialist studies of the 1848/9 revolutions can easily be tempted to interpret events in a normative fashion by applying the traditional tripartite structure, beginning with the revolutions, followed by the counter-revolutions and concluding with a period of reaction. Such an undoubtedly valid interpretation cannot be seriously challenged. However, I would suggest that this traditional sequence of events perhaps encountered a philosophical undercurrent which had originated a generation earlier and was to come to an end in the 1830s with the deaths of Goethe and Hegel. If this view, normally adopted by historians of philosophy and German literature, were to be applied to the history of the German revolutions, then the entire period from Pre-March up to the formation of the German nation state could be understood as one unit, defined by the desire for political power, economic modernization and the search for a national identity. In short, the period from the 1830s up to 1871 and beyond could be interpreted as an epoch in opposition to the realm of ideas (*Weltgeist*), paving the way for Bismarck's execution of *Realpolitik*. If seen in such a light, the revolutions become part of a wider power struggle, an early phase of Germany's road towards modernization and an attempt by the middle and lower social strata to gain political influence. Such an interpretation would invariably view the Frankfurt experience of German liberalism as a failed experiment. With its roots in German idealism and wedded to the concept of personal freedom as illustrated in the plays of Lessing, Goethe and Schiller and expressed in the philosophy of Kant and Fichte, it, nevertheless, allowed itself to be drawn into the new age of *Realpolitik*, and in its acceptance of compromise, abandoned many of its idealist principles in the pursuit of political gain and national identity. One brief example may throw further light on such a reading of history: the famous *Staatslexikon* in its 1845 edition emphasizes that 'revolutions have not only a materialist, but also an idealist starting point' in which the 'intellectual and ethical tensions are directed against a condition which is only perceived through them as oppressive'.[6] At the same time, the entry acknowledges the materialist nature of revolutions in that they come about and cannot be made, anticipating Marxist views in this respect. The entry indicates a change of direction, away from the idealism of Hegel and towards Marxist materialism. Such a reading might also explain why liberal principles often seemed safer with left-Hegelians like Ruge, Jacobi and Freiligrath, possibly even with conservative 'humanists' such as Grillparzer, rather than in the hands of the liberal protagonists Gagern, Bassermann and Dahlmann. However, in order to remain sufficiently close to received views on the German revolutions, this philosophical interpretation has not been taken much further in this study.

These considerations inevitably lead to the question of the cause of the revolutions. Before too much excitement is generated, the author feels obliged to admit that he is unable to furnish a clear set of causes to explain the year of European revolutions in 1848. One important consideration, though of little analytical value, is to suggest that revolutions – like many other human actions, too – lent themselves to imitation. The revolutionary energy of the Paris events of February 1848 was so vibrant, so infectious in its political and social aspirations that it crossed the Rhine quite effortlessly, especially since the Swiss civil war had strengthened general confidence in a positive outcome. This 'infection theory', though by no means satisfying our intellectual curiosity, would certainly help to explain the great diversity in revolutionary aims and objectives. While Munich citizens, wishing for the expulsion of Lola Montez, the ageing king's mistress, were ready to strike an alliance with the clerical parties, the revolutionaries in Baden aspired after a new peasants' war and attempted to play out the grand duke against noble landlords and bankers. The Viennese meanwhile wished to bring down the hated 'Metternich system' and Berliners were angered by an oppressive military presence in their city. There is, of course, much more to each of these examples given, including several common demands such as an insistence on constitutional government and the long-held 'romantic' desire for a German nation state.

Equally important were the various social and economic reasons. Germany, too, suffered from the Europe-wide potato famine; the plight of farmers on their small-holdings was pitiful, forcing large numbers of agricultural workers, artisans and traders into emigration. And yet, if measured by the scale of other countries, Ireland should have had a particularly ferocious revolution. Similar observations apply to the industrial proletariat, which one might have expected to become the actual revolutionary engine and which certainly played a key role in some revolutionary centres. In general, however, Germany had not yet reached the peak of its industrial revolution and its workers were insufficiently organized to play a very significant role in the revolutions.

Some experts maintain that revolutions are not so much started by a vibrant force of 'agitators', but are the result of decadent and incompetent or feeble governments. There is some evidence of weakness among German governments which helps to explain the early success of many revolutions, but it would be misleading to suggest that German potentates of this time were particularly illiberal or incompetent. Many of the southern German states had given prominence to liberal politicians and had introduced reforms which certainly went in the general direction of constitutional government.

The desire for national unification was perhaps the strongest force, already clearly defined at a public meeting in early March at Heidelberg, and the

Schleswig–Holstein conflict did much to inflame national passions. Yet it never reached the fervour of a 'levée en masse', and the first national German parliament in Frankfurt contributed towards the extinction of the revolutionary flame rather than to its rekindling.

All in all then, the reader will have to accept that no conclusive reason for the outbreak of the revolutions can be found. This does not mean that our interest in the revolutions should be diminished. Indeed, the divisions between liberals and socialists, a rapidly developing bourgeoisie and a declining peasantry and artisanship, as well as diverse religious factions, contribute to make this historical event a fascinating subject for detailed study, not to mention the reception of the revolutions during the subsequent 150 years.

The classical approach to the German revolutions tended to focus on their revolutionary potential and on the underlying social and economic reasons for their initial successes, a theme which deserves some prominence when examining the early phases of the revolutions. However, following the approach adopted by Wolfram Siemann and other contemporary German historians, more prominence has been given to the development of a democratically inspired German mind, more evident perhaps in the regions of the southwest than in Berlin or Vienna and in the serious constitutional reforms undertaken by Frankfurt parliamentarians. Throughout the book, brief biographies of leading activists from different political backgrounds have been included; these accounts will not only serve to illustrate abstract and often theoretical versions of specific issues, but may also highlight the particular dilemmas which confronted many protagonists or at least demonstrate the constraints under which they were forced to operate.

Structure of the book

The first two chapters will be of particular interest to the student with little knowledge of German history, but are not essential for the more advanced student. Chapter 3 analyses the roles of Hecker and Struve in their radical attempts to seize the initiative in Baden and chapter 4 examines how this initiative was taken over by the two dominant capitals of Vienna and Berlin, where, although the socio-economic potential for revolution was most advanced, political leadership was lacking. In both chapters, an analysis of the social and economic conditions is vital for an understanding of both the success and the failure of these particular revolutionary movements. Chapters 5 to 7 analyse the various attempts to introduce parliamentary democracy, not only within the various established parliaments, but also by adopting democratic procedures at grass-roots level in clubs and associations. Particular attention has been paid to the work of the National Assembly, leading to a discussion of the 'dilemma' of the German revolutions and the various attempts at compromise, not only between committed republicans and monarchists, but also between supporters of a 'greater Germany' and those advocating a 'smaller Germany' solution. The Imperial Constitution, the National Assembly's main achievement, is examined, together with the struggle for its defence in the face of the hostile regrouping of old powers, a struggle which concluded with the defeat of revolutionary energies by a reactionary establishment. Chapter 8, rather than being seen as an epilogue to the revolutions, should be read as an attempt to determine the extent to which the revolutions contributed to Germany's modernization, despite having failed in their broader objectives. Chapter 9, intended to follow the German tradition of a *Forschungsbericht* (research report), soon developed into a study of the reception of the revolutions over the past 150 years. In this capacity it turned into an interesting alternative to the more traditional conclusion to such a book, moving beyond the debate on the perceived success or failure of the revolutionary aims. The results which emerge indicate the existence of a continuous interest in the events of 1848/9, retaining them as a touchstone for subsequent democratic initiatives, not least within the recent context of seeking to establish a successful, western-style political culture for the re-united German Federal Republic.

Author's acknowledgements and editorial policy

It is editorial policy to avoid German technical terms and quotations in German and I have adhered to this wherever possible. However, in some instances I felt the need to give the German equivalent in parenthesis. Unless otherwise indicated, all quotations taken from a German source have been translated by me. A very simple table of events supports the first two chapters, followed by a more general table which highlights major developments during the 'year of revolutions'; this may help readers to view the German revolutions in their wider European context.

Finally, I wish to thank my colleagues and students for their welcome interest in my studies and for their support and guidance. My particular thanks go to the staff of Oxford's libraries, above all to those of the Bodleian Library; I could not have attempted my research without access to their invaluable collection. I am indebted to my own university for granting me sabbatical leave and thereby affording me the time to conduct my research. My deepest gratitude, however, is reserved for my wife, who has read and corrected various drafts and wrestled with my somewhat idiosyncratic English.

H. J. Hahn, Oxford, December 2000

Notes

1 Dieter Langewiesche, 'Die deutsche Revolution von 1848/49 und die vorrevolutionäre Gesellschaft: Forschungsstand und Forschungsperspektive, Teil 2', *Archiv für Sozialgeschichte*, 31 (1991), p. 331.

2 Veit Valentin, *Geschichte der deutschen Revolution 1848–49*, vol. 2 (Berlin, 1931), p. 613.

3 Cf. in particular David Blackbourn and Geoff Eley, *The Peculiarities of German History. Bourgeois Society and Politics in Nineteenth-Century Germany* (Oxford University Press, 1984).

4 Cf. Helmuth Plessner, *Die verspätete Nation. Über die politische Verführbarkeit bürgerlichen Geistes* (Stuttgart, 1959), a study which had a deep impact on German scholars of the 1960s and 1970s.

5 Carl von Rotteck and Carl Welcker eds, *Das Staatslexikon. Encyklopädie der sämmtlichen Staatswissenschaften für alle Stände*, 2nd edn (Altona, 1845), vol. 11, pp. 550–62.

6 Karl Marx, *Das Kapital*, Afterword to the second German edition, here in my own literal translation. *Das Kapital, Ökonomische Schriften*, H. J. Lieber and B. Kautsky eds, vol. 1 (Stuttgart, 1971), p. xxxi. cf. also Chapter 8.

7 Wolfram Siemann, *The German Revolution of 1848–49*, trans. by Christiane Banerji (London, 1998).

Chapter 1

German society in transition (1789–1815)

The impact of the French Revolution of 1789

The events of July 1789 had profound repercussions throughout Europe; the *Thermidor*, Napoleon's subsequent rise to power and military successes brought about major changes within the Holy Roman Empire, which finally led to its demise and to far-reaching political and social changes. The modernizing effect of the 'Age of Napoleon' on the German-speaking countries and its influence on specifically German concepts of patriotism and liberalism made a significant contribution to the rise of the 1848 revolutionary movement.

There is no doubt that such a politically and economically outdated system, symbolically held together by the medieval notion of the Holy Roman Empire, failed to assimilate the new ideas of the Enlightenment, despite the fact that the French Revolution had initially made a major impact on its various cultural circles. Germany's ensuing modernization therefore remained incomplete, since a political force comparable to that of the French *citoyen* had not developed within her territory. Constitutional and political reforms emerged as a reaction to, or as a result of, the perceived French hegemony, resisted and often hampered by the continued existence of a corporate society. The burgeoning literary and philosophical elite, whilst successful in reviving German thought and culture, contributed in only a minor way to a new political reform movement. The series of wars against France strengthened feelings of patriotism and nationalism, but with no political structures to direct them, these sentiments languished in romantic dreams of the revival of the old *Reich*, engendering a fierce hatred of anything French and intrinsically rejecting the modernist ideas of the Western Enlightenment. With the influence of Goethe and Schiller still largely confined to the princely court of Weimar and the philosophy of Kant scarcely known beyond university circles, the formation of a public mind was not possible until the end of this period. The situation changed with the so-called 'Wars of Liberation' against Napoleon, but the new romantic and patriotic spirit failed to promote modern ideas of citizenship or liberal democratic principles.

Intellectual responses to the French Revolution of 1789

The generally held view among historians used to be that German society at the end of the eighteenth century was so antiquated, fragmented and damaged by the catastrophe of the Thirty Years War that a public mind, generated by open intellectual debate, could not develop. This assessment has been revised in recent years. The response of Germany's cultural elite to the Revolution, though uneven, was generally positive and was received by a wider public. In 1784 Ludwig Wekhrlin recognized the importance of public views generated by German literary circles.[1] The American War of Independence had made a profound impression within such circles, promoting more than mere discontent with the domestic situation. A varied response emerged to the tempestuous period 1789–1815, which can be generalized as follows.

The older generation of writers and philosophers, associated with adapting the ideas of the French Enlightenment to German conditions, were generally in favour of events west of the Rhine. Friedrich Gottlieb Klopstock, then in his late sixties, welcomed the revolution as the century's most noble deed, regretting only that its origin was in France, not Germany. His ode to La Rochefoucauld celebrates immortal France as the liberator from despotism and harbinger of peace, while consoling himself that Germans took part in the American War of Independence and that Germany had ushered in the Reformation.[2] Christoph Martin Wieland was slightly more critical, but was moved to address the French National Assembly as a world citizen. Expressing his admiration for their general policies, particularly the new type of patriotism, he, nevertheless, urged the Assembly to exercise greater circumspection in its proposed 'palingenesis' of the monarchy into a republic.[3] The various uprisings in Geneva, Aachen, Liège and Brabant were eagerly discussed throughout Germany and Joachim Heinrich Campe's *Letters from Paris* during the Revolution were widely read.[4] The constitutionalist A.L. Schlöser took the opportunity to criticize all forms of despotism: 'The incidents in France in these days are a strong lesson for all oppressors of mankind, in every region of the world and amongst all classes.'[5]

The younger, neo-classical generation, now at the zenith of its fame, was not quite so easily moved to take an active interest in these tumultuous events. Immersed in the revival of Greek classicism and wedded to the truth of absolute beauty, they remained strangely dubious about the news from France. Goethe, though not a supporter of the Revolution and deploring the rule of the masses, acknowledged its ideals of freedom and equality and recognized its deep effect on his own life,[6] recalling years later:

> It is true, I could not be a friend of the French Revolution, for its terror reached me too closely and outraged me daily and hourly, whereas its benign consequences

could not then be foreseen. Furthermore, I could not remain indifferent to the fact that artificial attempts were made in Germany to bring about similar events which in France had been the consequence of great necessity.[7]

During the first war of coalition against the French Republic he paid tribute to the spirit of the French troops, recognizing that a new chapter in world history had dawned.[8] Later still, he was to see Napoleon as some victorious demi-god, though this view was not entirely objective, since Napoleon had granted Goethe an audience and expressed his admiration for the author of *Werther*.

Although Goethe's friend, Wilhelm von Humboldt, was in Paris during the Revolution, he took scarcely any heed of the upheaval, concentrating instead on visits to churches and museums[9] in contrast to his companion, the enlightened pedagogue Campe, who welcomed the Revolution as 'the greatest and most general blessing for mankind since Luther's improvement of the creed'.[10] Even Schiller, whose revolutionary plays *Die Räuber* (1779), *Kabale und Liebe* (1783) and *Don Carlos* (1787) championed freedom of thought and pilloried the despotism of German princes, came to reject political issues in favour of the more general aspects of history and the laws of aesthetics. Although an honorary citizen of the French Republic, he had turned against the Revolution, condemned the establishment of the *Mainz Republic* (1791–2) and was appalled at the imprisonment and execution of Louis XVI.[11] Indeed, the course of the Revolution also led him to criticize some aspects of the Enlightenment: he blamed the rationalist age for the loss of wholeness in modern human existence, believing it could only be regained within a new synthesis of art, morality and politics. And yet his *Aesthetische Briefe* return to the theme of revolution, albeit on a higher, philosophical level and clearly under the influence of Kant's philosophy: whilst affirming the importance of the state as guarantor of order, individual citizens must move beyond their dependence on the state in order to maximize individual freedom. Although this realization of freedom is part of an historical process, violent revolution is not rejected out of hand:

> Man has roused himself from his long indolence and self-deception and . . . is demanding restitution of his inalienable rights. But he is not just demanding this . . . he is rising up to seize by force what, in his opinion, has been wrongfully denied him.[12]

This revolutionary pronouncement, cloaked in a philosophical context, reminds us of the Heinrich Heine *bon mot* that Robespierre's revolution consisted of chopping off the head of a king, whereas Kant's philosophical revolution rid mankind of its own Creator.[13] Such a philosophical, indirect and abstract involvement in the revolution is evident in Schiller's *Wilhelm Tell* (1804), a play much criticized by the literary left for its protagonist's apparent lack of heroism and petit-bourgeois demeanour.[14] And yet, the references to human rights and to political freedom clearly draw on the French Revolution, as does the appeal to fraternity at the clandestine *Rütli* meeting and the Bastille-like storming of the tyrant's fortress. Furthermore, this choice of a Swiss source might even be seen as encouragement to Germans to follow the Swiss example. The Helvetian Republican government had already used the theme as a symbol of its own victory (May 1798) and followed the French example of introducing freedom trees in its cities.[15]

The younger generation of writers and philosophers, mostly still at university, greeted the Revolution with unbounded enthusiasm. The philosopher Fichte welcomed this historic moment, when individual freedom would be realized, but he still regarded the state as the guarantor of such freedom and expressed his total admiration for the French nation, to which he was prepared to dedicate his *Wissenschaftslehre*.[16] Friedrich Schlegel counted the French Revolution among the three 'tendencies' which influenced the Romantic age,[17] while his friend Joseph Görres rushed to Paris to support France's annexation of the Rhineland.[18] The three leading Romantics from the Tübingen theological seminary, the poet Hölderlin and the philosophers Hegel and Schelling, were equally enthusiastic. They sang the forbidden *Marseillaise*, devoured revolutionary pamphlets and planted the symbolic freedom tree. Of the three, Hegel remained closest to the spirit of the revolution, referring to it as 'a glorious dawn' in his 'Philosophy of Spirit'.[19] Not unlike Goethe, he, too, greeted Napoleon enthusiastically as the executor of the revolution.[20] In equally jubilant mood, Hölderlin composed several poems in celebration of the event and urged his sister to pray for a French victory against Austria so that the abuse of princely power would be diminished.[21]

The range of intellectual responses to the 1789 Revolution has revealed the influence of events in France on the German intelligentsia. It will become apparent, however, that many of the younger representatives, particularly those of the Romantic generation, revised their views in the post-Thermidorian age and embraced a Germanic mythology and strident nationalism. It would appear that the more sceptical generation of Goethe and Humboldt was wiser in its initial assessment, recognizing that Germany was not yet ready for such an upheaval. First and foremost, there was the impediment of the old Empire with its corporate social order, time-honoured privileges and protective measures. In addition, there remained scores of monarchs and ecclesiastical leaders and an increasingly damaging power struggle between Prussia and Austria, with Frederick the Great having become a virtual counter-emperor.[22] By the end of the eighteenth century, many leading legal and literary figures openly questioned the constitutional meaning of the *Reich*.[23] Obviously, the overthrow of one king in a centralized and corrupt state may be possible, while the removal of the multiheaded hydra of the Holy Roman Empire was a different matter. Furthermore, it must be emphasized that among her leaders were some enlightened, modern monarchs, not least the Emperor Joseph II. Another leading example was Karl Friedrich, Margrave of Baden, who asserted, in 1783, that the wellbeing of the ruler was inalienably linked to that of his country. Recent research has suggested that many German regimes were unstable and that a series of riots in the Rhineland, the Mosel valley, the Saarland, the Palatinate, parts of Saxony, Mecklenburg and Silesia were such a threat to the political order that by 1794 the whole country was on the brink of collapse.[24] It would appear, however, that this assessment is too simplistic: the middle classes were still politically too heterogeneous and economically far too weak to emulate their French counterparts; discontent with the presence of French and Prussian troops caused reluctance to join forces with the French. Individual potentates were not immediately seen as the source of oppression, which instead was put down to warfare and disunity. Change had to come from outside and it arrived in the shape of Napoleon.

The struggle for supremacy between Austria and Prussia

This analysis of the various military and political actions between 1792 and 1806 will focus on those aspects which may have had a bearing on subsequent events, leading – in one way or another – to the German revolutions of 1848. Table 1.1 attempts to give a survey of events, although it cannot convey the full complexity of the situation.

There is no doubt that the rivalry between these two powers significantly contributed to the collapse of the Holy Roman Empire. Originating during the Seven Years War (1756–63), hostilities continued to smoulder despite various attempts at conciliation, such as the Treaty of Reichenbach (1790) and the Declaration of Pillnitz (1791). Both powers seemed to underestimate the threat from revolutionary France, since they remained preoccupied with seventeenth-century absolutist policies of territorial expansion, regardless of historical and cultural contexts. Indeed, Prussia saw the outbreak of the Revolution as an opportunity to make further territorial gains at a cost to France. Austro-Prussian rivalries continued in the Netherlands, where Prussian troops sought to gain political advantage at the expense of Austria. Both countries seemed more interested in gaining territory from Poland and the Ottoman Empire and in forming a coalition with Russia than in events west of the Rhine. The first coalition war revealed continuing tensions: the three coalition armies were poorly co-ordinated; Austrian and Prussian troops fought separate battles, with the rest of the Empire inactive or neutral until March 1793, when the Imperial Diet, becoming fearful of French successes, declared the hostilities an imperial war. Of the various

Table 1.1 Table of events, 1792–1806

Date	Participants	Events	Results
1792–1796/7	Prussia, Austria, Hesse-Kassel vs. French Republic	**First war of coalition:** Duke of Brunswick leads army against Gen. Lazare Carnot. **Cannonade of Valmy** (20/9/92): allied advance stopped. Defeat of Austrian contingent at Jemappes (6/11/92)	French victory: loss of Austrian territory in Low Countries. Loss of Speyer and Mainz.
1793	Prussia and Russia	Second Polish division	Territorial gains for Prussia and Russia, but not Austria.
23/3/1793	Britain, Spain and Hl. Roman Empire vs. France	Imperial war declaration against France. Archduke Carl of Austria defeats Gen. Dumoriez	Recapture of Austrian territory in Low Countries and of Mainz.
13/10/1793	Austria vs. France	Austrian victory by Gen. Wurmser at Weissenburg	Austrian occupation of Alsace.
December 1793	France vs. Austria	Counter-attack by Gen. Hoche	Austria loses the Alsace.
1794	Prussia + France	Separate armistice	Ten years of peace for Prussia.
26/6/1794	Britain + Austria vs. France	Defeat at Fleurus (Holland)	Recapture of Alsace by Austria.
5/4/1795	Prussia, Austria, Hanover, Hesse-Kassel and France	Peace Treaty of Basel	Neutrality of Prussia, Austrian loss of Netherlands and territories left of Rhine.
1795	Austria, Russia, Prussia	Third Polish division	Extinction of Poland: divided up between Russia, Austria and Prussia.
1796/7	Austria vs. France	Gens. Carnot and Bonaparte vs. Archduke Carl. French victories in northern Italy, Austrian victories at Amberg and Würzburg	Ultimately gains for France.
October 1797	Austria – France	Peace of **Campo Formio**	Belgium and Lombardy to France, Venetian Rep. to Austria. Archdiocese of Salzburg to Austria.
1797	Switzerland	France creates republics of Helvetia and Rome	French domination in southern Germany and Italy.
1797/8	Hl. Roman Empire, France	**Congress at Rastatt** (Imperial Peace Congress)	Territories left of Rhine > France, secularization of ecclesiastical *Reich* territory with exception of electorates of Cologne, Mainz and Trier.

Table 1.1 (cont'd)

Date	Participants	Events	Results
28/4/1799	Austria vs. France	Murder of French delegates	Start of Second War of Coalition.
1799–1801 March– June 1799	Austria, Hl. Roman Empire, Russia (Britain)	**Second war of coalition:** Archduke Carl defeats French troops in Germany and Switzerland; Russian Gen. Suvarov defeats French troops in northern Italy	French retreat across Rhine. Nov. 1799: Russia withdraws from war.
June 1800	Austria vs. France	Napoleon's victory at **Marengo**	Austria withdraws from northern Italy.
3/12/1800	Austria vs. France	Gen. Moreau's victory at Hohenlinden	French troops in Bavaria.
9/2/1801	Austria/Hl. Roman Empire, France	Peace treaty of **Lunéville**	Austria loses all her Italian provinces except Venice, also all territory left of the Rhine, but is compensated with *Reich* territory.
25/2/1803	France + Hl. Roman Empire	*Reichsdeputationshauptschluß* (Final Recess)	Dissolution of 112 *Reich* principalities.
18/5/1804	France	**Napoleon is crowned Emperor**	Presages end of Hl. Roman Empire.
10/8/1804	Austria	Francis II becomes Emperor of Austria	Presages his resignation as 'German' emperor.
May 1805	France vs. Austria	Napoleon = king of Italy	French annexation of Italian territory.
1805–6	Austria + (Russia & Britain) vs. France and southern German states	Battle at Ulm and French occupation of Vienna. 2/12/1805: Napoleon defeats Austrian & Russian armies at Austerlitz	Prussia surrenders Ansbach, Neuchâtel and Cleve, but gains Hanover. Austria surrenders Venice, Tyrol and southern German territory.
12/7/1806	France, Bavaria, Baden, Württemberg	Southern German states enter **Confederation of the Rhine** with France	Bavaria and Württemberg become kingdoms, Baden ➤ Great Dukedom.
6/8/1806	Hl. Roman Empire	Francis II abdicates as Hl. Roman Emperor	**End of Hl. Roman Empire.**
Oct. 1806	France vs. Prussia	French victory at **Jena and Auerstädt**	Prussia becomes French satellite state.

Note: Names and figures in **bold** refer to major events of the period.

imperial states, Württemberg and the Palatinate, sensing a French victory, declared their neutrality.[25] By the autumn of 1794 the second partition of Poland benefited Prussia and Russia to the disadvantage of Austria. Consolidating his gains, Frederick William II of Prussia sought peace with France and withdrew his troops from the imperial armies. Most German princes were content to be compensated for territorial losses in the west by territorial gains elsewhere, at the expense either of Poland or of some Italian state, or by the secularization of imperial ecclesiastical territory. Austria, for instance, was compensated for losses west of the Rhine by a secret codicil to the Treaty of Basel (April 1795).[26] While Prussia gained ten years of peace, Austria now found herself defending an enormous frontier, extending from the Low Countries down the Rhine valley and into Italy. After some early successes, the outdated Austrian forces suffered several major setbacks, culminating in the defeat of Austerlitz (December 1805). Led by an incompetent, often disunited political leadership, Prussia also began to make an effort to stem French advances, but it was too late. She had failed to benefit from her peace and had been unsuccessful in gaining new allies, even provoking war with Britain as a result of Hanover passing to Prussia by the Treaty of Schönbrunn. With Napoleon's dual victory at Jena and Auerstädt, Prussia's fate was sealed.

Events in Switzerland and other non-imperial German-speaking territories

Switzerland had seceded from the *Reich* in 1499 to become established as a loose federation of individual city states with more or less absolutist rulers. She was soon immersed in religious conflict. As a consequence of such instability, the French Revolution invoked a much stronger response in Switzerland than in Germany. Several incidents of unrest aided the city states of Berne, Schaffhausen and Zurich in regaining their dominant positions. The situation in Basel was complicated, since part of its territory, the bishopric of Basel, belonged to the Empire and was protected by Austrian troops. Here, in March 1791, the Rauratian Republic was declared, to be annexed two years later by the French. In 1797, French violation of Swiss territory within the Basel bishopric led to war with Zurich and to a collapse of the old order (March 1798). The Helvetian Republic was proclaimed by ten of the twenty-two cantons, with a representative republican constitution guaranteeing equality before the law. The newly established centralization caused unease in several of the more rural cantons with the result that Switzerland, too, became drawn into the European wars. Following several *coups d'état*, in September 1802 the Helvetian Republic ceased to exist, replaced under Napoleon's influence by the Helvetian Confederation, a mediated compromise consisting of nineteen cantons. The citizens' rights, established earlier, remained intact, despite the return of several members of the old aristocracy. The federation maintained its neutrality during the French wars against Austria and Prussia, but had to support Napoleon's campaign against Russia. Napoleon's defeat and the subsequent Vienna Congress abolished the Helvetian Confederation and re-established the pre-revolutionary system.

Nevertheless, events in Switzerland indicate that republican tendencies had a major impact on the region. Switzerland remained an important source for democratic and republican stimuli throughout the first half of the nineteenth century and subsequently became a haven for German republicans during and after the 1848 revolutions.

The emergence of a 'Third Germany'

The growing rivalry between Prussia and Austria and the earliest hostilities were an indication that the old structures of the Empire were out of joint and could no longer provide sufficient protection for the smaller states. Although several of the campaigns against France did not involve the Empire, the territories of the Rhineland and of the central and southwestern states suffered from military action and from political uncertainty. Baden alone faced an influx of 10,000 French immigrants, more than the whole of Prussia and Austria.[27] These immigrants formed their own military forces, acting at times as if they were an army of occupation. In addition, the smaller states had to endure billeting by Austrian and French armies on their territories throughout the three coalition wars. Baden therefore sought a closer association with France, concluding an armistice in 1796. Württemberg and the Palatinate had already declared their neutrality in 1792, at the outbreak of the first coalition war. Economic co-operation, too, was closer between Baden and France than with most other German states, the result being that Baden, Württemberg and later Bavaria were generously compensated for the territorial losses they incurred across the Rhine. This type of territorial horse-trading caused some political unease, especially amongst Baden's wealthier classes, and, when the Helvetian Republic was established, there was some attempt to accede to the new state, an initiative soon suppressed by Austrian intervention.[28] Bavaria, too, became increasingly wary of plans to integrate her territory within Austria's borders. Similar anxieties were expressed by many of the smaller ecclesiastical principalities, fearing loss of independence, nominally still guaranteed by imperial law, but already openly violated by Emperor Francis II.

In general, the policies of the two major German powers seemed to indicate that their own self-interest not only outweighed common imperial interests, but also ignored the new patriotic impetus which had emerged

9

within literary and philosophical circles. This outlook can also be illustrated by their lukewarm response to attempts at creating a militia along the lines of the French 'levée en masse', which had produced an army of some 850,000 citizen soldiers. Friedrich Christian Laukhardt, a military expert, deplored the lack of commitment among German politicians to this idea, particularly in Prussia and Austria. He concluded that 'the great states of Austria and Prussia are reckoned incorrectly [as belonging] to Germany or to the Roman Empire', otherwise they would share 'a single interest for the welfare of the fatherland'.[29] After Austria's defeat at Austerlitz and only months before the establishment of the Rhenish Confederation, Karl Dalberg, Archbishop and Imperial Chancellor, called upon Francis to abdicate the imperial crown in favour of Napoleon. In a letter to the French ambassador, he proposed the restoration of Charlemagne's empire, 'composed of Italy, France and Germany', to the exclusion of Prussia and Austria.[30] Dalberg's suggestion conveys a romantically antiquarian tone: with the Final Recess (*Reichsdeputationshauptschluß*) of 1803 the imperial order had been all but abolished. The imperial deputation, in negotiation with the French government at Regensburg, reorganized German territory on a more far-reaching scale than at any time in German history. By a process of 'secularization' all ecclesiastical territories were abolished, with the exception of the seat of the Teutonic Order and the Electorate of Mainz, which became secularized but independent. In addition to changes on the left bank of the Rhine, three electorates, nineteen bishoprics and forty-four abbeys were abolished. In a further process, known as 'Mediatisierung', 112 free imperial cities and countless smaller territories were incorporated into existing German states. Only the cities of Bremen, Lübeck, Frankfurt, Nuremberg and Augsburg succeeded in retaining their independence for a little longer. The main beneficiaries of these changes were the central and southern German states, particularly Baden, Württemberg and Hesse-Darmstadt. They owed their new importance to Napoleon, who had created a strategic buffer zone between his own country and Prussia and Austria. The establishment of the Confederation of the Rhine in July 1806 was the natural consequence of this policy, establishing a 'Third Germany' in all but name and undermining the two larger powers of Austria and Prussia. The abolition of the Holy Roman Empire was now a mere formality, since, as the young Hegel observed, by forfeiting the power to defend itself, it had already lost its significance as a state.

Constitutional and socio-economic reforms

A survey of the various reforms implemented will demonstrate that they contained many elements often associated with French revolutionary aims.

Commentators have frequently tended to focus on the Prussian reform programme, ignoring or playing down reforms introduced in other German states. It can be demonstrated, however, that between 1806 and 1815 many important aspects of reform were common to other individual states and that their impact on modernity and democracy generally decreased from west to east. Furthermore, a closer analysis would indicate that many German states were well prepared for reform, even if a number of the new democratic principles had not yet been fully understood. Several of the more enlightened princes were involved in modernizing their own states and the fate of the newly independent United States of America was closely observed.[31]

The most far-reaching reforms were seen in those territories which had come directly under French control. In 1792, the French National Convention introduced its own democratic constitution in all occupied lands, and Napoleon, though revoking the most extreme revolutionary laws, introduced his own *Code Napoléon* in all the territories on the west bank of the Rhine, in the kingdom of Westphalia, in the Grand Duchy of Berg and in Frankfurt. The constitutions of these states were intended as showcases for the revolutionary aspirations of the period, promoting civil equality, religious tolerance, trial by jury in an open court and the abolition of serfdom, guilds and aristocratic privilege. However, other measures ensured plenty of scope for anti-French feelings: a levy was imposed for the local maintenance of French troops, religious practices were in fact often suppressed and members of the dissolved guilds resented their diminished status. A general spirit of opposition, however, contributed in its own way towards developing political awareness, nurturing a general climate of revolt.

Within the Confederation of the Rhine, French pressure was brought upon governments to impose the *Code Napoléon*, though its implementation did not necessarily guarantee an improvement of democratic rights. In Württemberg, the old corporate states, despite their deficiencies, were a force for decentralization against an absolutist duke. French intervention, however, abolished them in favour of a centralized state under the new king, Frederick I, leaving the seigniorial rights and privileges of the landed gentry intact.[32] Baden and Bavaria fared slightly better, thanks to their enlightened ministers Freiherr von Reitzenstein and Count Maximilian Montgelas. The latter, of French background, but a free knight of the Empire, was an excellent civil servant who appreciated the French reform spirit of true patriotism: the 'patri' should bestow citizenship and, above all else, provide a fair and incorruptible legal framework.

Reforms in Prussia and Austria

While Prussia was all but eliminated at the Treaty of Tilsit (1807), Austria suffered relatively little after the disaster of Austerlitz. Austria shared many of the problems of the other German states, despite retaining some of the benefits of Joseph II's reforms. She had submitted to French domination, had to pay high reparation charges and had to concede significant territorial losses. Unlike Prussia, however, these were less crucial to Austria's survival, since they were largely restricted to areas well beyond the Habsburg heartlands. Her losses in the Netherlands, Italy, southern Germany, the Adriatic and West-Galicia actually simplified the burden of administration,[33] whereas Prussia's losses along the country's new borders included Westphalia, the Rhine provinces and her Polish acquisitions. The Treaty of Tilsit 'had reduced Prussia as an effective power to about the rank of the duchy of Oldenburg'[34] and over 80 per cent of her remaining territory was occupied by a French army, which controlled all major fortifications and strategic military routes. Her war indemnities were such that a revival of her depleted economy was out of the question and the reduction of the Prussian army to 42,000 troops made any prospect of a military counter-offensive impossible.

Both Prussia and Austria had monarchs of a similar nature, at heart indecisive, timid, romantic and reactionary. The difference between the two countries lay in their geographical and national make-up, but even more crucially in their leading politicians. While Austria sought to pursue a policy of neutrality and at times even acted as conciliator between the tsar and Napoleon, Prussia was served by men of strong national passion. Austria's chief minister, Prince Clemens von Metternich, was a diplomat of the old school, opposed to the emergence of any national or popular movement. He therefore chose to accept French supremacy as a means of keeping Vienna's reformist party in check. Rivalries within the Habsburg court hindered the emergence of any clear-cut reform policy and preserved a more conservative approach, strengthening the position of the nobility. However, a militia was established and certain legal reforms were contained in the Civil Code of 1811, though amounting to little more than bureaucratic refinements and failing to dent the ancient privileges or modernize the outdated administration.

The Prussian reform movement has traditionally been seen as a 'creative revolution',[35] a 'revolution in a positive sense',[36] as 'defensive modernization'[37] and as a key to the new liberal movement prior to March 1848, but modern historians have tended to revise this positive image. Playing down the apparent contrast between Prussian successes and Austrian failures, they point instead to the successful reforms in the former French-occupied

Confederation of the Rhine.[38] There is some justification in this, particularly since the traditional view was somewhat coloured by nationalist historians. The agrarian reforms, introduced by Prussia's chief minister, von Stein, were intended to establish civil equality, social mobility and economic freedom, but these measures were criticized as 'a relic from the dark ages'.[39] In reality, peasants were not protected. Transformed from serfs into unprotected agricultural labourers, they were obliged to compensate landowners either in financial or in territorial terms and fell victim to 'Bauernlegen', that is, confiscation of their territory, which, though officially outlawed, increased after 1807.

The reform of municipal government (November 1808) was intended to give townspeople control over the administration of what, in many cases, were garrison-town authorities. The reform established elected town mayors, magistrates and restricted the power of the guilds, thus introducing an element of competition and free enterprise, but these measures did not extend to rural communities. Stein also failed to apply this democratic principle to a planned national assembly.[40]

The army reforms, carried out after Stein's enforced dismissal by Napoleon, abolished corporal punishment and rejuvenated the officer corps in a rigorous attempt to break the dominance of the aristocracy. The most important aspect of the reforms possibly consisted in General von Scharnhorst's endeavour to create a citizens' national army, despite opposition from Frederick William III and Prime Minister Karl August von Hardenberg. Although the nobility was still over-represented in the officer corps, the reforms were significant in view of Prussia's traditional role as a military state.

Distinguished historians have questioned the liberal and democratic dimensions of the reform programme, going so far as to suggest that 'neither Hardenberg nor Stein could establish ways to represent a nation that was apathetic or hostile towards his political goals'.[41] Although there is little tenable evidence to suggest much progress towards a greater liberalism, the transformation of the country's academic and literary elite should not be underestimated. Their emerging nationalism, with an undercurrent of sentimental romanticism, was undoubtedly fuelled by anti-French resentment against the real hardship inflicted by French hegemony. Other forces, however, were committed to the Enlightenment and to the ideals proclaimed during the French Revolution. The philosopher Fichte welcomed the liberating tendencies of the 1789 Revolution and, in his *Addresses to the German Nation*, advocated a free and independent German nation state. Although chauvinistic in its hatred of everything French, the patriotic spirit of poets such as Arndt, Jahn and Körner heralded Prussia's position as the champion of a future German nation state. An analysis of Stein's own attitude will illustrate the impetus towards a spiritual renewal in the face of the widespread destruction, deprivation and hardship resulting from the Treaty of Tilsit. Stein defined the objectives of his reforms as follows: 'The chief idea was to arouse a moral, religious and patriotic spirit in the nation, to instil into it again courage, confidence, readiness for every sacrifice in [sic] behalf of independence from foreigners and for the national honour.'[42] Scharnhorst expressed similar sentiments, insisting that 'one had to instil into the nation a sentiment of self-awareness', views reminiscent of Fichte's *Addresses*.

The far-reaching education reforms of Wilhelm von Humboldt must also be seen as part of this intellectual renewal. Though steeped in neo-classical tradition, they promoted independence of mind, freedom of thought and encouraged character building. With this ethos, the new University of Berlin developed into a national institution for all Germans, attracting outstanding talent and emerging as a centre of German patriotism under its first *Rektor*, Fichte. If Humboldt's achievements, together with the new literary climate, are seen in conjunction with the Stein–Hardenberg reforms, a somewhat different picture from that painted by many modern historians will emerge: while it is certainly true that a majority of Prussian citizens were primarily concerned with sheer survival in the face of the country's grim economic situation, a powerful intellectual elite had begun to manifest itself, capable of developing a public opinion and inspiring a German patriotic conscience which was now centred on Prussia, whilst its rival Austria was still steeped in a pre-revolutionary sentiment.

The wars of liberation and the restoration of the old order

While there has been a tendency among past historians to overemphasize the role of German nationalists in the struggle against Napoleonic domination, it should be recognized that this struggle was a crucial element in Germany's national awakening. It is true that the rulers of the Confederation of the Rhine, whose troops had been all but annihilated during Napoleon's Russian campaign, remained loyal to France. Austria under Prince Metternich meanwhile kept her options open, remaining undecided whether to support Russia against France, and King Frederick William III of Prussia and his chancellor, Hardenberg, remained irresolute and inactive. The uprising against Napoleon was inspired by the enthusiasm and efforts of the Prussian reformers. Stein, Scharnhorst, Clausewitz and General Yorck von Wartenburg took the initiative. By August 1812, Stein, still in the service of Tsar Alexander, had begun to organize a German legion and the following January he raised a militia in Eastern Prussia, using his influence with the tsar to secure the military liberation of Germany. The national mood was captured by Ernst Moritz Arndt, whose *Catechism for the German Soldier* (1813) and many other patriotic songs earned him the title of poet of the war of liberation. Many others, such as 'Turnvater' Jahn, produced fiercely patriotic literature, continuing in the tradition of Fichte, Kleist and the early Romantics.

Against this background General Yorck took the decision, in December 1812, to remove his army from French control and join the campaign against Napoleon, a move initially opposed by Frederick William. Later, on the advice of Chancellor Hardenberg, the king reluctantly changed sides, first moving his court from Berlin to Breslau, beyond the reach of French troops. He grudgingly decreed the establishment of a militia (*Landwehr*) and a reserve (*Landsturm*), thereby mobilizing a *de facto* citizens' army, an unprecedented decision for a Prussian king. Furthermore, on 17 March, three months after Yorck changed sides, the king made his famous proclamation 'To my people',[43] which virtually amounted to a new pact between the monarch and his subjects. Some four months earlier, Stein had already demanded a German constitution, in a memorandum which declared that if the German princes did not join the national cause, they would forfeit any claim for recognition or restoration of their rights by the allied armies.[44]

Though individually perhaps not very impressive as far as numerical involvement[45] and political clout were concerned, these events, in essence, amounted to something of a national revolutionary uprising. This perceived threat was soon to be countered by the victorious allies. The protracted negotiations at the Congress of Vienna (November 1814–June 1815), where most of the assembled diplomats thought in terms of eighteenth-century absolutism, succeeded in restoring a pre-revolutionary order. Stein attended many of the proceedings as adviser to the tsar, but his plans for an all-German constitution or for the revival of a modernized, more liberal Holy Roman Empire came to nothing. They were opposed not only by Metternich, fearful of the rise of a national movement, but also by virtually all the great powers at Vienna, and even more so by the smaller southern German states, who did not wish to see their sovereignty subordinated to the interests of a new democratic nation state. When, very much at Metternich's behest, the Holy Alliance between Russia, Austria and Prussia was formed, its first article declared:

> In accordance with Holy Scripture which commands all men to consider themselves brothers, the three monarchs will remain united through the bonds of a true and indissoluble brotherhood, viewing each other as compatriots and considering themselves as fathers *vis-à-vis* their subjects and armies, in order to protect religion, peace and justice.[46]

This statement amounts to a mockery of the Rights of Man of a quarter of a century before, which had proclaimed the equality of all men and the general right to freedom. Based on the feudal order of the Holy Roman

Empire, the Constitution of the German Federation (June 1815) was no less reactionary. It exclusively recognized the crowned heads of its thirty-eight individual states as sovereign representatives of their people, ignoring any concept of liberalism or patriotic nationalism. While the kings of Britain, Denmark and the Netherlands were members, vast areas of 'German' territory, particularly in Austria and Prussia, were not represented in the Federation. Its Frankfurt Diet was organized in accordance with pre-revolutionary principles, carefully preserving a balance of power, but oblivious of the emerging political will of the people. Neither Prussia nor Austria introduced regional parliaments or constitutional monarchies and, as will be discussed in the next chapter, patriotic institutions, programmes and demands were suppressed or abolished.

Notes

1 Rudolf Vierhaus, 'Deutsche Urteile über den Ausbruch der Französischen Revolution', in Jürgen Voss ed., *Deutschland und die Französische Revolution* (Munich, 1983), p. 3.

2 Friedrich Gottlieb Klopstock, *Ausgewählte Werke* (Darmstadt, 1969), pp. 142f.

3 Ch. M. Wieland, 'Kosmopolitische Adresse an die französische Nationalversammlung', in B. von Jacobi ed., *Werke*, vol. 10 (Berlin, Leipzig, Vienna, Stuttgart [1900]), pp. 38–57.

4 Vierhaus, 'Deutsche Urteile', p. 7.

5 Staatsanzeiger, vol. 14 (1789), p. 466, n. 4.

6 Goethe's letter to F. H. Jacobi, 3 March 1790, in J. W. von Goethe, *Briefe der Jahre 1786–1814*, Ernst Beutler ed., vol. 19 (Zurich, 1949), p. 159.

7 J. P. Eckermann, *Gespräche mit Goethe*, H. Steger ed. (Munich, 1949), p. 60 [4 January 1824].

8 J. W. von Goethe, *Werke* (Hamburger Ausgabe), 4th edn, vol. 10 (Hamburg, 1972), p. 235.

9 Anna von Šydow ed., *Wilhelm und Caroline von Humboldt in ihren Briefen*, vol. 1 (Berlin, 1906), pp. 49f [letter to Caroline, 4 August 1789].

10 J. H. Campe, *Briefe aus Paris zur Zeit der Revolution* (Braunschweig, 1790), p. 324; in Claus Träger ed., *Die Französische Revolution im Spiegel der deutschen Literatur* (Leipzig, 1975), pp. 184f.

11 F. Schiller, *Werke (Nationalausgabe)*, J. Peterson *et al.* eds, vol. 26 (Weimar, 1992), pp. 170–2, 177–83, 271f [Letters to Körner, 21 December 1792, 8 February 1793, also 17 July 1793].

12 Schiller, *Werke*, vol. 5, 2, pp. 24f. [On the Aesthetic Education of Man, letter 5, trans. by E. M. and L. A. Willoughby].

13 Heinrich Heine, *Sämtliche Werke*, vol. 8, 1 [Düsseldorfer Ausgabe], M. Windfuhr ed. (Hamburg, 1979), p. 82.

14 Ludwig Börne, *Gesammelte Schriften*, vol. 4 (Hamburg/Frankfurt/M., 1862), pp. 315–25.

15 N. Flüeler *et al.* eds, *Die Schweiz vom Bau der Alpen bis zur Frage nach der Zukunft* (Zurich, 1975), pp. 72f.

16 J. G. Fichte, *Briefwechsel, Kritische Gesamtausgabe*, Hans Schulz ed., vol. 1 (Leipzig, 1925), p. 449.

17 A. W. Schlegel and F. Schlegel, *Athenaeum*, Gerda Heinrich ed. (Berlin, 1984), pp. 93f [Fragment Nr. 216].

18 Golo Mann, *Deutsche Geschichte des 19. und 20. Jahrhunderts* (Frankfurt/M., 1969), p. 86.

19 G. R. G. Mure, *The Philosophy of Hegel* (Oxford University Press, 1965), p. 181.

20 Georg Lukács, *Goethe and His Age* (London, 1968), pp. 138 and 177.

21 Träger ed., *Die Französische Revolution*, p. 148.

22 Karl Otmar von Aretin, *Das Reich, Friedensordnung und europäisches Gleichgewicht 1648–1806* (Stuttgart, 1992), p. 30.

23 von Aretin, *Das Reich*, p. 19, but cf. also John G. Gagliardo, *Reich and Nation: The Holy Roman Empire as Idea and Reality 1763–1806* (Bloomington, IN, 1980), p. 127, who quotes several German constitutionalists of the time defending the system, suggesting that the imperial order protected Germans against the two extremes of wealth and poverty.

24 David Blackbourn, *The Fontana History of Germany 1780–1918. The Long Nineteenth Century* (London, 1997), pp. 50f.

25 Gagliardo, *Reich and Nation*, p. 92.

26 James J. Sheehan, *German History 1770–1866* (Oxford, 1989), p. 224.

27 Voss ed., *Deutschland und die französische Revolution*, p. 98.

28 Ibid., p. 115.

29 Quoted after Gagliardo, *Reich and Nation*, p. 56.

30 Note of 19 April 1806, quoted after Gagliardo, *Reich and Nation*, p. 275.

31 R. Vierhaus, 'Politisches Bewußtsein in Deutschland vor 1789', in Helmut Berding and Hans-Peter Ullmann eds, *Deutschland zwischen Revolution und Restauration* (Düsseldorf, 1981), p. 167.

32 Sheehan, *German History*, p. 272.

33 Blackbourn, *Fontana History*, p. 80.

34 Guy Stanton Ford, *Stein and the Era of Reform in Prussia, 1807–1815* (Gloucester, MA, 1965), p. 126.

35 Statement by Minister Johann Struensee, quoted from Sheehan, *German History*, p. 294.

36 Statement by Hardenberg, quoted from Sheehan, *German History*, p. 305.

37 R. Engelsing, *Analphabetentum und Lektüre* (Stuttgart, 1973), p. 127.

38 Sheehan, *German History*, p. 291 and Blackbourn, *Fontana History*, p. 81.

39 Theodor von Schön, quoted from Rassow, *Deutsche Geschichte*, Martin Vogt ed. (Stuttgart, 1987), p. 360.

40 Cf. Christian Engeli and Wolfgang Haus eds, *Quellen zum modernen Gemeindeverfassungsrecht in Deutschland* (Stuttgart, 1975), quoted from Sheehan, *German History*, p. 302.

41 Sheehan, *German History*, p. 307.

42 Quoted from Ford, *Stein and the Era*, p. 123.

43 Cf. Rassow, *Deutsche Geschichte*, p. 356.

44 Cf. Ford, *Stein and the Era*, p. 295.

45 The Prussian army was thus increased from 42,000 to 280,000 men. Cf. Blackbourn, *Fontana History*, p. 88.

46 Quoted from Walter Mönch, *Deutsche Kultur von der Aufklärung bis zur Gegenwart*, 2nd edn (Munich, 1971), p. 258.

Chapter 2

The 'Holy Alliance' and *Vormärz*: the demise of the German *ancien régime* and the preface to the revolutions

Much has been written about the historical origins of revolutions and few commentators can improve on Rudolph Stadelmann's observation that revolutions are not brought about by the suppression of the people, nor by 'structural changes of the old order'.[1] Stadelmann considers the ideological aspect far more important, since 'oppression creates discontent and opposition only where it is perceived as an injustice'.[2] Political awareness has, therefore, to be raised, in order to create the necessary critical analysis of existing social and economic conditions, together with the prospect of their replacement by more satisfactory and promising ones. To take the argument one step further is to understand why revolutions – almost by definition – are normally judged as failures. The search for a more just society and for fairer economic conditions will inevitably involve utopian elements. The intoxicated spirit of optimism which propels the revolution can only give way to the inevitable 'hangover' that follows. Such remarks are not meant to be cynical or pessimistic: a permanent state of elation is neither desirable, nor sustainable, but who could condemn the bacchanalia for the brevity of their exaltations?

The question as to why the 1848 revolutions ended in failure is therefore of little consequence and should be replaced by the consideration of their achievements, in particular as far as the constitution was concerned. The repeated demand for public participation in government, encompassing a desire for democracy and the will to appropriate the new concepts of the Enlightenment and thereby also of modernism, was the single most important issue leading to the revolutions. Economic considerations, whatever their undoubted importance has been for the shaping of modern Germany, must take a secondary place here. While the economic importance of the railways for efficient communication and transport should not be underestimated, they were no less significant as a potent symbol of the new progressive age. The economic crises of the 1840s, too, were less notable for the misery and starvation which they inflicted than for the growing awareness which they inspired, that a different political order might provide a better outcome.[3]

These introductory remarks are intended to map out the direction to be followed in this chapter: the interrelationship between a rather backward social and economic situation within the German Confederation and an increasing perception of this socio-economic *malheur*, alongside a new understanding of its political causes. Such an approach is more in line with Hegelian than with Marxist philosophy, giving priority to the spirit rather than to its material foundation. Wolfram Siemann relates the European revolutions to four causes: middle-class demands for political participation, the growing desire for national self-determination, the pre-industrial crisis in the crafts exacerbated by a rapid population growth and the agrarian problems between 1845–7.[4] This chapter will cover these topics in a slightly different form: the first two issues will be subsumed in a study of the nature of the German Confederation, while the two remaining points will be investigated in particular relation to Berlin, the Rhineland and southwest Germany. A final section will discuss the unrest during 1830 in other parts of Europe, notably Switzerland, which impacted more heavily on the German situation than any other European country.

The German Confederation, a battle-ground for forces of reaction and modernization

Napoleon's defeat sowed the seeds of conflict among the victorious powers. The more progressive elements within Prussia, associated with Stein, as well as politicians from the former Rhenish Confederation and a majority of the German intelligentsia found themselves in opposition to the forces of reaction, embodied in the Holy Alliance of the sovereigns of Russia, Austria and Prussia.

The Congress of Vienna, pre-revolutionary in nature and dominated by crowned heads and their personal political advisers, favoured these reactionary forces. The Congress was in the last throes of absolutism, its *ancien* nature measurable by the spectacular nature of its intrigues and cabals and by the very manner in which whole territories and peoples changed 'ownership'.[5] The decisions taken at Vienna reflected in every respect the spirit of eighteenth-century absolutism: territory was divided up among the victorious nations regardless of linguistic and cultural ties, with major players such as France and Britain anxiously preserving a balance of power in order to further their own imperial interests, with scant regard for the modernizing tendencies which the French Revolution and the wars against Napoleon had fostered. Metternich's declared aim was to prop up 'rotten buildings',[6] considering any new departure from time-honoured practice as revolutionary. The English Tory, Sir Thomas Cartwright, British ambassador at the Frankfurt Diet, established in 1815, remarked that the very word 'revolutionary', as used by members of the Diet, 'is often applied to every opinion indiscriminately which is not strictly in unison with . . . the Austrian system'.[7]

The more progressive statesmen and activists such as Stein and Humboldt found themselves little more than bystanders. The Romantic historian and scholar Joseph Görres criticized the emerging political order as a deplorable, misshapen, unrepresentative monstrosity, created by expediency rather than design.[8] Two aspects, in particular, were actively discouraged.

The voice of the people The concept of a people's army (*Bürgerwehr*) had fired the popular imagination, as a Prussian equivalent to the revolutionary *levée en masse*. Whatever its actual military impact, and granting that it lagged far behind its French equivalent, it was, nevertheless, perceived as a very popular uprising in German history, well documented in popular literature.[9] The fame of the *Lützow* Free Corps lived on in student associations and such militias were to play an important role during the 1848 revolutions. These popular aspirations were bitterly disappointed by the settlement at the Congress. Although the actual *Bundesakte* (1815) produced a confederation of German states, its Article Thirteen stipulated that every federal state had to introduce a constitution based on corporate principles.[10] This clause was disregarded by Austria and Prussia, causing perhaps the most serious discontent prior to 1848.

The patriotic and national issue The divisions of Italy and Poland were seen as anachronisms, reflecting the very nature of the Habsburg Empire, its multinational make-up no longer corresponding to a new landscape and failing to respond to the aspirations of those of its subjects who had fought for Germany's liberation from Napoleon. The patriotic agenda had been undermined at the Congress: von Stein's plan for a 'Third Germany' had been rejected; instead, Hardenberg's Forty-One Articles had been adapted by Metternich, removing the proposal for an independent court of law and diluting national representation at Frankfurt. The kings of England, Denmark and the Netherlands were among the thirty-eight potentates of the Confederation who exercised power, while the suggested bicameral representation was shelved. Austria held the chair of the Diet and remained the strongest force. Essentially, the Confederation was even weaker than the old Empire; it had no central executive power, had lost all its *Reich* territory and was seen by the people not to reflect their aspirations for a German nation state. For Humboldt and many other patriots the end result was a shadow of what had been hoped for.[11]

The history of the Confederation can broadly be divided into two halves: the period from its inception to the outbreak of the July Revolution (1815–30) and the subsequent period until 1848.[12] The first stage was particularly reactionary in nature, with Metternich in the ascendancy until 1818, and Austria maintaining her strong position despite declining support from Western powers. After 1830 there was a weakening of Austria's influence and a strengthening of Prussia's role, with tensions between Austria and various smaller German states and the re-emergence of the national issue.

The period of reaction (1815–30)

Even a cursory glance at these events (table 2.1) will illustrate the major tendencies of the period, as well as their interrelationships. Liberal forces united against Metternich's oppressive system: students, university teachers, journalists and individuals from every range of the middle-class spectrum united in demanding more freedom. The Italian *Risorgimento* was in permanent conflict with Austria, even during its struggles with Pope Gregory XVI and the Vatican. Austrian suppression of Italians, Poles and Belgians enraged German democrats, who already saw Austria and her allies as oppressors of their own national sovereignty. When the Schleswig–Holstein crisis broke (1844), the nationality issue centred on German-speaking territories, and, although hostilities did not break out until 1848, the existing political tension found the widest resonance throughout Germany, in particular at singing festivals (*Sängerfeste*) in Würzburg (1845), Cologne (1846) and Lubeck (1847).[13]

Space permits only a brief discussion of the two related aspects, the constitutional issue and the Prussian Customs Union (*Zollverein*). The first modern constitution within Germany had been introduced in Westphalia (1807), under the influence of Napoleon, who saw this as a means of deterring its citizens from ever wishing to return to the stringent Prussian rule.[14] The constitution replaced the old feudal order, introduced nominal equality before the law, ended serfdom and centralized power, and though not unchallenged,[15] it became an important reference point during the Pre-March period. After 1815 new constitutions were adopted in most other states of the former Rhenish Confederation, notably in Baden, Württemberg and Bavaria. Baden acquired a model constitution, taking the advice of, amongst others, the liberal Freiburg constitutionalist Karl Rotteck:[16] its lower house was based on the representation of individuals, not 'communities' (*Stände*) as was usually the case. Elections were held via electors (*Wahlmänner*) and candidates had to prove that they were in receipt of a certain level of income. In the upper house, however, prominence was given to corporate institutions and in particular to the old nobility. In most other states elections were

Table 2.1 Table of events, 1814–47

	Participants	Events	Results
Nov. 1814–June 1815	Russia, Prussia, Austria, France, Britain, most smaller German states	Vienna Congress	Return to pre-revolutionary positions, but no restitution of ecclesiastical and *Reich* territory.
8/6/1815	Austria, Prussia, Hanover, Bavaria, Württemberg	Setting up constitution for German Confederation (*Bundesakte*)	Confederation of 39 (later 41) independent sovereign states to maintain foreign and interior security of Germany and to guarantee the states' inviolability.
7/8/1815	Switzerland	Dissolution of *Mediationsakte* and replacement by *Bundesvertrag*	A return to a more reactionary, less liberal form of government.
18/10/1817	*Burschenschaften*, in part. Jena branch	Wartburg Festival	Demand for a German fatherland, for freedom, against resolutions of Vienna Congress and against German Confederation.
May 1816	Saxony-Weimar, Karl-August	Liberal constitution	Corporate representation in parliament, equality before the law.
Aug. 1818	Baden, Ludwig	Lib. constitution	Taxation via parliament, equality before the law, following the pattern of most German constitutions.
1818	Bavaria	Lib. constitution	Equality before law, freedom of conscience, introduction of corporate principles.
1819	Württemberg, William I	Lib. constitution	Constitutional monarchy.
Sept. 1819	German Federation: Metternich	Karlsbad Decrees	Suppression of academic freedom, disbanding of *Burschenschaften* and *Turner*, persecution of 'demagogues'.
July 1820	German Federation: Metternich	*Wiener Schlußakte*	Federal laws enjoy priority over laws of individual states. Federal intervention in case of political disorder.

Table 2.1 (cont'd)

	Participants	Events	Results
July 1820	Carbonari, Ferdinand I, Austria	Uprising in Naples	Austrian provinces threatened by unrest in Sicily and Sardinia.
1820	Ferdinand VII of Spain	Absolutist reign	Abolition of Cortes, return of Jesuits.
Jan. 1821	Austria, Ferdinand I	Congress of Laibach	Abolition of Sardinian/Sicilian constitution, absolutist reign of Ferdinand I.
March 1821	Radetzky, Carbonari	Battle of Rieti, rebellion in Milan	Defeat of Carbonari, return of Ferdinand I to Naples.
1822	Holy Alliance, France *et al.*	Congress of Verona	Complete re-establishment of Ferdinand VII.
1822	Metternich, versus Wangenheim, Württemberg	Metternich memorandum	Isolation of Württemberg within German Confederation because of its liberal policies.
Nov. 1825	Russia (Tsar Nicholas I)	Rebellion of Decembrists	Defeat and punishment of rebellious liberal officers, return to absolutism.
1821–29	Greece, Turkey *et al.*	Greek War of Independence	Turkish defeat at Navarino (1827), setting up of Greek monarchy (1832), death of Lord Byron (1824).
July 1830	France ➤ Europe	July Revolution	Charles X deposed, reign of Louis Philippe.
July 1830	Aachen, Berlin, Breslau, Hamburg	Civil unrests	Minor skirmishes of police with demonstrators (journeymen, some workers).
August 1830	Belgium, Holland	Uprising against Dutch rule	Independence of Belgium under Leopold of Saxony-Coburg, very liberal constitution.
Summer 1830	Swiss Protestant cantons	Demonstrations	Introduction of liberal constitutions in 11 cantons.
Sept. 1830	William II (Hesse-Kassel)	Civil unrest in Kassel	Introduction of liberal constitution.
Oct. 1830	Charles III of Brunswick	Revolution	Burning down of royal palace, Charles III replaced by his brother William.
Nov. 1830	Poland, Russia	Warsaw Uprising	Nicholas I defeats Polish revolutionaries (25/2/1831) and abolishes Polish independence.

Table 2.1 (cont'd)

	Participants	Events	Results
8/1/1831	Hanover, Göttingen University	Protests	For a liberal democracy, 1833 introduction of liberal constitution.
Feb. 1831	Carbonari; Bologna, Parma	Confrontation with France	Restitution of Vatican state, strengthening of reactionary forces.
Sept. 1831	Saxony: Frederick August II	Civil unrest	Unrest in industrial towns, change of government, introduction of liberal constitution.
27/5/1832	Students, journeymen	Hambach Festival	Protests against Metternich and German Federation; solidarity with France, Poland, Greece, Italy. Demands for a united German fatherland.
April 1833	Frankfurt: radical students	Civil unrest	Attempted storming of Frankfurt Assembly, arrest of revolutionaries by Federal forces.
1837	Göttingen University	The Göttingen Seven	Abolition of Hanover constitution by Ernst August; seven leading professors are sacked and expelled from Hanover.
1832–4	Portugal	Civil war	Economic depression, introduction of constitutional monarchy.
1833–9	Spain	Civil war	Introduction of liberal reforms.
1840	Frederick William IV of Prussia	Accession to Prussian throne	Liberal policies, professorships for patriotic professors, reform plans for a German Federation.
1832–47	Switzerland	Sonderbund	Seven liberal cantons versus Catholic, reactionary cantons.
March 1845	Sonderbund versus Freisinnige	Battle of Maltes	Defeat of liberal troops by Sonderbund during seige of Lucerne.
Nov. 1847	Sonderbund versus Freisinnige	Battle of Giesilikon	Defeat and dissolution of Sonderbund. Introduction of modern liberal constitution for Swiss Federation.

even less 'democratic'. The upper chamber usually consisted of the nobility, the higher echelons of the clergy and of appointed academics. While there was nominal equality before the law, special rights and privileges frequently qualified it. Although public expenditure and certain legislative powers were in the hands of parliament, in every case the sovereign's power remained virtually undivided and undiminished. By the 1830s most member states of the Confederation, with the exception of Austria and Prussia, had adopted fairly liberal constitutions. Austria was by far the least liberal state, aptly described as Europe's China,[17] since censorship laws ensured that she remained insulated from her more liberal neighbours. It was Metternich's declared aim to exclude the estates (*Landstände*) from all constitutional issues, thereby retaining the opportunity of playing one group off against another. Power remained in the hands of the state council, a quasi-absolutist *camera*, answerable only to the emperor.[18]

The situation in Prussia was less autocratic, partly because of recent memories of the popular uprising against Napoleon, but more particularly because of Prussia's attempt to initiate a Customs Union, which involved a more conciliatory attitude towards those constitutional states which might otherwise have been wary of a closer union with Prussia. Hardenberg, Gneisenau and Humboldt favoured this more liberal stance, while Stein shared some of Metternich's misgivings regarding any change in the role of the estates.[19] During the Congress of Vienna, King Frederick William III had proposed a constitutional commission to consider the formation of 'a representative organ of the people', whereby provincial delegates would elect a representative state body in Berlin, consisting of civil servants and elected deputies from the estates. However, after 1815 the king seemed to forget his promise and, under the influence of his more reactionary counsellors and the *Junkers*, the issue was allowed to lapse. In his capacity as minister for estate affairs (*ständische Angelegenheiten*) Humboldt produced a memorandum in which he outlined his concept of a constitution.[20] When his plans were rejected, not least because of the intervention of Metternich, who feared that they might incite revolution, Humboldt felt compelled to tender his resignation. Nevertheless, the Prussian administration benefited from the quality of its civil servants, prompting the liberal historian B. G. Niebuhr to suggest that 'freedom depends much more on the administration than the constitution'.[21] This observation is perhaps less contradictory than it might at first sound. The German concept of a fair and competent administration, of *Rechtsstaatlichkeit*, goes back to the Prussia of Frederick the Great. Indeed, several scholars have pointed out that the majority of German states were not significantly less advanced in this area of political culture than other European states, including Britain.[22] A fair and incorruptible administration shared the major aims of an elected government in limiting the arbitrary rule of the sovereign and curbing the special privileges of elites and institutions. Higher civil servants gained advanced conditions of service, rendering them secure from monarchic whims. As James J. Sheehan put it: 'The emergence of constitutional government and the consolidation of bureaucratic authority were part of the same historical process, frequently advocated by the same people, opposed by the same enemies, and seeking to advance the same goals.'[23] In this sense, Prussia's bureaucratic regeneration accomplished a political revolution which transformed a society of subjects into one of citizens. While these observations on the prevailing conditions in Prussia are certainly accurate, the reactionary period between 1815 and 1830 saw an inevitable deterioration of the administration, emphasizing the interrelationship between constitution and government. In addition, the Prussian civil service was largely taken over by aristocrats and this may further explain the fury of the liberals at the king's failure to honour his promise of a constitution. Similar observations apply to Austria, except that her *camera* administration was even more pronounced. As a consequence, 'deep pessimism crippled the most able officials' pleasure in their work, formalistic routine and a reluctance to take responsibility triumphed'.[24] The success of Prussia and Austria in over-riding the constitutional issue was sealed at the Congress of Aachen, but their reactionary opposition to the dominant issue of the age was doomed to end in defeat.

From reaction to protest: the role of the intelligentsia

The role of the intelligentsia was particularly crucial in maintaining support for the constitutional issue. The general unrest and disappointment which marked the period between 1815 and 1848 owes much to the prevailing hostility of the intelligentsia to the outcome of the Congress of Vienna. While it has become fashionable to play down the intellectual input during this phase, the testimony of both supporters and opponents seems to paint a different picture. Among the latter was the Prussian historian Heinrich von Treitschke, who commented on the 'Romantic' period, suggesting that 'German liberalism sprang, not from the class interests of the wealthy and self-conscious bourgeoisie, but from the academic ideas of the professors'.[25] Frederick William IV was even more damning; in his eyes elementary school teachers had caused the revolution:

> All the misery that has come upon Prussia during the bygone year is your fault alone, the fault of pseudo-education, of irreligious mass-knowledge, intended to eradicate faithfulness from the minds of my subjects and to turn their hearts against me. I am not afraid of the gutter, but I do fear the unholy doctrines of a modern and frivolous world-wisdom with which you poison and undermine my bureaucracy which has hitherto been my pride and joy.[26]

Historians tend to divide this period between the rather sentimental and historically minded bourgeois years of the *Biedermeier* and the more progressive, forward looking pre-revolutionary time of the Pre-March *(Vormärz)*. Two historical events will serve as an illustration of each period: the *Wartburg* Festival (1817), backward-looking and romantic in nature, and the *Hambach* Festival (1832), forward-looking and progressive in tone. Generations of historians, guided by monarchical or anti-republican sentiments, seemed to play down the importance of a wider academic input to the upheavals of this period; the re-appraisal of the intellectual role was to the merit of East German historians.[27] From the mid 1960s, West German historians and literary critics also began to address these matters in an attempt to revise the franco-phobe, nationalist and anti-republican interpretations of previous generations.

Earlier forms of intellectual opposition to the Confederation had their origins in the patriotic struggle against Napoleon, tending to foster a strong nationalist bent and harking back to the lost Holy Roman Empire. One such group, associated with the famous 'Turnvater' Jahn, became known as the *Burschenschaften*. This national student fraternity was reconstituted from existing regional fraternities (*Landsmannschaften*) in June 1815 and originated at Jena, a university long associated with Romantic philosophy and politics. It marked a protest against the emerging nature of the German Confederation, which was seen as a betrayal of the national issue. The fraternity supported the democratic sentiments of Fichte, Arndt, Jahn and other romantic patriotic writers and raised the national tricolour of black, red and gold. The *Wartburg* Festival, celebrating the tercentenary of Luther's Reformation and the fourth anniversary of the battle at Leipzig, was their high point. Recalling Luther's burning of the papal bull, demonstrators burnt their own symbols of oppression: an Austrian corporal's baton, a Hesse pigtail, a Prussian uniform, several books by reactionary authors and a copy of the final declaration of the Congress of Vienna. The demonstrators displayed a strange mixture of enlightened eighteenth-century attitudes and romantic irrational sentiments. In the context of the festival, the *Burschenschaften* published their 'principles and conclusions'. These aimed to enlighten their fellow citizens about the true nature of the fatherland and the state of public affairs, 'to purify and strengthen their minds for nation and fatherland' and bring about a new awareness of 'morality, politics and history'.[29] A minority of students and young intellectuals abandoned such romantic notions: the Gießen University law tutor Karl Follen spoke up for a democratic nation state wedded to the principles of the French Revolution, including the concept of political assassination.[30] Such ideas motivated the Jena theology student Karl Sand to murder the reactionary writer August von Kotzebue (March 1819), who had mocked the national movement and was widely suspected of being a Russian spy. The implications of this murder, together with the *Wartburg* Festival, provoked a major backlash. Metternich summoned delegates to a Confederation meeting at Karlsbad, where a comprehensive system of censorship and university controls were imposed. An official was appointed to each university, responsible for 'the strictest enforcement of existing law and disciplinary instructions'.[31] Individual governments were obliged to expel subversive university teachers and students, who were denied re-entry to other universities. The *Burschenschaften* were declared illegal and censorship was strengthened by a subsequent law which decreed that every document of less than twenty sheets had to be examined.[32] The climax of such reactionary policies and of Metternich's influence was the Vienna Convention (*Wiener Schlußakte*), accepted by the German Diet in July 1820. By granting the Confederation the right of intervention in order to safeguard public order (Article 26) it limited the autonomy of individual states and restricted individual state constitutions (Article 58). Once again the constitutional issue was of paramount concern, as the English delegate reported to foreign secretary Castlereagh:

> Such is the effect of hope completely frustrated hitherto, and of the non-accomplishment of the promise of a representative constitution, solemnly given to them in the hour of danger to lead them to efforts, which they made as zealously, as successfully.[33]

The intellectual and political climate changed after the French July Revolution. The views of independent writers, academics and some university professors assumed greater prominence. Romantic nostalgia gave way to more direct political agitation. The nature of the new literature adopted a more specific tone:

> Our faith is at one with the faith of mankind; fine talk and sweet dreams are over. . . . I wanted to write about literature and have begun with politics. Of course! It is the defining mark of modern literature that it is the child of politics, or, in plain German, the child of the French July Revolution.[34]

The earlier dominance of beauty and truth over political reality met with increasing scepticism, as did Hegel's formula of the unity of reason and reality. This general move away from imaginative subjectivity towards material objectivity became an important topic for philosophy and literature. The new generation, no longer captivated by the beautiful, the heroic and the ingenious, turned their attention instead to the ugly, unwashed and exploited proletarian, often anticipating the growing power of the working classes. Ferdinand Freiligrath foresaw the new potential of the fourth estate:

> We are the power! Our hammers will rejuvenate this old and rotten thing, the state,
> We who till now, by God's wrath, are the proletariat![35]

What at first appeared to be the familiar ground of academic debate was soon to acquire eminent political significance. As Karl Marx was to put it: 'Philosophers hitherto have only interpreted the world, the point is, however, to change it.'[36] The time had come for writers to put their words into action. No longer content to look backwards, their new journals were forward-looking, with such titles as *The New Century* or *Young Europe* and they themselves were labelled as the 'Young Germany', a new generation who welcomed the new age of technology and the advent of the railway.

At the same time, a more moderate climate emerged from within the universities. This liberal faction was positioned between the conservative camp of Carl Ludwig von Haller, Adam Müller and the Gerlach brothers and the radical wing of the Young Germany movement and the growing working-class movement of Wilhelm Weitling. Karl Theodor Welcker, professor of constitutional law at Heidelberg and editor of the popular *Staatslexikon,* described the 1830s as a distinctly political period, requiring the establishment of corporate bodies capable of participating in state politics. This liberal movement extended across the Confederation and gained vital stimuli from France and Switzerland.

The *Hambach* Festival exemplified this new political atmosphere; it not only embodied the political and liberal response to the French July Revolution and political unrest in Aachen, Berlin, Hamburg, Hesse and Brunswick, but also became the organized focus of a new international dawn. The fresh interest in international affairs also inspired a new patriotism, voiced by Johann Georg Wirth, the chief organizer of the festival, and echoed in the speech of Philip Jakob Siebenpfeiffer, a tailor's son, Baden civil servant and a much under-rated political poet:

> We shall help to free Greece from her tyrannical yoke, we toast the re-emergence of Poland and we become angry when the despotism of kings cripples the fervour of the peoples of Spain, Italy and France, we anxiously watch the progress of the Reform Bill in England, we praise the strength and wisdom of the Sultan who is involved in the rebirth of his people, we envy the North Americans their good fortune, which they themselves have bravely brought about.[37]

The major cause of the Hambach demonstration was an increase in press censorship, an issue which in progressive circles had long been considered an anachronism. The governments of Bavaria, Württemberg and Baden had taken a fairly relaxed attitude to existing censorship laws, but, after the French July Revolution, these attitudes hardened. The ensuing clash between the Confederation and its three dissenting states developed into a conflict over the old monarchic principles and the new liberal and constitutional ideas. The English delegate at the Frankfurt Diet saw that demands for an 'unrestricted press in Germany has now become a cry for Revolution' and advocated instead some other restrictive measures to inhibit the ultimate aim of the liberal opposition, 'the Unity of Germany with republican Institutions'.[38] The impact of the *Hambach* Festival unnerved the Bavarian government, who sent half its army, some 8,500 troops, to the Palatinate in order to quell the unrest. The 30,000 participants, nearly half of whom were students and professors, but also including many craftsmen and businessmen, were subject to a wave of persecutions and a wholesale political news blackout was imposed within the Confederation. At Metternich's behest the Confederation established a Central Bureau of Political Investigation and called upon the Holy Alliance to renew its stance against revolutionary unrest. Although these measures intimidated the smaller states within the Confederation, they failed to subdue the population at large. A politically active public mind had become established, industrial and commercial leaders, 'who had found their ideas and their railroads obstructed'[39] by the old traditions, were demanding a more progressive, liberal climate and ordinary people began to join with the new spirit of political dissent.

Two further incidents may illustrate how constitutional violations, though technically restricted to individual states, could take on a national significance. Queen Victoria's accession to the British throne (1837) severed the union between the crowns of England and Hanover. When Ernst August, Duke of Cumberland, succeeded in Hanover, he suspended the liberal constitution of 1833 in favour of a personal oath of allegiance. The resulting protests, particularly at the University of Göttingen, led to the dismissal of seven eminent professors, 'The Göttingen Seven', amongst them Gervinus, Dahlmann and the Grimm brothers. This repressive move resulted in a nationwide wave of sympathy for the professors; funds were raised on their behalf and the university of Königsberg awarded honorary doctorates to two of their number.

Within the same year a constitutional conflict involving the catholic church threatened the peace of the Prussian Rhine province. The Prussian authorities intervened in an internal catholic dispute, anticipating Bismarck's *Kulturkampf* of the 1870s. Adhering to a papal decree on mixed marriages, the Archbishop of Cologne, Freiherr von Droste-Vischering, had renounced a secret arrangement between his predecessor and the Prussian government. He was arrested and charged with high treason but, again, a national wave of protests forced the Prussian government to agree to far-reaching concessions.

Religious strife

Religious controversy was to play a major role during the Pre-March period, with the churches supporting both reactionary and liberal factions. The state church of Prussia was protestant and, with a predominantly catholic

Rhineland Westphalia, conflicts such as that over Archbishop Droste-Vischering were not uncommon. His distant relative, the poetess Annette von Droste-Hülshoff, witnessed a riot in Münster, where the Prussian army attempted to subdue thousands of stone-throwing citizens, chanting 'down with Prussia' and 'long live the archbishop'.[40]

The protestants themselves were deeply divided. The neo-conservative, protestant orthodox wing became the focus of all reactionary tendencies, adhering closely to Luther's doctrine of the church's subordination to the state. The mouthpiece of this reactionary faction was the editor of the *Evangelische Kirchenzeitung*, Berlin theology professor Ernst Wilhelm von Hengstenberg, a close friend of the crown prince with direct links to his *camarilla*. His staunchly anti-liberal, anti-rational circle opposed any form of constitutionalism and promoted a fiercely anti-Jewish hate campaign, accusing Jews, as well as catholics, pantheists and atheists, of Jacobin revolutionary activities.[41] The opposing faction consisted largely of young-Hegelian intellectuals who influenced the wider liberal wing of protestantism. Best known amongst them was David Friedrich Strauß whose *Life of Jesus* (1835) contained strong anti-orthodox elements which revolutionized theology. Others in the same mould were Bruno Bauer and Ludwig Feuerbach, who added a secular and, more importantly, a politically radical dimension to protestantism. Loosely associated with these liberal groups were the *Lichtfreunde*, 'Association of Protestant Friends', who gained strong support among the protestant laity in Prussia. By 1845 feelings had become so strong that the Berlin City Council presented a petition to the king, accusing the church's orthodox wing of a 'hypocritical presumptuousness and thirst for power' which threatened to turn religion into an '*instrumentum regni*'.[42]

The catholics were no less divided, though their reactionary wing was more associated with Vatican policies than predominantly German matters. Although Archbishop Droste-Vischering initially enjoyed little public support, the situation changed when his cause was taken up by bishops elsewhere. Some catholic German states, notably Bavaria, used this incident to express anti-Prussian sentiments, but soon found themselves in opposition to the liberal wing of catholicism. The latter were based within the *Deutsch-Katholiken* (German catholics), who, like the *Lichtfreunde*, found broad support amongst the lower middle classes. These German catholics resented papal authority and rejected 'superstitious' practices such as pilgrimages and the devotion to saintly relics. Particularly prominent in the Rhineland, with centres in Bonn and Trier, they also had supporters in Baden, as evident in the Offenburg dispute over the dismissal of Professor Kuhn, a disciple of Carl von Rotteck.[43] The liberal wings of protestantism and catholicism alike tried to play down doctrinal differences, being tolerant on the issue of mixed marriages and seeking links with the emancipated Jewry. Such dissent found an echo among other disaffected social groups, especially among middle-class activists and within journeymen associations, as a wider political awareness continued to develop.

The 'Young Germany' writer and critic Ludwig Börne observed that the writer was some kind of mediator, moving radical intellectual ideas on to a wider public platform, thereby creating the preconditions for revolution.[44] Whatever the validity of Börne's view, there can be no doubt that a wider dissemination of the critical views of the intelligentsia was necessary in order to harness the growing political awareness in Germany:

> The accession in 1840 of Frederick William IV, of whom liberal reforms had been expected, had brought only renewed disappointment. From that point on, the necessity for political action became continually more urgent for Germans. . . . they had no parliament, no trial by jury, no rights of free speech or assembly; and the new king . . . made it quite plain that he would give them none of these things.[45]

Although educated middle-class Germans, known as *Bildungsbürger*, were not renowned for their political astuteness, their continuous insistence on the constitutional issue and on political participation provided a wider public with a topic, which was of such universal relevance, that it became part of a common platform. The constitutional issue culminated in the basic demands of March 1848, including the right to a constitution based on popular suffrage, press freedom and on a clear division between the judiciary and the administration.

The nationality issue and the formation of political groups

Even the complex national unity issue revolved around the constitutional nature of the Confederation. Uprisings in Poland, Greece, Italy and Spain, all of which involved member states of the Confederation, had a profound impact on public opinion and sharpened national awareness. France's revival of old claims to German territory left of the Rhine in 1840 provoked fierce anti-French sentiments. The fanatically patriotic songs of Nikolaus Becker, Max Schneckenberger and Ernst-Moritz Arndt were popular throughout Germany, much to the dismay of German exiles such as Heine, Herwegh, Ruge and others. Although Hoffmann von Fallersleben's *Lied der Deutschen*, adopted as Germany's national anthem in 1922, falls into this context, his liberal and democratic tone indicates a critical attitude towards the more hysterical forms of nationalism. The populist nationalist movement gained further support in 1842 from an association formed to complete the building of Cologne cathedral, which had remained unfinished since 1248. For a time the whole movement led to a somewhat more liberal climate in Prussia, to a relaxation of censorship, to the establishment of newspapers such as the *Rheinische Zeitung* and the *Königsberger Zeitung* and to a revival of Gymnasts' Associations (*Turnerschaften*). It was a period of festivities throughout Germany, usually commemorating national heroes or heroic events: Gutenberg's invention of modern printing was celebrated in Mainz (1837), Schiller was celebrated in Stuttgart (1839), Dürer in Nuremberg (1840), Bach in Leipzig (1843), Goethe in Frankfurt (1844) and even the victory of the Germanic prince, Arminius, over the Romans (9 AD) was commemorated at Detmold in 1840. These national celebrations culminated in the *Deutsche Sängerfest* of 1845. This took place against the background of the Schleswig–Holstein crisis, which became a catalyst for a wider national movement that no longer recognized the political make-up of the Confederation and was particularly seized upon by liberals and democrats such as the *Hallgarten* circle in southwest Germany.

By the autumn of 1847 quasi-political parties began to emerge, initially confined to the southwest, with a democratic association in Offenburg and a liberal one in Heppenheim. As political associations within the Confederation were illegal, they continued to assume the guise of gymnastic and cultural associations.[46] Membership was largely from the upper middle classes, with a high proportion of academics, civil servants, businessmen and guild officials.[47] They moved into the political sphere in the hope that their own interests would be promoted by a democratic and prosperous society, no longer restricted by petty privileges and officious regulations. Journalists and political radicals often criticized them for lack of real political involvement, a preoccupation with political rhetoric rather than action. Such criticism failed to recognize the momentum of industrialization and the growing political influence of a modern bourgeoisie. A good example of this is the Berlin *Bürgergesellschaft* of 1846, whose official aims were described as the 'promotion of intellectual and social contact of the citizens of Berlin'.[48] While many left-wing liberals supported the society, the police watched its activities nervously, particularly suspicious of any discussions of a social or economic nature. After only a few weeks the society was banned and attempts to gain a new licence failed. Not even the Berlin police, however, could stop the promotion of public lectures on broader aspects of public concern.

In the southwest, the liberal bourgeoisie deflected the cruder forms of nationalism into regionalism and also opted for economic unification as a prerequisite to national union. Public houses became important venues for clubs and associations, perhaps best known was the *Salmen* in Offenburg, where the 'Constitutional Friends' of Baden met in September 1847. Under the direction of Struve and Hecker, they published the Offenburg Programme, with demands such as the abolition of the *Karlsbad* Decrees, complete press freedom, academic freedom, parliamentary control of the army, freedom of assembly and a constitution with far-reaching democratic rights.[49]

In Baden the development of political parties was more focused than elsewhere in Germany, her proximity to France and Switzerland being of some, though not exclusive, importance. More recent research has indicated that the formation of parties with specific programmes was more widespread than hitherto assumed, not only in the major centres of political activity (Vienna, Berlin, Frankfurt), but also in the provinces.[50] The popularity of such political centres and meeting places is evident, indicating the existence of a high degree of often rather sophisticated political awareness.[51] The programme of the Heppenheim liberals in the southwest (October 1847) contained all the elements of a party-political programme and was also openly revolutionary in its rejection of the German Confederation, believing that the economic ties of a Customs Union would result in a strong and united Germany.[52]

The re-emerging Gymnasts' Associations now broadened their base to include craftsmen and clerical workers. In the Rhineland, Carnival Associations seceded from their more conservative central organizations to develop democratic and revolutionary concepts.[53] Secret communist cells were formed in the Rhine and Main regions, establishing contacts with more radical branches in Paris, Brussels and London.

Another politically active force was the militia. In contrast to the conservative, strictly monarchist veteran associations, these civil guards (*Bürgerwehren*) were more liberal in outlook, especially in the southwest. Recruited from among 'well established citizens, experienced in the use of weapons',[54] they had originally been established as a police force to stem civil unrest. The militias in Prussia were often of a rather more conservative nature, becoming politically active only after March 1848.

Political literature during the *Vormärz*

Newspapers and pamphlets played a major role in the development of political awareness with attitudes towards censorship changing rapidly within the period 1830–48. The 'Sixty Articles' of 1834 had given censorship a high priority: individual states were advised to restrict the number of political papers and to be alert to printed material in German published outside the Confederation. The availability of foreign language publications was restricted.

The official authorities need not have feared an imminent revolutionary uprising. Georg Büchner's famous *Der Hessische Landbote*, distributed in 1834, failed to make an impact on the peasants of Hesse who simply handed over the pamphlets to the police. Büchner himself only narrowly escaped arrest; his collaborator Pastor Weidig was detained and the Human Rights Society (*Menschenrechtsgesellschaft*) was banned. Despite such censorship, the public appetite for printed materials rose. Between 1821 and 1840 book publications in Prussia increased by 150 per cent; even newspapers such as the rather mundane *Vossische Zeitung* managed to double in circulation and small provincial papers were prepared to get involved in 'political agitation'.[55] Many writers avoided the censorship laws by adopting more devious methods. Karl Gutzkow, censored as a member of Young Germany, advised Büchner to escape the shotgun barrel of the censor by smuggling out his ideas on freedom.[56] Some cities, such as Leipzig, which depended on the book trade, gained the reputation of operating a rather liberal censorship. In many police states, censors could be by-passed or duped, and writers, publishers and booksellers perfected the art of remaining one step ahead of the authorities. The Swiss publishers Schlöpfer and Fröbel were particularly effective in disseminating banned literature across the German border, including Hoffmann von Fallersleben's *Lied der Deutschen*.[57] By the end of the 1830s censorship had lost much of its effectiveness. Arnold Ruge's radical *Hallische Jahrbücher für deutsche Wissenschaft und Kunst* went into publication in 1838, followed in 1842 by Marx's *Rheinische Zeitung*. Both papers were frequently censored, but not before their contents had been widely circulated. Georg Gervinus' *Deutsche Zeitung*, published in Heidelberg in 1845, gained wide support among liberals and became an important medium for democratic politics. In the southwest, Heidelberg, Mannheim and Konstanz established themselves as important publishing centres. The *Mannheimer Abendzeitung*, Gustav Struve's *Deutscher Zuschauer* and Joseph Fickler's *Seeblätter* in Konstanz had a deep impact on the region, strongly influencing the Offenburg Declaration of September 1847.[58]

The contribution of journeymen and industrialists provides another element in the pre-revolutionary climate. A recognition of the political maturity of this group and of the impact of journeymen's writings can be deduced by a Confederation decree (January 1835), forbidding them to travel into areas of political unrest. One paragraph states explicitly that 'strict police surveillance' will be exercised over travelling journeymen, 'especially with regard to their associations'.[59] Journeymen's logbooks and personal effects were often examined; in 1844 seventy-nine journeymen, returning from Switzerland to Heilbronn, were questioned and investigated regarding 'communist ideas'.[60] The life of the average journeyman was hard, only a minority of them managed to become master craftsmen and own their business. A humorous, but socially accurate description of the lives of journeymen is given in Gottfried Keller's short story *Die drei gerechten Kammacher* (1855). Even master craftsmen often lived in great poverty; in

Baden only 9 per cent had any capital of their own and could afford to employ a journeyman.[61] In rural areas they usually owned smallholdings and supplemented their income through subsistence farming. It was the established practice for journeymen to travel during the summer months, providing the opportunity to become familiar with political and social conditions beyond their own regions. Journeymen in particular trades seemed more aware than others: tailors, silk weavers and vintners tended to be better informed than carpenters and masons.

Of particular importance was Wilhelm Weitling (1808–71), a tailor journeyman from Magdeburg whose travels took him to France where he made contact with German exiles. He joined their *Bund der Gerechten* and wrote his best-known book, *Die Menschheit wie sie ist und wie sie sein sollte*. He spent much of his time in Switzerland, where he was imprisoned, expelled to Prussia and subsequently moved to London and Brussels, where he met Karl Marx. Like so many other revolutionaries, he ended his life as an immigrant in the United States. Influenced less by Marx than by Proudhon and by fundamentalist protestant sects, he gave priority to the destruction of the existing social and economic order rather than to the development of a new utopian society. Weitling's fame, as one of the first proponents of communism, spread across Germany; his work is an important testimony to the revolutionary awareness of his class.

Yet it would be misleading to assume that the revolutionary spirit was more prevalent among the 'proletariat' than among the prosperous entrepreneurs. Industrialists – self-made men such as Ludolf Camphausen, August Borsig or Werner Siemens – were also in favour of change, since trade restrictions and traditional work practices hindered business expansion. Most of them were liberals and, as such, promoted free trade, supported the Customs Union, railway construction and general education. The Eßlingen Citizens' Association (*Bürgerverein*), just one example, consisting of some 160 members, included forty-eight independent tradesmen, eight factory owners, sixteen businessmen and twenty academics, mostly doctors or teachers.[62] The industrial bourgeoisie was the most active and vocal constituent within the association, open to new progressive ideas and was anything but class conscious.

Social and economic conditions within the Confederation

Some excellent studies have been published on individual regions within the Confederation and this section will summarize their most important findings rather than carry out a detailed analysis. A particular emphasis will be given to the importance of early industrialization in the German revolutions of 1848/9, to an examination of the concept of the 'Bürger' and working-class structures and concluding with the question of how far economic depressions and food shortages may have affected the revolutionary course.

Traditionally, historians tended to see 'the Revolution' as the product of Germany's middle classes.[63] More recent studies of specific German regions have interpreted events as an anti-capitalist revolt, rooted in the lower social classes. Current thinking attempts to reject these contradictory approaches and investigates a plurality of social and political forms of unrest, covering several different social strata. At the heart of this question lies a sociological problem: terms such as 'bourgeois' or 'middle class' cannot be readily applied to the German situation. In the early period of industrialization, differences between craftsmen and factory workers or even 'entrepreneurs' were fluid. In 1841 Austria-Hungary had 240 steam engines, mostly employed in the mining industry and in spinning, and, although Prussia had more than treble this amount, none of these plants was large by today's standards. The Krupp factory employed about 140 workers, Borsig in Berlin had more than a thousand,[64] but a genuine working-class movement did not develop until the second half of the century. In general terms the least liberal states also tended to be socially and economically underdeveloped. This was certainly true of Austria which had fallen even further behind during the 1830s, while the Rhineland was perhaps the most progressive region, followed by Berlin, Silesia, Saxony and the Saar.[65] Former free towns also displayed entrepreneurial initiative. In the southwest, the city of Eßlingen (Württemberg) had twelve factories employing a total of 1,500 workers and Heilbronn increased its work force substantially when its paper manufacturing changed from pulp vats to machine production.[66] Energy resources were still limited to water and wood-burning; in 1840 Württemberg had only one steam engine with a capacity of 16hp (approx. 12kw).[67] Textile manufacturing was still partly on a domestic basis with relatively few factories. Metal and machine-tool industries only began to develop in the 1840s, when railroad construction was in progress and the first German-made steam engines and locomotives were produced.[68]

In general, industrial growth was gradual, enabling the labour force to adjust to new conditions. Even so, the dominance of guilds tended to hinder industrial expansion. This situation should be borne in mind when assessing the forward-looking, progressive attitudes of craftsmen and journeymen and the role attributed to them during the revolutions. In those areas where the dominance of the guilds had been broken and where mass poverty had become endemic, reflecting the social implications of early industrialization, the hostility of the guilds towards industrialization can be understood, particularly in relation to the use of child labour and the preponderance of the 'truck system'.

Germany was still an agrarian society with more than 70 per cent of its population living in rural areas: large agricultural estates existed alongside subsistence farming, emerging factories alongside cottage industries. German pig-iron production was only a small fraction of British capacity and cotton and wool manufacturing lagged similarly behind.[69] The contrast between relatively advanced and other, more backward regions was stronger in Germany than in Britain, decreasing only in the 1840s with the advance of the railways.

Population growth was very uneven across Germany, varying considerably even within individual states. A simplified summary suggests that between 1815 and 1850 the population of the Confederation grew by around 55 per cent, with this growth strongest in Prussia and weakest in Austria. The annual average growth rate of 1.57 per cent was anything but spectacular, but could generally be sustained, though obviously not at a constant level. A variety of reasons contributed to this steady growth: improved farming methods, an increase in manufacturing productivity, improved hygiene and easier mobility with better transportation. Infant mortality, nevertheless, remained high, increasing slightly between 1815 and 1850. The growth in illegitimate births was significant throughout the nineteenth century; between 1790 and 1866 they more than trebled, largely through legal restrictions on marriage, secularization and urbanization. Mortality rates tended to be higher in big cities than in rural areas, but none of these trends is significant enough to suggest that industrialization was the decisive factor. Emigration to America or to other parts of the Confederation was strongest from the southwest; reaching a peak in the 1850s, with an average emigration rate of 14.85 per cent in Baden and 20.38 per cent in Württemberg.[70]

The sociological problem of defining the 'middle classes' has already been mentioned and requires some clarification. Academics played a particularly significant role both in shaping a middle-class structure and within the revolutionary movement. The Humboldtian reforms in Prussia, whereby academics gained high-ranking positions within the civil service, affected most German-speaking territories. During the 1820s, the position of 'middle-class' academic civil servants was increasingly threatened by reactionary members of the nobility and further destabilized by an emerging academic proletariat. State officials harassed professors and civil servants, who were often in danger of losing their positions, while young academics faced the problem of having to wait, often for up to a decade, before gaining a salaried position.[71] As a result, this group began to emerge as a critical mass within the politically aware bourgeoisie. University professors in particular were prominent throughout the *Vormärz* period. When the Frankfurt Parliament was established, nearly 12 per cent of its members were professors, with a similar percentage of high-ranking civil servants from an academic background and an astonishing 27 per cent of legally qualified academics.[72]

The impact of this academic middle class, a term used here to cover professors, high-ranking civil servants and members of the legal profession, has been hotly debated in recent years. Rüdiger Hachtmann represents historians who question the validity of the term 'middle class' as applied to the revolution, suggesting that a fundamental change in socio-economic circumstances was the major reason for the outbreak of the revolutions.[73] He therefore rejects the epithet 'bourgeois' to describe the driving force of the revolution, crediting instead a plurality of different social strata with having brought it about. Dieter Langewiesche, on the other hand, believes that middle-class activists with a strong academic background articulated the essential revolutionary concepts.[74] It can be demonstrated that the two positions are not irreconcilable: evidence suggests that 1848/9 saw a number of revolutions happening concurrently, producing sharply differing factions, each with its own agenda. While middle-class academics primarily supported constitutional reform, social and economic issues were supported by a diverse coalition of peasants, journeymen and a working-class proletariat that defies any simple modern categorization.

If the definition of a German middle-class bourgeoisie is problematic, the task becomes virtually impossible in relation to the working classes, when many a master-craftsman made ends meet by subsistence farming, and journeymen may have found employment only as unskilled labourers. Even a description of the work place is not easy: what in the 1840s was described as a 'factory' would in today's terms be called a workshop. James J. Sheehan gives a clear description of the state of affairs:

> The development of 'class consciousness' grew . . . from political and social conflicts that were often based on but did not necessarily flow from, people's work experience and economic situation. Family relationships, the social ties arising from neighbourhood associations, and a shared sense of political oppression and social injustice were equally important for the creation of common values among workers from different parts of the economic system.[75]

This situation continued, especially in rural areas, until well into the twentieth century, and it is not immediately evident how such a socially ill-defined class structure produced the revolutionary energies of this period. Indeed, craftsmen, journeymen and home-workers, conservative and reactionary in their outlook, often held Luddite views, demanding the restoration of guilds and supporting family enterprises and cottage industries. In short, they remained all too unaware of the advantages of a proletarian class consciousness and its implications for organized labour. The initiative remained with writers and academics; Heine recognized that it was one thing to advocate emancipation for the proletariat, but quite another to idealize this 'underclass', whose ugliness and 'wickedness', he believed had to be overcome through education and social welfare.[76] Robert von Mohl, constitutional reformer and later member of the Frankfurt Assembly, deploring the dependency of the proletariat, proposed legislation for the protection of workers and the establishment of co-operatives.[77] Many 'Young Germany' writers described the abysmal housing conditions and industrialists such as Friedrich Harkort sought to devise measures for their general improvement. Even the churches advocated laws for the protection of children in factories.

Such problems intensified during the hungry forties, when Europe experienced a series of poor harvests, further exacerbated by the potato blight and a severe economic crisis. The resulting unrest, although widespread, was not sufficiently well organized to precipitate a full-scale revolution. The best-known incident was the uprising of the Silesian weavers in 1844, celebrated in many poems and street ballads. The uprising itself was by no means the most serious one, but the employment of Prussian troops to restore order gave it a particular prominence. In many other regions the starving population stormed bakeries, flourmills and food shops, while poaching, coffee smuggling and the theft of firewood became common place. Annette von Droste-Hülshoff's narrative *Die Judenbuche* portrays such delinquency in association with a general decline in law and order. The fundamental causes of such crime were the infringements of traditional rights over the use of common land, changes in forestry cultivation and the insistence on outdated duties and tax laws. Vintners in the Rhineland and the Palatinate were in uproar over unreasonably high taxation.[78] The number of bankruptcies increased dramatically, nearly doubling in Cologne between 1845 and 1847, where almost 20 per cent of the population was dependent on some form of charity.[79]

The Swiss civil war

As the legacy of 1789 and the modernizing influence of Napoleon had inspired an earlier generation, events beyond Germany's borders continued to provide an impetus towards revolution. Although imbued with revolutionary awareness, workers and peasants were still too disparate and disorganized to constitute a revolutionary force. The middle strata of society were similarly divided, with many civil servants hoping for a peaceful resolution of the constitutional issue, while the more extreme left-wing intellectuals and writers were mostly in exile or too small in number to present a real challenge. Events in Italy, Switzerland and France changed all this. A critical momentum was established to propel the various groups into action, though none of them was yet ready to take over government, should the opportunity arise. Before examining the various revolutions within the Confederation, it is helpful to give a brief overview of the Swiss civil war as the overture to a succession of revolutions which ended the first half of the nineteenth century and the old order in Europe.

For some considerable time Switzerland had been a haven for exiled political activists, a centre for subversive publications and a link between Germany and political developments in Italy and France. The Swiss civil war had its origin in religious conflict and it is significant that this conflict had a veritable domino effect throughout the Confederation. The poet Ferdinand Freiligrath celebrated the Swiss conflict as 'the first shot' of the 'German' revolution, but historians have been reluctant to agree: Swiss historians, perpetuating the country's most powerful national myth, tend to play down this event in favour of the William Tell legend.[80] A closer examination will illustrate that there were, indeed, links between the Swiss and German struggles. Confessional differences existed between catholics and protestants within the Prussian Rhineland and also in the Palatinate. Other issues crucial to both the *Sonderbund* war and the German struggles revolved around the nationality question and the search for a democratic constitution.

Switzerland, too, had been affected by the reactionary period following the defeat of Napoleon. At the Congress of Vienna Switzerland had nominally gained her neutrality, but her constitution (*Bundesvertrag*) was far less liberal than earlier constitutions in effect since 1798 and shared many of the reactionary undemocratic features of the various constitutions of the Confederation. In 1817 Switzerland was even obliged to join the Holy Alliance.[81] Many of the country's patriotic features had been suppressed, giving rise to powerful local protest groups. The French July Revolution resulted in a number of liberal groups returning to the political arena, but only in some cantons, producing severe tension between liberals and conservatives. In 1832 seven cantons formed a liberal, distinctly anti-clerical association which led to the formation of a conservative federation by the more reactionary, catholic cantons of Uri, Schwyz, Unterwalden, Basel-city and Neuenburg. The liberals demanded stronger 'national' ties, sovereignty of the people and a considerable weakening of the influence of the guilds. Metternich supported the conservatives and in 1845 the cantons of Lucerne, Zug, Freiburg and Wallis joined them to found the *Sonderbund*, as a secret alliance designed to establish a separate, centrist Swiss state.[82] Lucerne even went so far as to recall the Jesuits, reopening their monasteries and entrusting them with the canton's education, a move guaranteed to provoke Europe's liberal protestants who tended to equate Jesuits with reactionary papal control, with anti-patriotic ultra-catholicism. Several volunteer corps under

41

the Berne politician and general, Ulrich Ochsenbein, moved against Lucerne, but were defeated with heavy loss of life.

By the summer of 1847 political fortunes began to change. The liberals gained a majority of seats in the federal diet (*Tagsatzung*) and demanded the dissolution of the *Sonderbund* and the expulsion of all Jesuits. They also demanded a modern constitution, a proposal wholeheartedly supported by the French-speaking areas.[83] The terms included an extension of the franchise, press freedom, judicial reforms and the establishment of jury trial. Radicals replaced the conservative government in Geneva and foreign powers, particularly Austria and Prussia, were advised not to intervene in the country's internal affairs. In November 1847 General Guillaume-Henri Dufour, a brilliant soldier, scholar, engineer and politician was put in command of the federal armies and, after a brief three-week campaign, the forces of the *Sonderbund* were defeated. The success of the democratic liberals resounded throughout Europe; the speed of the victory and British support for the Swiss liberals thwarted any intervention by Austria and Prussia. Elsewhere, democratic liberals looked for similar successes in their own countries. The outbreaks of the French and German revolutions only weeks later gave the Swiss sufficient opportunity to rewrite their federal constitution; it was the work of pragmatists, in marked contrast to the Frankfurt efforts. The new constitution (*Bundesverfassung*), fashioned on the American model,[84] was based on compromise, but moderately liberal, containing a balance of federal and centrist elements and aimed towards reconciliation. It aided the development of the Swiss economy by abolishing customs and curbing the influence of the guilds, thus achieving a degree of prosperity in peace and neutrality. As Switzerland receded from the scene, the focus shifted to Paris from where the revolutionary wave was soon to engulf the German Confederation and the rest of continental Europe.

Notes

1 Rudolph Stadelmann, *Social and Political History of the German 1848 Revolution*, trans. by James G. Chastain (Athens, OH, 1975), p. 4.
2 Ibid., p. 5.
3 On the relationship between economic crises and political initiatives cf. R. Vierhaus, ' "Vormärz" – Ökonomische und soziale Krisen, ideologische und politische Gegensätze', *Francia*, 13 (1985), pp. 355–68.
4 Wolfram Siemann, *The German Revolution of 1848–49*, trans. by Christiane Banerji (London, 1998), pp. 45f.
5 James J. Sheehan, *German History 1770–1866* (Oxford, 1989), pp. 393–411.
6 Sheehan, *German History*, p. 392.
7 Quoted from Günther Heydemann, *Konstitution gegen Revolution* Die britische Deutschland- und Italienpolitik 1815–1848 (Göttingen and Zurich, 1995), p. 219.

8 *Rheinischer Merkur* (1815). Quoted from M. Behnen, 'Deutschland unter Napoleon. Restauration und Vormärz', in M. Vogt ed., *Rassow, Deutsche Geschichte* (Stuttgart, 1987), p. 368.
9 Cf. H. A. and E. Frenzel, *Daten deutscher Dichtung*, vol. 1 (Munich, 1966), p. 250.
10 Ernst Rudolf Huber, *Deutsche Verfassungsgeschichte seit 1789*, 3rd edn. vol. 1 (Stuttgart, 1988), pp. 88–100. A reading of the *Bundesakte* as well as of the *Wiener Schlußakte*, would suggest that the creation of individual constitutions for each member state was indeed an important objective for the negotiating powers. However, if related to the rest of these documents, it becomes obvious that Article 13 and its variations were little more than an exercise in 'political correctness'.
11 Anna von Sydow ed., *Wilhelm und Caroline von Humboldt in ihren Briefen*, vol. 4 (Berlin, 1910), pp. 553ff.
12 A third period (1848–66) falls outside the scope of this debate; however, the Confederation had only a nominal importance during this last stage.
13 A perceived threat from France to the territory west of the Rhine in the summer of 1840 had led to similar sentiments, but at that time Austria had at least not been hostile to the anti-French party.
14 E. Fehrenbach, 'Verfassungs- und sozialpolitische Reformen und Reformprojekte in Deutschland unter dem Einfluss des napoleonischen Frankreich', in Helmut Berding and Hans-Peter Ullmann eds, *Deutschland zwischen Revolution und Restauration* (Düsseldorf, 1981), p. 66.
15 David Blackbourn, *The Fontana History of Germany 1780–1918, The Long Nineteenth Century* (London, 1997), pp. 74f.
16 H. Rosenberg, *Bureaucracy, Aristocracy and Autocracy, The Prussian Experience, 1660–1815* (Cambridge, MA, 1958), p. 161.
17 Karl Marx and Friedrich Engels, in Hans Jessen ed., *Die deutsche Revolution 1848/49 in Augenzeugenberichten*, 2nd edn (Düsseldorf, 1968), p. 28.
18 V. Press, 'Landstände des 18. und Parlamente des 19. Jahrhunderts', in Berding and Ullmann eds, *Deutschland*, pp. 144–6.
19 Ibid., p. 146.
20 'Über die Einrichtung landständischer Verfassungen in den preußischen Staaten' [1819], in A. Flitner and K. Giel eds, *Wilhelm von Humboldt, Werke*, vol. 4, *Schriften zur Politik und zum Bildungswesen* (Stuttgart, 1964), pp. 433–501.
21 Huber, *Deutsche Verfassungsgeschichte*, vol. 1, p. 217.
22 Cf. Sheehan, *German History*, pp. 426–32; Blackbourn, *Germany*, pp. 82f; Siemann, *German Revolution*, pp. 20–4.
23 Sheehan, *German History*, p. 426.
24 F. Walter, *Österreichische Verfassungs- und Verwaltungsgeschichte von 1500–1955* (Vienna and Graz, 1972), p. 126.
25 W. H. Dawson, *Treitschke's History of Germany in the Nineteenth Century*, trans. by E. and C. Paul, vol. 2 (London, 1916), p. 245.
26 Berthold Michel and H. H. Schepp eds, *Politik und Schule von der Französischen Revolution bis zur Gegenwart*, vol. 1 (Frankfurt/M., 1973), p. 313.
27 H. Scheel, 'Deutsche Jakobiner', *Zeitschrift für Geschichte* 17 (1969), pp. 1130–40.
28 Franz Schnabel, *Deutsche Geschichte im 19. Jahrhundert*, 2nd edn (Freiburg, 1949), pp. 240–8.
29 K.-G. Faber, 'Görres, Weitzel und die Revolution (1819)', *Historische Zeitschrift*, 194 (1962), pp. 37–61.

30 K.-G. Faber, 'Politisches Denken in der Restaurationszeit', in Berding and Ullmann eds, *Deutschland*, p. 275.

31 Huber, *Deutsche Verfassungsgeschichte*, vol. 2, p. 101.

32 Ibid., p. 102. Cf. also Humboldt's memorandum to Frederick William III, warning against the limitation of Prussia's autonomy and expressing his concern about the restriction of academic freedom in *Schriften zur Politik und zum Bildungswesen*, pp. 501–21.

33 Heydemann, *Konstitution*, p. 43.

34 Georg Herwegh, *Werke in einem Band*, 3rd edn, H.-G. Werner ed. (Berlin and Weimar, 1977), p. 318.

35 *Von unten auf!* In Ferdinand Freiligrath, *Werke in einem Band*, 3rd edn, W. Ilberg ed. (Berlin and Weimar, 1976), p. 90.

36 Karl Marx, *Early Writings* (New York, 1975), p. 423.

37 Quoted from Tim Klein ed., *1848. Erinnerungen, Urkunden, Berichte, Briefe* (Leipzig, 1914), p. 44. For a good survey of events and additional literature cf. J. Sperber, *Rhineland Radicals. The Democratic Movement and the Revolution of 1848–1849* (Princeton, NJ, 1991), pp. 113f.

38 Quoted from Heydemann, *Konstitution*, p. 224.

39 Edmund Wilson, *To the Finland Station* (London, 1966), p. 127.

40 Annette von Droste Hülshoff, *Historisch kritische Ausgabe*, Winfried Woesler ed., vol. 8,1, *Briefe 1805–1838* (Tübingen, 1987), pp. 286–99, in part. pp. 290f. [letter of 9 February, 1838]; cf. also Sperber, *Rhineland Radicals*, pp. 43–52.

41 Rüdiger Hachtmann, *Berlin 1848. Eine Politik- und Gesellschaftsgeschichte der Revolution* (Bonn, 1997), pp. 104, 541–7.

42 Quoted from Hachtmann, *Berlin 1848*, p. 105.

43 Franz X. Vollmer, *Offenburg 1848/49. Ereignisse und Lebensbilder aus einem Zentrum der badischen Revolution* (Karlsruhe, 1997), pp. 42f.

44 Ludwig Börne, *Sämtliche Schriften*, vol. 2 (Düsseldorf, 1964), p. 268.

45 Wilson, *Finland Station*, pp. 125f.

46 Dieter Langewiesche, 'Die Anfänge der deutschen Parteien', *Geschichte und Gesellschaft*, 4 (1978), pp. 324–61.

47 Wolfgang Kaschuba and Carola Lipp, *1848 – Provinz und Revolution* (Tübingen, 1979), p. 127.

48 Hachtmann, *Berlin 1848*, p. 95.

49 Vollmer, *Offenburg*, p. 21.

50 Siemann, *German Revolution*, p. 85.

51 From the host of literature on this topic cf. in particular Klaus von Beyme, 'Partei, Fraktion', in *Geschichtliche Grundbegriffe*, vol. 4 (Stuttgart, 1978), pp. 677–733; Otto Dann ed., *Vereinswesen und bürgerliche Gesellschaft in Deutschland* (Munich, 1984), pp. 11–50; Dieter Langewiesche, 'Die Anfänge'; Siemann, *German Revolution*, pp. 86–94.

52 Walter Grab ed., *Die Revolution von 1848/49. Eine Dokumentation* (Stuttgart, 1998), pp. 27–30.

53 Sperber, *Rhineland Radicals*, pp. 97–9.

54 *Stadtratsprotokoll Eßlingen*, quoted from Kaschuba and Lipp, *1848*, p. 164.

55 Ibid., p. 143.

56 Quoted from W. Siemann, 'Ideenschmuggel. Probleme der Meinungskontrolle und das Los deutscher Zensoren im 19. Jahrhundert', *Historische Zeitschrift* (1987), p. 86.

57 Ibid., p. 90.
58 Cf. Vollmer, *Offenburg*, pp. 9, 40f.
59 Huber, *Deutsche Verfassungsgeschichte*, vol. 2, pp. 150f.
60 Kaschuba and Lipp, *1848*, p. 136.
61 Siemann, *German Revolution*, p. 26.
62 Kaschuba and Lipp, *1848*, p. 127.
63 Prominent examples are Thomas Nipperdey, *Deutsche Geschichte 1800–1866. Bürgerwelt und starker Staat*, 6th edn (Munich, 1987); Michael Stürmer, '1848 in der deutschen Revolution', in Hans-Ulrich Wehler ed., *Sozialgeschichte heute. Festschrift für Hans Rosenberg zum 70. Geburtstag* (Göttingen, 1974).
64 Hachtmann, *Berlin 1848*, p. 78.
65 Cf. Sheehan, *German History*, pp. 498f.
66 Kaschuba and Lipp, *1848*, pp. 44, 67.
67 Ibid., p. 46.
68 Sperber, *Rhineland Radicals*, pp. 65f: The exception being Solingen with its manufacture of cutlery and other steel wares. In 1840 only 5 per cent of locomotives were built in Germany, by the 1860s this figure had risen to 80 per cent.
69 Sheehan, *German History*, p. 451.
70 Ibid., p. 461.
71 Siemann, *German Revolution*, p. 122. The figure includes grammar school teachers.
72 Ibid., p. 20.
73 Hachtmann, *Berlin 1848*, p. 17.
74 Langewiesche, 'Wege zur Revolution', in Otto Borst ed., *Aufruhr und Entsagung, Vormärz 1815–1848 in Baden und Württemberg* (Stuttgart, 1992), p. 434.
75 Sheehan, *German History*, p. 494.
76 H. Heine, *Sämtliche Werke*, vol. 15 [Düsseldorfer Ausgabe], M. Windfuhr ed. (Hamburg, 1979), *Geständnisse* (1853/4), p. 31.
77 Sheehan, *German History*, pp. 647f.
78 Sperber, *Rhineland Radicals*, pp. 53–86.
79 Sheehan, *German History*, pp. 638f.
80 Thomas Hildbrand and Albert Tanner eds, *Im Zeichen der Revolution. Der Weg zum Schweizerischen Bundesstaat 1798–1848* (Zurich, 1997), p. 7.
81 Alfred Kölz, *Neuere schweizerische Verfassungsgeschichte. Ihre Grundlinien vom Ende der Alten Eidgenossenschaft bis 1848* (Berne, 1992), p. 182.
82 Ibid., pp. 457f.
83 Ibid., p. 462.
84 Ibid., p. 562.

Chapter 3

The March and April revolutions in the 'Third Germany'

Academic studies of the 1848/9 revolutions in Germany have, in the main, concentrated on Vienna and Berlin or have been preoccupied, particularly in recent years, with events in southwest Germany, in the Rhineland or other specific regions. In order to appreciate the complexities of the revolutions during this period, it is important to understand the interrelationships between all the various centres, rural and urban, and to recognize the importance which the various social components of their populace had on the aims and activities of individual revolutionary groups. This chapter will concentrate on events in the 'Third Germany'; the revolutions in Vienna and Berlin will be fully discussed in chapter 4.

The impact of the French February Revolution

While revolutionary events in Switzerland and Italy could not fail to have a significant impact on developments in Germany, it was the French February Revolution which actually triggered off the first wave of revolutions throughout Germany. The Rhineland cities were the first to learn of the Paris revolution; the tone of excitement was conveyed in a letter by the moderate liberal Dahlmann: 'Plus de Bourbons. Vive la république. You need not know any more.'[1] Learning of the Paris Revolution on 27 February, the radical republican Friedrich Hecker reported from the Mannheim Assembly that the radicals 'jumped from their seats, embraced each other, raising their glasses in jubilation: "let's quickly set to work on Germany's liberation, let us act now, let us bring to life what has been desired for such a long time, what has been talked about, discussed and debated". – Thus I heard hundreds and more voices in unison.'[2]

Other cities soon caught this mood. Berlin, which had remained calm during the 1830 revolution, saw this revolution as striking 'a deep blow against their own lives'.[3] A feeling of insecurity, too, plagued Vienna. The Saxon diplomat Count Vitzhum reported that Count Metternich apparently had no solution to the overall confusion; a general feeling of imminent war was in the air, with the Austrian chancellor appearing 'weak, stone-deaf ... hemmed in by exhausted phrases and sayings, a childish old

Table 3.1 Table of events, 1848–49

February 1848	Publication of Communist Manifesto (Karl Marx and Frederick Engels)
25 Feb.	Paris: abdication of Louis Philippe and declaration of French Republic.
late Feb./ early March	Popular gatherings in Mannheim, Heidelberg, Cologne and other cities, resolutions by liberal and democratic politicians in Baden and Hesse, demanding a wholesale reform of the German Confederation, together with civic rights.
3 March	Frankfurt: German Diet abolishes censorship.
5 March	Heidelberg: assembly of 51 eminent figures, demanding a national parliament.
6 March	Bavaria: Ludwig I promises far-reaching political reforms and civil liberties.
early March	'March Ministers' gain office in Saxony, Hanover, Hesse, Württemberg, Baden.
12 March	Delegation of Seven issues invitation to public figures to meet with a view to establish a National Parliament in Frankfurt.
13 March	Vienna: outbreak of revolution, resignation and flight of Metternich.
14 March	Vienna: establishment of a National Guard, press freedom introduced in Austria.
16/17 March	Saxony and Prussia: censorship abolished.
18 March	Berlin: popular uprising with mass demonstrations and street fighting.
19 March	Berlin: withdrawal of troops, declaration by Frederick William IV 'To my beloved Berliners'; establishment of civil guard.
20 March	Berlin: release of Polish political activists and general amnesty for all political prisoners.
21/22 March	Berlin: proclamation by Frederick William IV 'To my People and the German Nation', promise of political reforms and a parliament.
24 March	Schleswig–Holstein: formation of a provisional revolutionary government in response to Denmark's annexation of Schleswig.
26 March	Heidelberg Assembly demands free elections to a German national parliament and a constitution on the North American model.
29 March	Berlin: establishment of Camphausen–Hansemann ministry.
30 March–3 April	Frankfurt: Pre-Parliament in session.
31 March	Frankfurt: democratic and revolutionary demands (Hecker and Struve) rejected; establishment of the Delegation of Fifty.
2 April	Frankfurt: German Diet abolishes all anti-democratic laws (including Karlsbad Decrees).
4 April	Vienna: resignation of Kolowrat government, replacement by Ficquelmont.
7 April	Frankfurt: German Federation recognizes elected National Assembly.

Table 3.1 (cont'd)

12 April	Konstanz: outbreak of first revolution in Baden (Hecker).
20 April	Baden: defeat of revolutionaries at Kandern, death of General von Gagern.
21 April	Schleswig–Holstein: General Wrangel appointed as chief commander.
24 April	Baden: Herwegh's 'German Legion' crosses Rhine to aid Hecker, defeat at Dossenbach.
27–30 April	Mannheim: fighting between republicans and government troops.
1 May	Elections to German National Parliament in Frankfurt and Prussian parliament in Berlin.
4 May	Vienna: resignation of Ficquelmont, replaced by Pillersdorf.
16 May	Austria: Emperor Ferdinand 'retreats' to Innsbruck (returns to Vienna on 12 August).
18 May	Frankfurt: opening of National Assembly (Paulskirche).
21/22 May	Mainz: confrontation between civil guard and Prussian troops.
22 May	Berlin: opening session of Prussian National Assembly.
26 May	Vienna: dissolution of Academic Legion results in street fighting; establishment of a democratic security committee.
1 June	Cologne: first issue of *Neue Rheinische Zeitung*, general editor, Karl Marx.
7 June	Berlin: Prince William returns from British exile.
13 June	Prague: uprising and bombardment of city by Windischgrätz.
14 June	Berlin: storming of the Armoury.
14–17 June	Frankfurt: first congress of democrats.
18/19 June	Berlin: congress of workers and craftsmen.
20 June	Berlin: resignation of Camphausen government, replaced by Auerswald-Hansemann.
29 June	Frankfúrt: Archduke John elected Regent and head of provisional German government.
5 July	Frankfurt: debate opens on the Basic Rights of the German people.
8 July	Vienna: Pillersdorf government resigns; Wessenberg becomes new prime minister.
22 July	Vienna: inaugural session of the Austrian *Reichstag*.
24–27 July	Frankfurt: National Assembly debates Posen, left wing delegates protest against anti-Polish sentiments.
21–23 Aug.	Vienna: National Guard suppresses earth workers' uprising.
23 Aug.– 3 Sept.	Berlin: General Workers' congress, foundation of Workers' Fraternity (Stephan Born). Workers Congress manifesto on social reforms presented to National Assembly.
26 August	Armistice of Malmö between Denmark and Prussia.
7 September	Vienna: Austrian Diet liberates peasants unconditionally (Hans Kudlich).
8 September	Berlin: resignation of the Prussian Auerswald-Hansemann cabinet.
16 Sept.	Frankfurt: National Assembly confirms Malmö armistice.
17/18 Sept.	Frankfurt: riots in protest at Malmö, assassination of Prince Lichnowsky.

Table 3.1 (cont'd)

21 Sept.	Baden: Struve proclaims a German Republic – outbreak of second revolution in Baden.
22 Sept.	Berlin: formation of Pfuel government. Donnersberg proclamation against Malmö.
26 Sept.	Cologne: state of emergency, closure of *Neue Rheinische Zeitung*.
6 October	Vienna: popular uprising, murder of Minister of War Latour.
7 October	Austria: Emperor Ferdinand escapes to Olmütz, Viennese citizens take up arms.
12 October	Vienna: Messenhauser appointed Commander in Chief of National Guard.
16 October	Vienna: Emperor Ferdinand appeals 'to my peoples'; Viennese students ask peasants for support.
17 October	Vienna: arrival of delegation from Frankfurt National Assembly (Blum, Fröbel *et al.*).
20 October	Vienna: Windischgrätz and Jellačić lay siege to the city.
26–30 October	Berlin: Second Congress of Democrats. Appeals for assistance for Vienna.
30 October	Austria: battle at Schwechat, Hungarian army withdraws and Vienna capitulates.
1 November	Berlin: new government under Count Brandenburg.
8 November	Berlin: coup d' état forces Prussian National Assembly to leave capital.
9 November	Vienna: execution of Robert Blum.
15 Nov.	Frankfurt: organization of Central March Association.
27 Nov.	Prussia: reconstitution of Prussian National Assembly in Brandenburg.
	Austria: reconstitution of Austrian Diet in Kremsier.
2 December	Austria: Emperor Ferdinand abdicates in favour of Francis Joseph.
5 December	Prussia: dissolution of Prussian National Assembly, imposition of a new constitution.
15 Dec.	Frankfurt: Schmerling abdicates as Minister President of provisional central government.
22 Jan. 1849	Prussia: first and second chambers of parliament elected under new constitution.
4 March	Austria: dissolution of Austrian Diet, imposition of an all Austrian constitution.
12 March	Frankfurt: Carl Welcker demands adoption of new Imperial Constitution.
27 March	Frankfurt: National Assembly accepts hereditary imperial monarchy.
28 March	Frankfurt: Election of Frederick William IV as German Emperor; publication of Imperial Constitution.
3 April	Berlin: Frederick William rejects offer of imperial crown from Frankfurt delegation.
5 April	Austria: recall of delegates from National Assembly.
14 April	Recognition of Imperial Constitution by 28 smaller German states.

Table 3.1 (cont'd)

21 April	Recognition of Imperial Constitution by second Prussian Chamber.
26 April	Prussia: Second Prussian Chamber dissolved by Prussian government.
3 May	Dresden: outbreak of Saxon revolution (Wagner, Bakunin).
6 May	Frankfurt: Central March Association calls for implementation of Imperial Constitution.
7 May	Prussia: final rejection of German Imperial Constitution and crown.
9 May	Dresden: city falls to Prussian and Saxon troops; end of Saxon revolution.
10 May	Frankfurt: National Assembly protests against suppression of Saxon revolution, resignation of Gagern cabinet.
14 May	Prussia: delegates recalled from National Assembly, uprising by Elberfeld citizens.
19 May	Baden: outbreak of third revolution, proclamation in support of Imperial Constitution.
26 May	*Dreikönigsbündnis* established (coalition between Prussia, Saxony and Hanover).
30 May	Prussia: introduction of three tier electoral system (*Dreiklassenwahlrecht*).
31 May	Frankfurt: National Assembly decides to move to Stuttgart (Rump Parliament).
13 June	Palatinate: start of Prussian invasion.
16 June	Stuttgart: Rump Parliament dismisses Imperial Regent Archduke John.
18 June	Stuttgart: Rump Parliament dissolved by Württemberg troops.
21 June	Baden: defeat of Badenese revolutionary army under General Mieroslawski at Waghäusel.
28 June	Baden: collapse of revolutionary government in Karlsruhe.
23 July	Baden: capitulation of revolutionary army in the fortress of Rastatt.

man . . . no longer strong enough in his head to weather the present storms'.[4]

A general anticipation of war with France aroused hope amongst liberals and democrats alike that the German governments would act in the national interest and that Prussia would revert to her reformist democratic course of 1813.[5] On the other hand, the fear of war provided a convenient excuse for the Frankfurt Federal Diet to appeal for national unity, in an attempt to restore order and discipline and to prevent the overflow of revolution from across the Rhine.[6] The legacy of 1789 was still a potent force in everybody's mind, and there was general relief when it became apparent that war between France and Germany would not become an issue.

The French February Revolution was very different from events a generation earlier. It gathered momentum with breathtaking speed: within hours of the first barricades being erected, the Guizot government fell; barely a day later Louis Philippe was forced to abdicate and flee the country. On 25 February, the third day of the Revolution, the Republic was declared. Such speed made any consideration of outside intervention impossible; it also took the new provisional government unawares, turning it into a victim of its own revolutionary fervour. The political force of the Paris streets, of a disenfranchised, impoverished proletariat, gained control. Socialist ideals became political reality. The socialist intellectual Louis Blanc and Albert Martin, a workers' leader, joined the provisional government and introduced public workshops in an attempt to alleviate unemployment. The government reduced daily working hours and recognized a universal right to work. Although more than 100,000 workers gained employment in these workshops, poor organization and exploitation by work-shy elements combined to give them a bad reputation. By June 1848, severe demands on the public purse and a general move to the right contributed to their abolition. A significant aspect in these developments was the decision by the provisional government to widen the franchise, so that every Frenchman over twenty-one was entitled to vote. This increased the electorate from 200,000 to some nine million voters, most of whom were illiterate, with no experience of the political process and a ready instrument for political manipulation. During the two months before the election, the instinctively conservative rural mass of small proprietors, royalists and politically and economically dependent peasants had time to take fright at the disorder and social experimentation in Paris. The elections of 23 April produced a new National Assembly, where the revolutionary party was outnumbered by eight to one and Louis Blanc and Albert lost their positions on the executive council. A further coup attempt by the extreme left, designed to re-assert the revolutionary leadership of the 'Paris mob' met with failure, in the face of the National Guard and other military forces assembled by General Cavaignac. The revolution had reached its final stage; reactionary forces gained control after heavy loss of life, amounting to several thousand casualties. The path was set for a new power struggle; Napoleon III, nephew of the great emperor, eventually gained power in 1851, bringing the Second French Republic to an end.

A brief comparison between the February Revolution in Paris and various March events in central Europe can elicit differences and similarities in almost equal proportion. The profound agrarian crisis in Europe of which the potato famine was only one dramatic aspect has already been discussed. A catastrophic harvest in 1846/7 led to dramatic price increases for wheat and other basic foods. A worker in Germany in 1835 worked a full day to earn the equivalent of two five pound loaves of bread; conditions had become significantly worse by 1847, when the same work earned only half the amount of bread.[7] Although the next harvest was better, starvation and general poverty continued into the winter of 1848, with debts outstanding and continued unemployment. Political events contributed to loss of orders and excess production resulted in a stock-market crisis. Shares on the Berlin stock market fell by approximately 5 per cent within half a day when events in Paris became public knowledge.[8] The economic and financial crisis, at least partly associated with the February Revolution, led to the dismissal of thousands of workers in various industrial centres.[9] While starvation was widespread in the countryside, the issue of public subsidies to ailing businesses became a matter of fierce argument. Liberals tended to favour subsidies; democrats opposed them, believing that they benefited capital rather than the workers.[10]

The Paris national workshops provided a new momentum for those governments which had previously attempted to combat unemployment through the commission of public works. On 9 March Berlin opened an employment office, but its complete ineffectiveness increased the unrest amongst workers and journeymen.[11] However, while the centralized French administration had established Paris as the focal point for innovation as well as unrest, Germany, with no universally accepted capital, looked uneasily towards Berlin, Vienna or Frankfurt.

While the French Revolution of 1789 had revolved around constitutional matters, allowing social issues to come to the fore by 1848, the German revolutionary impetus was weakened by a bifurcation into constitutional and socio-economic aspects. The more moderate, liberal and middle-class elements dominated attempts to set up a national parliament in Frankfurt, whereas the more radical, socialist wing, supported by workers, journeymen and farmers, was largely excluded, leaving their concerns to 'revolutionaries' in the provinces. Two factors seem to converge here. On the one hand, the evident division between the constitutional and the social issue, itself the result of Germany's late development, on the other hand, the natural pattern, inherent in most revolutions, where a moderate and liberal faction is overtaken by a more radical one. A third issue which confronted Germany, the Schleswig–Holstein problem, highlighted the national and patriotic theme. This particular problem was to complicate matters further, positioning the German revolutions somewhere between their French models of 1789 and 1848. The German Confederation's declaration of war on Denmark was endorsed by an enthusiastic national upsurge; volunteers joined regular troops, urged on by fiery declarations, often expressing imperialist political aims and demanding a national German navy. The whole issue thus deflected from the constitutional and the social themes, at least until the unsatisfactory conclusion of the Malmö peace treaty (26 August 1848) served to merge the national with the constitutional agenda.

While a comparison of the German and French revolutions must not be given too much weight, a few observations might throw further light on the importance of these revolutions for Germany's subsequent history. The success or failure of any revolution is difficult to assess; it seems an inherent feature of most revolutions that they produce anti-revolutionary dictatorships. Anti-revolutionary stages are apparent at different times on both sides of the Rhine. What seems to be more crucial is the impact on social and political developments which are associated with any revolution. Events in Paris gave some prominence to the political role of the new proletariat which had evolved with industrialization, something the German revolutions could not achieve, given the territorial and social disruptions. However, the German revolutions initiated the collapse of the old European order, opening the door for Italy, Hungary, Bohemia and also Germany herself to develop a national identity and to experience an element of democratic self-representation. If seen from this perspective, the question of failure or success recedes behind the more important recognition that developments, begun in the early 1830s, brought to a climax in 1848 and continuing well into the twentieth century, consisted of both national and democratic–republican elements. The German upheavals of 1848 can then be viewed as a pivotal force within a wider European struggle for national identity and not merely as a limited constitutional and democratic development.

Observations on the social strata in the 'Third Germany'

The following observations should be read in conjunction with comments made in chapter 2; they will serve to examine the differing political actions in the German regions, to be discussed in this chapter. Two disparate groups in particular will be discussed here, peasants and a rural underclass, on the one hand, artisans and an urban proletariat in towns other than Berlin and Vienna on the other. Observations on a middle-class bourgeoisie in the making will be left to a later chapter.

The rural population

While in numerical terms, the rural population accounted for more than three-quarters of Germans with a considerable economic influence, their political impact was vastly under-represented. Even during the revolutions, the importance of the rural population decreased sharply once the National Assembly was established. Three factors in particular determined life in the country during the 1840s. Firstly, the social and economic impact of the peasant emancipation from serfdom kept small farmers locked into an economic and social dependency on the lower nobility in general and on foresters, magistrates and tax collectors in particular. Peasant labour services continued in many regions, particularly in Austria, and hunting rights and other residual feudal privileges were slow to die. Furthermore, farmers had to 'compensate' the gentry for these new freedoms, which frequently resulted in the creation of some form of rural proletariat. Consequently, rural anger was chiefly directed against local exploitation by their former 'patrons', while attitudes towards their respective sovereigns tended to be positive or at least neutral. Grievances were particularly strong in the least liberated areas of the southwest, parts of the Rhineland, Thuringia and Silesia, whereas northern and eastern Germany accounted for a high proportion of wealthy and independent farmers whose economic conditions had improved significantly during the first half of the nineteenth century.[12]

Secondly, overpopulation, particularly in rural areas, contributed to a tense situation, especially during the 'hungry forties', when crop failures such as the potato famine exacerbated economic problems. However, changes in farming, in particular the three-field rotation system, prevented a disaster on a par with the famine in Ireland. Indeed, higher yields exceeded the population growths, but they in turn led to a high degree of specialization, with whole villages specializing on just one crop or tending to a division between rich cattle farmers and subsistence farming.[13]

Thirdly, land had become a commodity and rising farm prizes encouraged an early form of agrarian capitalism. Small farmers tended to be among the losers. Welcker's entry in the *Staatslexikon* quotes an example from Westphalia where the profit gleaned from one acre of arable land amounted to only six Pfennigs, whereas the feudal duties payable were more than two-hundred fold of this profit.[14] In Saxony, only an estimated 22 per cent of peasant households were self-supportive[15] with similar figures for Bavaria and the southwest, a situation which was made worse by the practice of partible inheritance which resulted in ever-decreasing smallholdings. These 'dwarf holders' were also deprived of access to former common land, where they once grazed their animals and gathered firewood or leaves for bedding their cattle. The journal *Die Gegenwart*, commenting on these problems believed that 'a very communist attitude among peasants regarding the property of the forests' had come about.[16] The socio-economic situation was worst in the southwest, among tenant or agricultural workers in the Rhineland and in the mountainous areas where soil quality was poor; it can be measured by an increasing number of emigrants to North America or other parts of Germany. As a result, these farmers lost their social position and became indistinguishable from agricultural labourers or cottagers. The grim reality of this life stands in strange contrast to the idyllic description of farming in the *Staatslexikon*: a noble occupation, the individual farmer is seen as a person on whom the foundations of every state can rest. At the same time, Welcker's liberal position makes it clear that he sees the need for new legislation to cope with new farming conditions and new property laws. It may well be that such attitudes encouraged farmers as well as lawyers to resort to the many legal claims which are recorded for this period.[17] In such times of divided fortunes memories of the peasant uprising of 1525 were awakened. Recent studies indicate that such memories had survived for centuries as an undercurrent to potential unrest.[18] Such recollections are one of the reasons behind the early radical involvement of the rural community in the southwest where the peasant population was among those who benefited from the revolutions. Noble privileges, such as hunting rights and patrimonial jurisdiction were abolished everywhere, laws which in the southwest had already been introduced by the 'March Ministries'.

Artisans and industrial workers

Artisans and industrial workers will be considered jointly here, though distinctions must be made between a 'proletariat' in the big cities[19] and non-agricultural workers in the provincial regions. Even with such a division, the emerging picture remains diffuse and several further distinctions will be necessary. A distinction should be made between traditional, still relatively prosperous craftsmen and those artisans who increasingly were forced to accept contract work, either working in cottage industries at home, involved in piecework under contract or as the comparatively new group of factory workers. The most traditional constituency of artisans were rural craftsmen, making up nearly half of all artisans. Their position remained relatively stable, well beyond the revolutions even into the 1950s, with their lives tied to agriculture, supplementing their earnings through smallholdings. Among this group were wheelwrights, blacksmiths, coopers, saddlers and masons; their method of production can be defined as 'proto-industry',[20] since it merged the working conditions in agriculture with those in industry. As a result, they tended to benefit from changes in agriculture, they were not threatened by the advancing industrial revolution and they often played an important role within their local community.[21] They were also not easily distinguishable from local traders or publicans, wishing to be part of their rural community, in contrast to those artisans who lived in smaller industrial towns who aspired towards a more 'bourgeois' lifestyle.

Other crafts again fared less well, either because of increasing rivalry with each other or because of competition from newly established factories. These workers were hardly a homogeneous group of wage-earners, but their ranks were swelled by other sectors of a newly emerging urban proletariat, consisting of migrating workers from rural communities, women and children; by 1848 their number had risen to a million. A large number within this category of craftsmen were weavers, tailors, cabinetmakers and shoemakers, but also travelling journeymen who had failed to settle after their customary 'year on the road'. Among the latter, many had 'temporarily' moved abroad; 20,000 journeymen lived in Paris, constituting the bulk of the 'German legion' of 1848, another 10,000 had moved to London, often involved in organizing a communist league.[22] Tailors, shoemakers and cabinetmakers represented the most numerous trades; they were also most prominent in any labour unrest and best represented in the organizations of the early labour movement.[23] Even master craftsmen often faced the prospect of going out of business in firms with no more than three or four workers, indeed more than half of them worked on their own. Journeymen suffered 'the threefold yoke of low wages, excessive hours and living in the master's household',[24] with no opportunity of having a family or founding their own business. Even worse was the life of those who worked under a putting-out system; they made up almost 40 per cent of the manufacturing work force.[25] Many of them lived in Silesia, Saxony, the Rhineland or in Württemberg, working under contract for newly established merchant capitalists and depending for their supplies of raw materials on the same people to whom they sold their products. Such practices caused a member of the Saxon parliament to speak of the 'autocrats of gold and speculation' and to observe that 'the political need of labour and labourer are directly connected with the material need of the worker.' He therefore demanded 'restoration of the imbalance between capital and labour, an abolition of the feeding power of mere money without work'.[26] Production techniques remained traditional, and the arrival of mechanical looms, still the exception rather than the rule, made matters even worse, leading to plummeting prices and starvation wages. The liberation of customs policies and the foundation of the Customs Union advanced industrial growth, leading at the same time to a further decline in craft production and to mass unemployment.

Since the early 1840s, the consumption of cotton rose steeply, as did the production of iron and coal and the use of steam power, with the introduction of railways signalling a rapid change. In general, however, industry in most regions still relied on wood, wind and water for its energies and on horses for transportation. The state rather than private enterprise took the lead in the construction of railroads, in mining and iron production, but private entrepreneurs took advantage of the changing infrastructure. They soon became dissatisfied with existing trade restrictions and excessive bureaucracy and demanded liberalization of the economy. The railways became not only a key factor for communication during the revolutions, they also afforded far greater mobility. Young unattached men supplied the majority of migrant railway construction workers, a volatile work force, often linked to seasonal workers in the rural communities. Although there were no reliable statistics for the whole of Germany until 1882, the population mobility in the 1840s was spectacular. This is also illustrated by emigration statistics to North America. Emigration rose sharply from 1845, fluctuating between 37,000 in 1845 to 80,300 in 1847, with a noticeable decline during the revolutions and a steep increase in 1850 to 83,200 emigrants.[27]

As will become apparent in the next two chapters, the revolutions significantly assisted the development of a more homogeneous new working class, forged during the demonstrations and the fighting on the barricades. Whereas the middle classes found their identity through political speeches, the workers established theirs in new forms of militancy.[28] However, both groups shared a common interest in education. The *Arbeiterverbrüderungen* (workers fraternities) in particular were established in order to raise living conditions and the general standing of their members, mostly journeymen and workers in different areas, but also some representatives of the middle classes and the intelligentsia.[29] They acted as co-operative self-help organizations, but put great emphasis on the emancipatory role of education previously enjoyed largely by the middle classes in their reading clubs or similar institutions. The Stuttgart branch for instance made it its declared aim 'to strive for a general and moral education of the worker and to give him . . . the full enjoyment of all civil rights as well as to further his material and intellectual interests most emphatically'.[30] The career of Robert Blum serves as a good example. Born in Cologne in 1807, the son of an impoverished craftsman, he moved to Leipzig in 1832, after a varied career, frustrated by the lack of educational opportunities. As a bookseller and journalist, Blum became heavily involved in the campaign for political rights in general and for workers' rights in particular.[31] He became the central figure in Leipzig's political struggles, intent on politicizing the masses and establishing links between the radically democratic and the liberal middle-class factions. Blum's efforts led to co-operation between the liberal German Club and his own democratic Fatherland League. In March 1848 he became a delegate to the Pre-Parliament and shortly afterwards was elected to its Executive of Fifty (*Fünfzigerausschuß*). Working-class associations, which were a minority during the spring and summer of 1848, increased in influence during the revolutions. The Communist Manifesto by contrast, published in February 1848, was only programmatic, looking towards a vaguely defined future rather than addressing the *status quo*.[32] Cologne, the centre of activities for

Marx and Engels at the time, formed the largest communist federation, but other workers' associations were politically more important. In July 1848 the various trade and craftsmen's associations met at Frankfurt, where a split developed between a small conservative group, mostly consisting of master craftsmen intent on re-establishing the guilds, and a progressive General Workers' Congress, largely supported by journeymen.[33] The latter's anti-capitalist agenda ensured that it became the largest working-class association and the nucleus of a future trade union movement, which was to develop in the 1860s. During August and September 1848, delegates from Hamburg, Prussia and Saxony, under the stewardship of Stephan Born, founded the General German Workers' Federation (*Allgemeine Deutsche Arbeiterverbrüderung*) at a gathering in Berlin. In essence more of a self-help organization than a political party, it aimed to integrate workers into the political establishment and to promote those social issues which were so blatantly neglected by the National Assembly.

The 1848 uprising in Baden and its impact on other German regions

Wolfram Siemann interprets the first stage of the German revolutions as a popular uprising, the result of a grass-roots movement with little input from the middle classes,[34] an opinion reinforced by many of the popular history works written for the 150th anniversary of the revolutions.[35] Comparisons between the different regions will indicate the extent to which the rural population supported these actions and will also seek to establish the dynamics of this first phase of the German revolutions. Friedrich Hecker's movement did indeed consist largely of peasants and impoverished craftsmen. Recent research of local developments would indicate that their grass-roots activities were closely associated with events in Switzerland and France, but that the revolution must also be seen in the context of liberal, parliamentary activities in Mannheim, Heidelberg, Offenburg, Konstanz and even Frankfurt. Indeed, the involvement of middle-class academics was considerable. In addition to the stewardship of Struve and Hecker, the enthusiastic response of the poet J. V. Scheffel, and the support of the parliamentarians Mittermaier and Brentano, of several doctors, teachers and country advocates cannot be ignored.[36] Hecker's relationship to his mentor, the constitutional lawyer J. A. von Itzstein was crucial to his political development, as was the tradition of the Heidelberg and Freiburg law schools and his connections with radicals of the stature of Jacoby and Blum.[37]

News of the French Revolution reached the Baden border post in Kehl on 26 February, from where it spread to Offenburg and Mannheim. The following day, Gustav Struve, nobleman, advocate and editor of the student magazine *Zeitschrift für Deutschlands Hochschulen*, who had already lent his voice to the Offenburg programme, organized a mass meeting in Mannheim. He had gained prominence when he took on the local censor and brother of a notoriously reactionary, anti-Semitic Badenese army officer, who not only upheld Metternich's authoritarian, illiberal regime, but also supported an extreme catholic position. Struve's efforts resulted in the dismissal of the censor and established Mannheim as a liberal and democratic stronghold. A petition was sent to the parliament in Karlsruhe, advocating an all-German initiative against the perceived threat of French or Russian aggression and seeking full self-determination, free education and political freedom for all social classes. Additional demands related to the creation of a militia with democratically elected officers, total press freedom, jury trial as in England and the establishment of an all-German parliament. Similar propositions were adopted in Heidelberg and Offenburg; since the second Baden chamber refused to accept them directly from the delegation, they were presented to the parliamentary representative Hecker on 1 March. These so-called 'March Demands' were also raised in many other German towns, and were partially adopted by the Federal Diet in Frankfurt. Immediate press freedom had been granted by Grand Duke Leopold of Baden, who by 15 March acceded to all the demands raised in the Mannheim petition.[38]

In the contrasting characters of Struve and Hecker, the liberal, constitutional elements met with the more radical, populist demands of the rural communities in Baden. Democratic and radical interpreters have represented Hecker as the symbol of the Baden revolution, as some kind of legendary Robin Hood figure, whereas to his more conservative, liberal contemporaries he was something of a bogeyman, the inspiration for *Struwwelpeter*.[39] Friedrich Hecker was, in fact, the son of a high-ranking government official. A pupil of the Mannheim *Gymnasium* and a product of the new, neo-classical, Humboldtian education, he studied law at Heidelberg, where the faculty had been profoundly influenced by the liberal constitutionalists Carl von Rotteck, Mittermaier and Welcker. Rather than enter government employment, Hecker chose to become an advocate and work on behalf of ordinary people. Fully integrated into Mannheim liberal circles, he became city councillor in 1842 and soon thereafter a delegate to the second parliamentary chamber in Karlsruhe. In 1845 he visited the democrats Robert Blum in Leipzig and Johann Jacoby in Königsberg, but his political affiliations led to his expulsion from Prussia. In 1847 his defence of Gustav Struve against censor Uria-Sacharaga marked the beginning of their friendship and collaboration. Both men made a decisive contribution to the Offenburg Declaration (September 1847) which anticipated the Mannheim Petition. In the same year, Hecker, supported by Struve, defended the Sulzfeld villagers who were demanding independence from feudal lords and their anachronistic rights.[40] As a radical democrat, he not only succeeded in mobilizing popular sentiment in the cause of the revolution, but was also a restraining influence when – together with liberals such as Mathy and Bassermann – he intervened against anti-Semitic excesses in the 'settling of accounts' with Jewish money-lenders.[41] Hecker's campaign on behalf of peasants and small craftsmen was successful; on 10 March the government announced the immediate abolition of all remaining feudal privileges. Further unrest in Sulzfeld and other villages in the Odenwald and Kraichgau led to the closure of local tax offices, to the seizure and subsequent destruction of tax registers, the dismissal of revenue collectors, the restoration of traditional common lands and the settlement of other disputed claims.

The radical democrats Hecker and Struve were intent on tackling both constitutional and social issues. Liberal activists, such as Bassermann, Mathy and Mittermaier were preoccupied with constitutional matters and the preservation of a monarchic order. Early results favoured the liberals; the 'March Ministries' in Baden, Württemberg and Hesse had formed new liberal governments, acceding to the demands of the Mannheim Petition. Riding on this wave of success, fifty-one representatives from Baden, Württemberg, Bavaria, Hesse, Prussia, Nassau and Frankfurt met in Heidelberg on 5 March and agreed on the formation of a national German assembly.[42] At its inaugural meeting in Frankfurt (31 March), the 'Pre-Parliament' (*Vorparlament*) was formed, but only after the rejection of Struve's radically democratic demands for a permanent national parliament. Neither he nor Hecker were elected to the Executive Committee and these setbacks provided the impetus for Hecker to call for revolution in Baden. Hecker's decision remains controversial; fellow radicals such as Blum accused him of undermining the success of the whole movement.[43] Viewed with hindsight, his 'poorly led ragtag army of journeymen, labourers, peasants and students'[44] was no match for regular military units from Württemberg and Hesse, commissioned by the German Confederation. Looking at events from within his own radical and republican base in Baden, Hecker had misjudged the national scene, but he cannot be accused of having misled the peasants in order to foster his own ambitions.[45]

From the perspective of the more radical camp in Baden, Hecker's revolution seemed to stand a chance. The popular mood was turbulent, regular troops were uneasy, and often reluctant to intervene on behalf of the authorities.[46] Even the famous *Staatslexikon* by Rotteck and Welcker declared: 'It is therefore obvious that radicalism, this most extreme form of democracy, has its most numerous supporters and its actual strength among the lowest strata of the population.'[47] The unlawful intervention of the liberal deputy Mathy in arresting Josef Fickler, editor of the radical Konstanz *Seeblätter*, served to indicate the need for speedy and decisive action, intimating that a counter-revolution was already in the offing and that Hecker would be the next target. Relying on popular support and hoping for backing from Switzerland and the German Legion in France, Hecker proclaimed the German Republic in Konstanz on 11 April, with the intention of marching on Karlsruhe. His hopes of raising four columns, however, were dashed when the citizens of Konstanz quickly lost their enthusiasm; only fifty-five men followed the call to arms under the command of Lieutenant Franz Sigel. Once *en route*, many more volunteers joined, some well armed, others equipped only with scythes and other make-shift weapons so that, at the height of the campaign, the revolutionaries consisted of some ten thousand fighters.[48] Further support was promised from Freiburg, Donaueschingen, Offenburg and Mannheim as well as from German exiles in France. However, the speed with which the Confederation managed to dispatch troops to Baden proved decisive in defeating Hecker. On 20 April contingents from Württemberg, Hesse and Baden, an army of some 30,000 men, confronted Hecker's troops near Kandern. Following an exchange of fire the commander of the federal forces, Friedrich von Gagern, brother of the liberal politician Heinrich, was killed. Hecker's forces were routed and, after a second defeat two weeks later, the revolution collapsed. Hecker fled to Switzerland, and when the Frankfurt National Assembly blocked his political comeback later that year, he emigrated to the USA where, during the 1850s, he supported the Republican Party in its campaign against slavery.[49]

Although revolutionary energies were strongest in the southwest, political unrest, to a greater or lesser degree, erupted in most German lands. Baden's revolution spilled over into Württemberg, the Palatinate and Hesse, but events in Vienna and Berlin overshadowed Hecker's campaign and led to a 'wait and see attitude'. Württemberg, where divisions between liberal middle-class activists, workers and the rural population seemed more pronounced than in Baden, experienced little actual unrest.[50] Many rural and working-class activists were discredited as alcoholics or petty criminals. Württemberg's liberal Römer government seemed particularly hostile to political gatherings.[51] Much of the unrest did not go beyond the looting of bakeries or breaking the windows of unpopular figures in authority, usually accompanied by a cacophony of 'caterwauling'. The one significant liberal protest took place at the university town of Tübingen and spread to the capital Stuttgart. On the 2 March, Ludwig Uhland, the distinguished poet and liberal parliamentarian, renowned for his patriotic poetry during the Napoleonic wars, addressed a huge gathering of students and townspeople. His speech emphasized the importance of the German 'Volk', of national unification and of popular participation in government, and his petition addressed issues almost identical to those of Mannheim and Offenburg.[52] Nassau, Hanau,

Hanover, Munich and Brunswick saw similar petitions. These similarities seem to indicate that communication between individual revolutionary centres was well organized and that these constitutional and liberal demands had widespread support, even among the 'underclass'.

Examples from other regions seem to indicate a comparable bifurcation between the social and economic demands of peasants and their lower-class counterparts and the constitutional and national issues raised by middle-class liberals. Wetzlar and the territories along the rivers Lahn and Dill offer a particularly interesting perspective. Wetzlar had been the seat of the Imperial Court and a free city until 1806. After 1815, Wetzlar's *Gymnasium*, established in the Humboldtian tradition, became a focal point for liberal and democratic activities, with strongly opposing factions among teachers and students. Several teachers, who had fought in the Wars of Liberation, were members of the *Burschenschaften* and fostered links with Turnvater Jahn.[53] As elsewhere in Europe, the rural population endured poor harvests, with local conditions exacerbated by considerable feudal burdens and inheritance laws which led to the division of farms. Trade and industry were underdeveloped with about 30 per cent relying on part-time work as weavers or following a trade, a large proportion making a livelihood as innkeepers (10 per cent), shoemakers (7.6 per cent) or tailors (6.3 per cent).[54] Nearly 40 per cent of households in Wetzlar were classified as poor.

Initially Wetzlar and the surrounding territory seemed less concerned about the revolution than Nassau, Hesse-Darmstadt or the Rhineland. Divisions between liberals and democrats were already in evidence and soon grievances among the rural population were to inspire more radical movements in surrounding areas. Incensed by their duke's arrogant, unyielding attitude, they refused to pay taxes, demanded their rights to common land, hunting and firewood and wanted elections for mayor and other local officers. By 18 April, the situation had reached a climax and crowds of armed peasants clashed with Prussian infantry and the local militia. The democrats of Wetzlar showed their sympathy for the peasants by releasing prisoners and erecting barricades to prevent troops from leaving their garrisons. Appeals to the liberal dominated Frankfurt parliament remained ineffective, the revolutionaries were condemned as 'communist agitators' for the insurrection.[55]

Events in the Rhineland have received much attention and can be summarized here.[56] The general pattern was similar to other regions, except that religious issues in this largely catholic province seemed to have played a more prominent role. When news of the Paris Revolution reached the Rhineland, fear of another French invasion caused some apprehension. Once these rumours proved unfounded, anxiety gave way to general rejoicing and the Marseillaise was taken up in preference to the much-despised

Hohenzollern anthem. Mass meetings, street demonstrations and petitions followed and in Darmstadt and Mainz liberal March Ministries replaced reactionary governments. The largest confrontation between revolutionaries and government loyalists erupted in Cologne, the capital of the Prussian Rhineland. Workers and journeymen initiated political action on 3 March, a day after the Women's Carnival, a traditional occasion for opposition to the forces in authority. The communist and charity physician Andreas Gottschalk and other prominent men led left-wing democrats. Their 'Pleas of the People' contained the usual March Demands, but also echoed those of Paris, including labour protection rights. An angry crowd stormed the council chamber, forcing the city fathers to flee. At the end of March eighteen city councils met in Cologne to discuss some co-ordinated approach. Initial attempts failed, and only after an angry confrontation with demonstrators were the province's representatives for the Pre-Parliament finally elected. A few days later Gottschalk founded the Democratic-Socialist Club which, in June, following high unemployment and an economic deterioration, demanded the formation of a German Republic.[57]

In Mainz, interdenominational services, including a Jewish representation, were held in the cathedral, with support from federal troops of the local garrison. Mainz, with its history of revolutionary unrest, obviously found it easier to organize a comprehensive protest movement than rural areas which had a scattered, less politically mature population. Just as the peasants' demands to exploit the forests and gain use of common land were not devoid of political awareness, so urban protests among workers and craftsmen were directed against tax collectors, grain speculators and factories which undercut local craft products with inferior goods. Some workers were more reactionary; fearing the impact of industrial progress, they attacked steamboats or damaged parts of the railroad. Protest in smaller towns was often restricted to 'caterwauling' or breaking windows, just as was the case in Württemberg. Civic guards, unlike their counterparts in Baden or Hesse-Nassau, tended to side with the authorities, and regular troops usually remained loyal to the government, especially those who had recently been posted from regions east of the river Elbe. The May elections to the National Assembly indicated some support for radical democracy, particularly in the southern Rhineland and the Bavarian Palatinate, whereas the more protestant regions around Elberfeld and Wuppertal and the Prussian Rhine province returned centre-right deputies. Following the pattern of so many other German regions, by June 1848 the democratic movement began to collapse. The old elites, aided by liberal and centre-right supporters gained the upper hand, fearful of a more radical turn of events which might undermine their own authority.

Saxony experienced only a brief revolutionary phase in the spring of 1848. Wedged between Prussia and Austria, the two most reactionary states of the German Confederation, its citizens may well have feared the worst, were they to challenge their existing regime. Its social and economic structure was unique in that half its population worked in the crafts or in industry. As in most other states, the Saxon monarchy made concessions to its people and established a new March. Ministry under Braun von der Pfordten.[58] Leipzig, famous for its book trade and publishing industry, was politically more enlightened than the capital Dresden, with its extensive bureaucracy. However, memories of the bloody repression of a peaceful demonstration in August 1845 were still alive, when clubs and societies had been closed down, writers had been persecuted and, despite Saxony's close constitutional links to Poland, Polish exiles had been expelled or extradited to Prussia. The potato famine of 1846/7 was worse than in most other German states, wages fell continuously while prices rose, with local rents going up by 25–30 per cent during that decade.[59] One parliamentarian observed: 'The alarming and frightening condition develops evermore menacingly, which will finally reveal nothing more than the gap between rich factory owners and poor labourers.'[60] Robert Blum, by now the major force in Leipzig's revolutionary scene, had inspired the masses and forged contacts between the radically democratic and the liberal middle-class factions, which led to collaboration between the liberal German Club and his own democratic Fatherland League.

Silesia, the last region to be discussed in this chapter, had a mixed population of German- and Polish-speaking citizens, poor agriculture and an outdated rural weaving industry. Silesia had experienced much unrest before 1848, an uprising of weavers in 1793 being only one of a long series of disturbances, the best known of which occurred in 1844, immortalized in the writings of Heine and Hauptmann. With few large towns and no radical university centre, unrest in Silesia was driven less by liberal demands than by purely economic considerations of poor living conditions and employment. In February 1848, just before the outbreak of the Paris Revolution, a secret circle of journeymen had been discovered in Breslau. Although their leaders were imprisoned and their publications confiscated, news of the Paris Revolution found a strong response in Silesia, even before turmoil erupted in Vienna or Berlin.[61] On 19 March, Breslau's city administrator and chief of police felt compelled to leave the city, fearful of violent demonstrations. Angry demonstrators in Breslau destroyed the railway line to Berlin, and neighbouring towns followed the pattern set by the provincial capital, storming bakeries and building barricades to prevent punitive actions by approaching troops. Journeymen demanded a civic guard of armed citizens, and unemployed members of the 'proletariat' exploited these urban disturbances, which in turn acted as a green light for rural unrest by peasants, who similarly ignored the liberal and moderate reform movements in favour of more radical, Luddite measures. Villagers of Langenbielau and Peterswaldau, centres of the 1844 weavers' uprising, took the lead, encouraged by local schoolteachers and village mayors, following the pattern in other regions, where wealthier and more educated individuals led these sporadic activities, with little evidence of organisation within clubs or associations. The similarity of the various demands registered, as well as their style and wording, indicates that these leaders, aware of agitation elsewhere, stayed in touch with revolutionaries up and down the country, and that the poorer, mountainous areas seemed more vocal than the prosperous village communities in the valleys.

The role of established protest groups

This section will illustrate how the press, various clubs and associations and – a novelty within this context – women contributed towards a dissemination of news and facilitated the formation of political factions during the spring and summer of 1848. As discussed previously, public opinion during the 1830s had achieved a high degree of organization, especially in towns and in middle-class circles. It can be demonstrated that the newly formed political public included all social classes, operating at a level which one would nowadays describe as grass-roots democracy and which has probably not achieved a similar degree of intensity since.

The very fact that calls for total press freedom tended to dominate the March Demands indicates how crucial the role and importance of this medium was seen to be. The Frankfurt National Assembly defined press freedom in a complex and detailed manner, including for instance the prohibition of economic and technical restrictions such as an insufficient supply of paper or artificially created transportation problems.[62] The vast majority of publications consisted of newspapers, in particular political organs specific to a social class or quasi-political association, such as Stephan Born's *Das Volk*, mouthpiece of the nascent trade union *Arbeiterverbrüderung*, Robert Blum's *Deutsche Reichstags-Zeitung* and Hecker's *Volksfreund*, influential in working-class and craftsmen's circles. Gervinus' *Deutsche Zeitung* represented the liberal-constitutional part and later became associated with the *Casino*. Prussia's conservative circles were served by the famous *Kreuzzeitung*, one of its journalists being the novelist Theodor Fontane, while the political wing of Rhineland catholicism offered the *Historisch-politische Blätter*.[63] Reading material for the most radical 'Jacobin' circles was either Karl Marx' *Neue Rheinische Zeitung* or the Berlin *Volksfreund*, edited by Gustav Adolf Schlöffel.[64]

It is clear that men of great charisma, intelligence and commitment were in the forefront of German journalism, establishing a tradition which has remained alive in Germany until very recently. In general, the number of papers in circulation rose sharply and the political press in particular achieved a level of penetration not experienced since. Even regions with no independent local paper received regular and detailed information on local and national events, either from the neighbouring regional press or through an official local publication, under the rubric 'edification and entertainment'.[65] Party political exchanges were hard-hitting and of a high standard. Prior to the Revolution, Austria had nineteen political papers, a number which in 1848 rose to 306, accounting for 80 per cent of all newspaper output.[66] Between 1847 and 1849 the number of high-profile papers for Austria's intelligentsia increased from seventy-nine to 215 and nearly doubled in many other German states.[67] Although the more popular titles achieved publication figures of little more than 20,000 copies, with a population density of less than half of today's, each newspaper was also read by many more people than would now be the case. Illiteracy in Germany had declined to approximately 20 per cent, with news publications and the dissemination of political opinion centred on reading-rooms, clubs and public gatherings. At the height of the constitutional debate, in the autumn of 1848, most German capitals received first-hand stenographer reports of proceedings at the Frankfurt Assembly.[68] A plethora of leaflets, posters, cartoons and popular street theatre, targeting the public on market days, at pilgrimages and other public events brought the revolution out on to the streets. Street ballads and songs provided further evidence of the well-informed and widespread nature of public opinion. Awareness of this grass-roots revolutionary culture is extremely significant, not least because it serves to illustrate the existence of a radical alternative to the more liberal, overwhelmingly middle-class representation at the National Assembly in Frankfurt.

Probably the most important feature of the early revolutionary phase was a new wave of political clubs and associations, building on earlier, less clearly defined organizations, established during the Napoleonic Wars and the *Vormärz*. Most political associations had been closed down in the aftermath of the Hambach Festival;[69] others had managed to continue in clandestine fashion, having transformed much of their political fervour into an often romantic notion of patriotism. Other groups avoided overt political activity by changing their original name to literary club or male voice choir. With the advent of the revolution the political side of these associations rapidly re-emerged. Political clubs and associations mushroomed, increasingly identified with very specific issues and taking on the role of quasi-political parties. The fastest growth occurred in those areas which had a background of some solid political or at least constitutional tradition, such as the majority of the southern German states, the Rhineland and certain other cities and urban areas. New voting rights, enfranchising some 75 per cent of the male population, led to a general politicization. A turnout at elections of between 40 and 75 per cent varied between regions but represents a significant figure, in view of the many impediments such as local political pressure, lack of electoral experience, not to mention poverty and excessive working hours. The proliferation of clubs, their astute political outlook, their contribution to election campaigns and reaction to developments at Frankfurt, indicate that a sophisticated, mature political culture had been established, comparable to that prevailing in neighbouring countries.[70] Political affiliation was no longer related to social background; clubs were organized according to democratic principles and membership was open to everybody. Robert Blum serves as an example of how the 'Kulturnation' of the 1800s had been honed into a politically mature society. In 1839 he edited a *General Theatre Dictionary*, and during the *Vormärz* he had held the view that, 'for us Germans, next to the church, the only public place [was] the theatre stage',[71] but by 1848 he had entered the political arena. His association for the promotion of public speaking (*Redeübungsverein*) now changed its name to the Fatherland Association (*Vaterlandsverein*) and became the first mass political organization with branches in many other German states.

Similar observations apply to the politicization of universities. In March 1848 debates and discussions, mostly led by students in the Berlin *Zeitungshalle*, soon spilled over into the area of the *Tiergarten*, drawing in an audience of diverse social and educational backgrounds.[72] Throughout the country reading clubs, male choirs and other musical organizations acquired a political agenda. The *Turnvereine* (Gymnasts' Societies) in particular devoted themselves to political activities where, in association with the *Burschenschaften*, they became breeding grounds for republicanism. In the aftermath of Hecker's defeat, many of these democratic clubs and associations were prohibited in Baden, only to re-emerge once the National Assembly had published its basic laws (28 December 1848), guaranteeing all Germans the 'unlimited right' to form associations.[73] This chapter will concentrate on the spring and summer of 1848, though an occasional glance at later developments may be necessary.

A division between democratic-republican and liberal-constitutional associations became evident in the period following Hambach. The democrats demanded a new political order, independent of the Confederation and any remaining links with the old system, leaving the final shape of the government still open; the liberals advocated constitutional reform, based on the existing political order. The democratic associations, taking the name *Volksverein*, believed in the sovereignty of the 'Volk', the roots of which can be traced back to Herder and Fichte. All the *Volksvereine* harboured a latent suspicion of the Frankfurt National Assembly and looked to Berlin for a national lead, gaining inspiration from free-lance journalists, philosophers and poets such as Julius Fröbel, Ferdinand Freiligrath, Ludwig Feuerbach and Andreas Gottschalk. The concept of *Volkssouveränität* (sovereignty of the people) gained particular significance in the person of Fröbel, who formulated policies critical of Rousseau's *volonté génerale* and of Marxist communism. The young Fröbel advocated material wellbeing, general education and universal freedom,[74] appealing to Silesian peasants, craftsmen and journeymen and to radical intellectuals.

The constitutional associations, searching for a 'third way' between republicanism and monarchism, only later defined themselves as liberals. Their clubs bore a variety of names, indicative of their connections with the bourgeoisie, constitutional monarchy or patriotic and national movements. The majority of their members were middle-class citizens, often wary of losing their privileges to the lower classes and the dispossessed. With strongholds in northern and central Germany, many of their leading figures were civil servants or high-ranking academics who formed an over-proportionally strong element in the Frankfurt National Assembly.

A good example of the rivalry and fluctuating fortunes of the two political associations can be gleaned from observing the situation in Wetzlar. The 1840s saw the establishment of many male voice choirs and gymnastics societies, with the former recruiting older, wealthier, liberal members and the latter more radical and democratic ones. By the summer of 1848 political differences between democrats and constitutionals began to form, reflecting an emerging polarization within the National Assembly. The democratic *Bürgerverein* recruited among academics and prosperous middle-class citizens, but also among craftsmen and a majority of the Jewish community. The constitutional association, drawing its membership from the *Casino* Club and old, wealthy patrician families, was much smaller, but also attracted a proportionally high number of academics.

Other factions were less important and their role can be summarized. The political influence of catholics in the Rhineland, the Palatinate and in Baden has already been discussed. In 1846 Pope Pius IX had encouraged liberal reforms and spoken up for an Italian Federation and in March 1848 the first of a number of Pius Associations, named after him, was formed. By now, however, this movement had become conservative and even anti-liberal: the associations supported church influence in education and the re-admission of the Jesuit Order. Other conservative or reactionary organizations gradually emerged during the summer of 1848. In Bavaria an association for the constitutional monarchy and for religious freedom was founded, attracting mostly catholic priests.[75]

Among the various other pressure groups, women's organizations are particularly noteworthy. A close study of the revolution in Baden would reveal the importance of the role of the wives of the revolutionaries: Marie Josefine Hecker, Amalia Struve and Emma Herwegh, whose courage, organizational talent, loyalty and resilience were decisive. Research during the last two decades has successfully countered traditional views of family life during the *Biedermeier*.[76] While the revolutions seem to have enhanced the social and political status of women, it is necessary to recognize that their action in radical politics goes back further, as evidenced in the *Staatslexikon* under the entry 'barricades': with reference to the French July Revolution, the author suggests that a defence with barricades can become 'impenetrable', if women and children throw paving stones or pour boiling oil and water against attacking soldiers from the windows of neighbouring houses.[77] The best-known women's representative is Louise Otto-Peters who founded the *Frauenzeitung* in April 1848 and who is often associated with the origins of German feminism.[78] Her *Allgemeine Deutsche Frauenverein* was influential in raising the general awareness of women's potential role in education. Women's participation in child rearing, and education in general, was now seen as an opportunity for upper-class women in particular to gain access to wider cultural and also political activities. Several of these women had been educated during the Romantic period, when they had enjoyed a certain degree of intellectual and social emancipation. Bettina von Arnim, Goethe's friend and sister of the poet Clemens Brentano, wrote on the subject of the poor in Hamburg, criticizing the government and police for many of their social problems.[79] Women's involvement in church activities provided further scope for political activities. In *Eine Reise nach Ostende* (1849), Malwilda von Meysenbug developed a utopian view of a society, coupled with severe criticism of the role of the church and its lack of compassion on social issues. Her secularized form of humanism culminated in a demand for total self-realization, and her ideas brought her into contact with Julius Fröbel and with Elisabeth Althaus and her circle of radical democrats. Meysenbug was acutely aware of male domination in society and demanded intellectual equality between the sexes.[80] The career of Mathilde Franziska Anneke offers another example of a liberated woman. By 1844 she had published an anthology of poems under her own name, acknowledging her social position as a divorcée. In 1848 she took over the financial and editorial side of the democratic-revolutionary *Neue Kölnische Zeitung* with its motto 'prosperity, freedom and education for all'. When this publication was banned, she went on to edit a paper for women. In 1849 she took part in the final phase of the Baden Revolution and, together with her second husband, managed to escape from the fortress of Rastatt. Anneke's passion for human rights turned her into an advocate of women's issues[81] and her radical feminist position caused her to depart from her early, edifying forms of religious poetry towards a fundamental critique of religion.

Nevertheless, it was in the nature of the social role of women at that time, that most activists remained unrecognized, in that much of their effort was restricted to working behind the scenes, producing banners for clubs and associations, flags for the militias, running soup kitchens and caring for the wounded and orphaned. Some of the more emancipated women from middle-class backgrounds did play a part in public debates at meetings and contributed to newspapers,[82] while working-class and lower-middle-class women were involved in the construction of barricades and in the provision of ammunition. Fanny Lewald had experienced the February Revolution in Paris and was impressed by the way women were accepted as a natural part of the revolutionary force, something as yet unheard of in Germany.[83] The foundation of democratic clubs, specifically by and for women during the autumn of 1848, indicates how women had gained a new confidence in their public role, while revealing by implication that many existing clubs, even on the political left, remained exclusively male territory.

Government responses and the establishment of the Pre-Parliament

We have already seen how most powers, following the unrest of March 1848, responded with a change of government, bringing liberally minded constitutionalists to power. The Prussian Rhineland led the way, followed by Württemberg, Nassau, Hanover, Bavaria, Saxony and Hesse. All these 'March Ministries' were headed by liberals who, during the Pre-March, had formed the opposition to the existing parliaments. Once in power, they felt the weight of government responsibility, striving to uphold the constitutions for which they themselves had fought only months earlier. In an attempt to prevent what they saw as the revolutions from getting out of hand, they felt compelled to slow down the political momentum and harmonize further development in preparation for a democratic national assembly. Such policies coincided with the political aims of their monarchs who hoped to preserve as much as possible of their former powers. Grand Duke Leopold of Baden for instance, fearful of the spread of revolution from France, agreed to the formation of a civil guard, complete press freedom and a jury system, in an attempt 'to calm the country and to hold it together through the establishment of a chamber which would support the government'.[84] The new Württemberg government under liberal prime minister Friedrich Römer proved more hawkish, closing several political clubs and even authorizing treason trials against followers of Hecker. Bavaria and Hesse, too, introduced anti-revolutionary measures to uphold law and order.

The situation in Munich was somewhat unique and cannot easily be placed within the overall context of events. It would be easy to focus on the enigmatic figure of Lola Montez, a Scottish–Creole dancer whose real name was Eliza Dolores Gilbert, and to interpret political events as the consequence of a bizarre sex scandal between this twenty-seven year old divorcée of dubious origin and a sexagenarian king. Early in 1848 Munich was shaken by disturbances, directed against King Ludwig and his government. Prince Karl von Leiningen, who later took a prominent role in the Frankfurt National Assembly, became the leader of a liberal reform movement; its March demands brought Bavaria into line with other states of the Third Germany.[85] However, when Lola Montez began to interfere in Bavarian politics, the scandal took centre stage, estranging the king from both his cabinet and army, and alienating him from his conservatives and clerical allies. At Lola's behest, the liberal government was sacked and replaced by a democratically minded administration which after only a few weeks also lost Lola's support. Reactionary clerics at Munich University initiated public demonstrations against Lola, eventually forcing her to leave Bavaria. Liberal democratic forces took advantage of the confusion: on 4 March demonstrators stormed the Munich armoury, two days later the king had to agree to the 'March Demands' and on 20 March he was forced to resign, the only German monarch who personally fell victim to the revolution.

Events in Bavaria were ominous for the other German states. Ludwig's explicit consent to a democratically elected national assembly was seen by other monarchs to undermine the old political order.[86] Heinrich von Gagern, the future president of the Frankfurt Assembly, complicated matters by suggesting that any federal body should be headed by a centralized imperial ministry under the Prussian crown. His brother Max, a diplomat in the service of Austria, was to seek approval for this centrist solution from other German courts. Such a proposal went in the face of republican demands which threatened to be over-ridden in the cause of internal unity. The fifty-one representatives at Heidelberg were forced to agree on a compromise, ensuring free elections to a national assembly, but rejecting a republic. Seven men of 'national reputation' were entrusted with the task of establishing such an assembly.[87] The outcome was the Pre-Parliament which met in Frankfurt from 31 March until 3 April. Its 574 delegates failed to represent the various German states 'in accordance with their populations',[88] as had been demanded at Heidelberg. None of the delegates had a democratic or popular mandate; the 141 Prussian delegates for instance had been recruited from among municipal councillors. The small state of Hesse-Dramstadt sent eighty-four delegates while only two represented Austria.

Though there can be no doubt as to the integrity of von Gagern, it is probably true to say that his political outlook was more romantic than revolutionary, closer to the ideas of von Stein than to those of the democrats.

71

Struve's democratic wing, represented by only eighteen members, proposed freely elected presidents for the individual states and an all-German federal constitution, based on the American model. This proposal was turned down and neither Struve nor Hecker could gain seats on the Committee of Fifty, which succeeded the Pre-Parliament on 3 April. Few of their social demands were met, though there was a promise of aid to the unemployed and universal state education. The Committee had no real power and could only voice opinions,[89] but was authorized to administer the forthcoming elections which resulted in the new all-German parliamentary assembly in Frankfurt. Its first president was Heinrich von Gagern, a choice which effectively excluded democrats from political power.

The democratic Offenburg programme had hoped to establish a distinctly democratic framework of government, comparable to modern constitutions in France and the United States and, indeed, more progressive than the constitution of today's Federal Republic. By comparison, the weak compromise solution proposed by the Pre-Parliament produced an Assembly which was vulnerable to a take-over by reactionary forces. This Assembly soon became involved in national and foreign affairs which made it reliant on Prussian and Austrian support. It proved far too conciliatory to federal considerations, and too strongly influenced by romantic notions of a medieval heritage and patriotic memories of the liberation wars against Napoleon. Almost from its inception, the national issue was seen to invoke a more enthusiastic response than any democratic consideration. Many of its leading representatives were members of the March Ministries. It was only natural that, in hoping to realize their particular political agenda, they would reject a radical programme which might jeopardize their own positions. In coming into office, like so many other political agitators, they shifted markedly towards a conservative, politically 'realistic' approach. In addition, a large number of representatives were civil servants, a majority of them with a legal background. Lawyers are, more often than not, upholders of authority and of the *status quo*; they tend to be 'etatist' in an Hegelian, and essentially Prussian tradition, conservative in the broadest sense of the word.[90] Birth and education had elevated them above the common needs of farmers and journeymen, had instilled in them an instinctive fear of revolution and nurtured a belief in the evolutionary progression of constitutional reform. In this context it is compelling to conclude that the National Assembly, from its very inception, would be ill equipped to bring about the changes which might have transformed Germany into a progressive democratic political and social entity.

Notes

1 Anton Springer, *Friedrich Christoph Dahlmann*, vol. 2 (Leipzig, 1872), p. 206.
2 Friedrich Hecker, *Die Erhebung des Volkes in Baden für die deutsche Republik im Frühjahr 1848* (Basel, 1848), p. 17.
3 'Berlin in der Bewegung von 1848', in *Die Gegenwart* (Leipzig, 1849), p. 538.
4 Carl Friedrich Graf Vitzhum von Eckstädt, *Berlin und Wien in den Jahren 1845–1852. Politische Privatbriefe*, 2nd edn (Stuttgart, 1886), p. 73.
5 Cf. letter by Beckerath to Mevissen (27 February), in Hans Fenske ed., *Quellen zur deutschen Revolution 1848–1849* (Darmstadt, 1996), p. 43.
6 Protokoll der zehnten Sitzung der Bundesversammlung, para. 108, in *Protokolle der Deutschen Bundesversammlung 1848* (Frankfurt/M., 1848), pp. 179f, in Fenske ed., *Quellen*, pp. 46f.
7 Cf. Irene Jung, Hans-Werner Hahn and Rüdiger Störkel, *Die Revolution von 1848 an Lahn und Dill* (Wetzlar, 1998), pp. 29f.
8 Rüdiger Hachtmann, *Berlin 1848. Eine Politik- und Gesellschaftsgeschichte der Revolution* (Bonn, 1997), pp. 131f.
9 Alfred Georg Frei and Kurt Hochstuhl, *Wegbereiter der Demokratie. Die badische Revolution 1848/49. Der Traum von der Freiheit* (Karlsruhe, 1997), p. 36.
10 The house of Haber, the largest bank in Karlsruhe and two other major banks had collapsed a year earlier, when the Frankfurt bank of the Rothschilds refused to honour their bills of exchange. Ibid., pp. 34f.
11 Hachtmann, *Berlin 1848*, p. 133.
12 K. Ries, 'Bauern und ländliche Unterschichten', in Christoph Dipper and Ulrich Speck eds, *1848. Revolution in Deutschland* (Frankfurt/M., 1998), p. 263.
13 D. W. Sabean, *Property, Production and Family in Neckarhausen, 1700–1870* (Cambridge, 1990), p. 50.
14 C. Welcker, 'Bauer' in Carl von Rotteck and Carl Welcker eds, *Das Staatslexikon. Encyklopädie der sämmtlichen Staatswissenschaften für alle Stände*, 2nd edn, vol. 2 (Altona, 1845), p. 212.
15 David Blackbourn, *The Fontana History of Germany 1780–1918. The Long Nineteenth Century* (London, 1997), p. 111.
16 *Die Gegenwart*, 5 (1847), pp. 274f.
17 Rotteck and Welcker eds, *Staatslexikon*, vol. 2, pp. 212f.
18 Cf. Ries, 'Bauern und ländliche Unterschichten', p. 262.
19 For a full discussion cf. chapter 4.
20 For a full explanation cf. T. Pierenkemper, 'Labour Market, Labour Force and Standard of Living: from Agriculture to Industry', in Klaus J. Bade ed., *Population, Labour and Migration in 19th- and 20th-Century Germany* (Lemington Spa, Hamburg, New York, 1987), p. 40.
21 Generalisations are, however, dangerous, since even within this group an increasing proletarization and creeping pauperism is noticeable. Cf. Wolfgang Kaschuba and Carola Lipp, *1848 – Provinz und Revolution* (Tübingen, 1979), p. 37.
22 Cf. minutes of meetings of the Paris Community of the Communist League on 8 and 9 March, in Karl Marx and Frederick Engels, *Collected Works*, vol. 6 (London, 1977), pp. 654–8.
23 F. Lenger, 'Beyond Exceptionalism: Notes on the Artisanal Phase of the Labour Movement in France, England, Germany and the United States', *International Review of Social History*, 36 (1991), p. 8.

24 E. Engelberg, 'Zur Forschung über Entstehung, Struktur und Entwicklung des Prole-
    tariats', in Hartmann Zwahr ed., *Die Konstitutierung der deutschen Arbeiterklasse von
    den dreißiger bis zu den siebziger Jahren des 19. Jahrhunderts* (Berlin, 1981), pp. 255f.
25 F.-W. Henning, 'Industrialisierung und dörfliche Einkommensmöglichkeiten', in
    H. Kellenheinz ed., *Agrarische Nebengewerbe und Formen der Reagrarisierung*
    (Stuttgart, 1975), p. 159.
26 'Verhandlungen in der 6. öffentlichen Sitzung der sächsischen zweiten Kammer', 21
    February, 1847, in J. Lasker and F. Gerhard eds, *Des deutschen Volkes Erhebung im
    Jahre 1848* (Danzig, 1848), pp. 252f. Quoted from Veit Valentin, *Geschichte der
    deutschen Revolution 1848–49*, vol. 1 (Berlin, 1930), p. 228.
27 P. Marschalck, *Deutsche Überseewanderung im 19. Jahrhundert. Ein Beitrag zur
    soziologischen Theorie der Bevölkerung* (Stuttgart, 1973), pp. 35–7.
28 T. Mergel, 'Sozialmoralische Milieus und Revolutionsgeschichtsschreibung. Zum Bild
    der Revolution von 1848/49 in den Subgesellschaften des deutschen Kaiserreichs', in
    Christian Jansen and Thomas Mergel eds, *Die Revolution von 1848/49. Erfahrung,
    Verarbeitung, Deutung* (Göttingen, 1998), p. 253.
29 Jürgen Kocka, *Lohnarbeit und Klassenbildung. Arbeiter und Arbeiterbewegung in
    Deutschland 1800–1875* (Berlin, 1983), p. 276.
30 Quoted from Martin Hundt, 'Zur Frühgeschichte der revolutionären Arbeiter-
    bewegung in Stuttgart', *Jahrbuch der Geschichte*, 7 (1972), p. 299.
31 Cf. Thorsten Maentel, 'Robert Blum', in Sabine Freitag ed., *Die Achtundvierziger.
    Lebensbilder aus der deutschen Revolution 1848/49* (Munich, 1998), p. 141.
32 W. Schieder, 'Die Rolle der deutschen Arbeiter in der Revolution von 1848/49',
    in W. Klötzer *et al.* eds, *Ideen und Strukturen der deutschen Revolution 1848*
    (Frankfurt/M., 1974), p. 46.
33 Wolfram Siemann, *The German Revolution of 1848–49*, trans. by Christiane Banerji
    (London, 1998), p. 90; cf. also Kocka, *Lohnarbeit*, p. 175.
34 Siemann, *German Revolution*, p. 68.
35 For example in Franz X. Vollmer, 'Es gilt, in Baden loszuschlagen', in *Zeitpunkte,
    Zeitmagazin*, Nr. 1 (1998), pp. 26–38. For further evidence cf. chapter 9.
36 Frei, Hochstuhl, *Wegbereiter*, pp. 68f.
37 Cf. Sabine Freitag, 'Friedrich Hecker: Der republikanische Souverän', in Freitag ed.,
    Die Achtundvierziger, pp. 51f.
38 *Allgemeine Zeitung*, 11 March 1848, in Hans Jessen ed., *Die deutsche Revolution
    1848/49 in Augenzeugenberichten*, 2nd edn (Düsseldorf, 1968), p. 40.
39 Helmut Fritz, 'Putsch der Tintenhelden. Wie ein Nervenarzt in seiner Kinderfibel
    Geheimcodes der Anarchie versteckte', *Merkur*, Nr. 10 (6 March 1998), pp. 36f;
    cf. also 'Das Guckkasten-Lied vom großen Hecker', reprinted in Heinz Rieder, *Die
    Völker läuten Sturm. Die europäische Revolution 1848/49* (Gernsbach, 1997), p. 76.
40 Frei and Hochstuhl, *Wegbereiter*, p. 49.
41 Ibid., p. 50.
42 Ernst Rudolf Huber, *Deutsche Verfassungsgeschichte seit 1789*, 3rd edn, vol. 2 (Stutt-
    gart, 1988), pp. 326–8.
43 Robert Blum to his wife, 13 April 1848, quoted from Ludwig Bergsträsser ed., *Das
    Frankfurter Parlament in Briefen und Tagebüchern* (Frankfurt/M., 1929), p. 352.
44 Blackbourn, *History of Germany*, p. 144.
45 Cf. P. Assion, 'Der Heckerkult', *Zeitschrift für Volkskunde*, 87 (1991/1), p. 60.
46 Sabrina Müller, 'Soldaten, Bürger, Barrikaden. Konflikte und Allianzen während der
    Revolution von 1848/49', in Jansen and Mergel eds, *Die Revolution*, esp. pp. 47–51.

47 Rotteck and Welcker eds, *Staatslexikon*, vol. 3. p. 325.
48 Siemann, *German Revolution*, p. 69.
49 Freitag, 'Friedrich Hecker', p. 58.
50 Wolfgang Kaschuba and Carola Lipp, *1848 – Provinz und Revolution, Kultureller Wandel und soziale Bewegung im Königreich Württemberg* (Tübingen, 1979), p. 171.
51 Ibid., pp. 184–6.
52 Ludwig Uhland, *Werke*, H. Fröschle and W. Scheffler eds, vol. 4 (Munich, 1980–4), p. 697.
53 Jung, Hahn and Störkel, *Die Revolution*, p. 36.
54 Ibid., pp. 24–6.
55 Ibid., p. 64.
56 Cf. in particular Jonathan Sperber, *Rhineland Radicals. The Democratic Movement and the Revolution of 1848–1849* (Princeton, NJ, 1991), pp. 145–54.
57 Jürgen Herres, 'Köln', in Christoph Dipper and Ulrich Speck eds, *1848. Revolution in Deutschland* (Frankfurt/M., 1998), p. 115.
58 Letter by King Frederick August II to King Frederick IV of Prussia, in Jessen ed., *Die deutsche Revolution*, p. 70.
59 Valentin, *Geschichte der deutschen Revolution*, vol. 1, p. 227.
60 Ibid., p. 227.
61 Cf. Helmut Bleiber, 'Bauern und Landarbeiter der preußischen Provinz Schlesien in der Märzrevolution 1848', in Walter Schmidt ed., *Demokratie, Liberalismus und Konterrevolution. Studien zur deutschen Revolution von 1848/49* (Berlin, 1998), p. 83.
62 Cf. also *Das Heppenheimer Programm der südwestdeutschen Liberalen*, in Huber, *Deutsche Verfassungsgeschichte*, vol. 2, pp. 324–6.
63 For an excellent introduction cf. Siemann, *The German Revolution*, pp. 110–19.
64 Hachtmann, *Berlin, 1848*, p. 311.
65 For a good survey in Hesse, cf. Jung, Hahn and Störkel, *Die Revolution*, pp. 129–52.
66 C. Elbinger, *Witz und Satire Anno 1848* (Vienna, 1948), p. 54.
67 Siemann, *German Revolution*, p. 113.
68 Franz Wigard ed., *Stenographischer Bericht über die Verhandlungen der deutschen constituierenden Nationalversammlung zu Frankfurt am Main* (Frankfurt/M., 1848/9).
69 Susanne Asche *et al.*, *Für die Freiheit streiten! 150 Jahre Revolution im Südwesten 1848/49* (Stuttgart, 1998), p. 26.
70 Siemann, *German Revolution*, p. 88; Blackbourn, *History of Germany*, p. 507.
71 Robert Blum, Carl Herleßsohn and Hermann Marggraf eds, *Allgemeines Theater-Lexicon oder Encyklopädie alles Wissenswerthes für Bühnenkünstler, Dilettanten und Theaterfreunde* (Altenburg/Leipzig, 1839), p. ix; quoted from Maentel, 'Robert Blum', p. 137.
72 Hachtmann, *Berlin 1848*, pp. 127f.
73 Franz X. Vollmer, *Offenburg 1848/49. Ereignisse und Lebensbilder aus einem Zentrum der badischen Revolution* (Karlsruhe, 1997), p. 144.
74 Rainer Koch, 'Julius Fröbel: Demokratie und Staat', in Freitag ed., *Die Achtundvierziger*, p. 152.
75 Manfred Botzenhardt, *Deutscher Parlamentarismus in der Revolutionszeit 1848–1850* (Düsseldorf, 1977), pp. 397f.
76 Cf. S. Bovenschen, *Die imaginierte Weiblichkeit* (Frankfurt/M., 1979); R. Möhrmann ed., *Frauenemanzipation im deutschen Vormärz. Texte und Dokumente* (Stuttgart,

1978); Anna Blos, *Frauen der deutschen Revolution 1848* (Dresden, 1928); Carola Lipp ed., *Frauen im Vormärz und in der Revolution 1848/49* (Moos, 1986); S. Paletschek, *Frauen und Dissens. Frauen im Deutschkatholizismus und in den freien Gemeinden 1841–1852* (Göttingen, 1990); Ann Taylor Allen, *Feminism and Motherhood in Germany 1800–1914* (New Brunswick, NJ, 1991); Carola Lipp ed., *Schimpfende Weiber und patriotische Jungfrauen. Frauen im Vormärz und in der Revolution 1848/49* (reprint Baden-Baden, 1998).

77 Rotteck and Welcker eds, *Staatslexikon*, vol. 2, p. 193.

78 Louise Otto, *Dem Reiche der Freiheit werb' ich Bürgerinnen. Die Frauenzeitung von Louise Otto*, Ute Gerhards *et al.* eds (Frankfurt/M., 1980).

79 Barbara Beuys, *Familienleben in Deutschland. Neue Bilder aus der deutschen Vergangenheit* (Reinbek b. Hamburg, 1980), pp. 368f.

80 Susanne Klabunde, 'Malwida von Meysenbug: Mit den Waffen der Freiheit und der Zukunft', in Freitag ed., *Die Achtundvierziger*, p. 230.

81 'Das Weib im Konflikt mit den sozialen Verhältnissen' [1847], in Freitag ed., *Die Achtundvierziger*, p. 218.

82 Sabine Kienitz, 'Frauen', in Dipper and Speck, *1848 Revolution*, pp. 272ff.

83 Hanna Ballin Lewis ed., *A Year of Revolutions, Fanny Lewald's Recollections of 1848* (Providence and Oxford, 1997), p. 85.

84 Grand Duke Leopold of Baden in a letter to Frederick William IV of Prussia, 1 March 1848, in Jessen ed., *Die deutsche Revolution*, p. 40.

85 Huber, *Deutsche Verfassungsgeschichte*, vol. 2, p. 505.

86 Cf. the proclamation of King Ludwig I of Bavaria, 6 March 1848, in Fenske ed., *Quellen*, p. 57; Letter by Radowitz to Frederick William IV on 9 March 1848, in Jessen ed., *Die deutsche Revolution*, pp. 42f.

87 Declaration of the Heidelberg Assembly in Huber, *Deutsche Verfassungsgeschichte*, vol. 2, pp. 326–8.

88 Ibid., p. 327.

89 Cf. Rudolph Stadelmann, *Social and Political History of the German 1848 Revolution*, trans. by James G. Chastain (Athens, OH, 1975), p. 54.

90 Cf. Ralf Dahrendorf, *Society and Democracy in Germany* (New York, 1969), p. 225.

Chapter 4

The revolutions in Vienna and Berlin

This chapter will cover the revolutionary events in the capitals of the two most important German states. In order to gain an overview of the course of the revolutions and a better insight into their dynamics, each revolution will be treated as an organic entity and a case study. References to developments elsewhere in Germany will be included only where they directly affect events in the two cities. This will not only afford a comparison of the two premier cities as seen from a revolutionary perspective, it will also allow an easier comparison with the Paris Revolution.

The revolution in Vienna: Social and economic conditions

This section will only be concerned with the situation in Austria, for a more general overview chapters 2 and 3 should be consulted. Ever since the Congress of Vienna, Austria had been considered the major force of reaction in Europe, especially by writers and critics. Her politically more-advanced writers refuted the stereotypical image of the Vienna of Austrian *Biedermeier*, with its contented bourgeoisie, residing in a peaceful, carefree city with a flourishing cultural life. Even stronger criticism emerged from within the Young Germany movement with Ludwig Börne, denigrating Austria as the China of Europe.[1] Among the many influential and widely read publications of the time which were critical of Austrian conservatism, was *Austria and Its Future*. Its author warned against the ossification of Metternich's system in the face of rising patriotism elsewhere. If progress was not forthcoming, 'four full-grown and fully armed nationalities will stand opposed to each other as enemies'.[2] Opposition to the regime of Prince Clemens von Metternich had grown steadily; his secretive and arbitrary system of government, supported by the most repressive and inquisitorial police methods in Europe could not last forever. By the late 1830s it had become fashionable in Vienna to ridicule the government, with opposition evident even inside the Viennese court. Count Franz Kolowrat, head of the empire's internal administration, though a conservative by nature, recognized the need for reform and opposed Metternich's uncompromising attitude, while Archduke John, future regent of Germany, also opposed Metternich from a liberal standpoint.[3] With the overthrow of Metternich the opportunity for reconciliation between the bourgeoisie and the court was much enhanced. The bourgeoisie depended on the court in matters of culture, entertainment and employment, either for the vast army of civil servants or commercially, where the court was the major customer of the supply of luxury goods, but also of general commodities. As a result, the Viennese middle classes considered the House of Habsburg with some affection. It is generally accepted that strong monarchist sympathies for the feeble-minded Ferdinand and nostalgia for his reformist great uncle Joseph II still played a decisive role with the public. Such sentiments stood in stark contrast to the Viennese hatred of the aristocracy and the clergy who were directly associated with the old regime. The liberal bourgeoisie were in favour of a speedy conclusion of the revolutionary uproar; their aim had been achieved with the overthrow of the Metternich system.

By contrast, the student body and many academics were far more radical. They had long been suspected of harbouring ideas of 'jingoistic Germanness, sovereignty of the people, national representation and other eccentric principles'.[4] The students' social backgrounds differed significantly from that of their fellow German students: more than 25 per cent of Vienna's students were sons of craftsmen and journeymen, another 14 per cent came from the ranks of lower civil servants.[5] They entertained links with the workers' communities throughout the Pre-March and showed commitment to their plight, while the bourgeoisie mostly ignored their conditions. The politically most prominent group of students came from the medical faculty or the arts, the students of technology enjoyed the closest contact with the working classes, whereas law students remained most distant. In general, these students also cultivated close contacts with the German student movement and were for a tighter union with the German-speaking territories.

Despite its antiquated political system and several economic downturns and social crises, Vienna's population had increased since 1815 by nearly 50 per cent, with more than 400,000 people accommodated within the city walls. The inner city remained the dwelling place of the middle classes, of artisans and domestic servants; the industrialized working classes and the mass of the unemployed lived on the outskirts. With an increase of only 11 per cent in Vienna's housing stock,[6] living conditions had worsened significantly. Work also deteriorated during the recent years of depression: on 25 February, the Vienna Stock Exchange experienced a major crash, when the Rothschild Bank withheld credit, leading to a fall of public funds by 30 per cent.[7] The subsequent credit squeeze brought silk manufacturing to its knees, having already suffered from the introduction of mechanical looms. The resulting unemployment and rising poverty was further exacerbated by the Europe-wide potato famine, causing large-scale starvation during the mid

1840s. An already critical economic situation was further depressed by a mass influx of unemployed workers from Bohemia. With a Dickensian system of child labour and unemployed skilled workers and journeymen, the situation remained volatile, as the Prague disturbances had shown, where workers protested against the introduction of mechanical calico printing. Machine wrecking was widespread, particularly in the summer of 1848, and courts tended to pronounce relatively lenient sentences, mindful of the 'poverty in the winter for the whole family, the excitement of the whole population and the dismissals caused by wage demands'.[8] As a result, a discontented industrial proletariat, which was to become one of the main forces of revolution, had developed on the outskirts of the city. Even sympathetic contemporaries, such as the writer Eduard Bauernfeld, were disturbed to hear the utopian ideas of Social Democrats: 'Who is to predict to what extent the utopian ideas of abolition of private property, of the community of property and the like will incite a wildly excited and uneducated mass of people?'[9] Though not yet organized, groups of workers began to express specific demands. The machine tool workers insisted on a reduction of the working day to ten hours, other groups demanded wage increases or a free Sunday. In general, wages were close to starvation level, with cotton workers worst off. On average, a day's earnings amounted to the equivalent of between two and four one-pound loaves of bread. Additional tensions arose between apprentices and journeymen on the one side and master craftsmen and their guilds on the other.[10] These figures serve to illustrate that Viennese workers cannot be collectively seen as a uniform group, they already began to form individual associations which aspired to an as yet rather elementary form of collective bargaining. Political rights, though not very high on their agenda, began to play a part: some opposed the new 'liberal' regulations that were to exclude them from service in the National Guard, which journeymen and domestic servants were permitted to join. Several of these groups were led by a reform-hungry academic intelligentsia, which centred on the University and the Polytechnic. The latter had been founded in 1815 in imitation of the Paris *Ecole Polytechnique* and – in Vienna's case – had become a benchmark for technological innovation. In 1840, members of the Polytechnic met together with industrialists and the Trade Association of Lower Austria to form the Legal-Political-Reading Club, whose official aim was to provide the educated, and in particular the legal profession 'with the most important and most interesting periodicals and the most significant artistic and scientific works'.[11] Another important centre for modernists was the Academy of Sciences, attracting physicians and medical students. The democratic press, too, took up the cause of the workers, demanding a ministry of public works, based on the Parisian model. The right to work became a central demand, as did the improvement of housing conditions.[12]

The simmering discontent in Vienna was to be crucially affected by external events. National uprisings in the northern Italian provinces, the peasant unrest in Galicia, together with the nationalist opposition movements in Hungary and Bohemia, all served to undermine the Imperial Court. The charismatic leader of the Hungarian opposition movement, Lájos Kossuth, was re-elected to the Hungarian Diet in 1847 and, introducing liberal reforms in his own country, became a particularly bitter critic of the old regime. His passionate campaign for Hungarian independence became the impetus for revolution throughout the empire; he became a celebrity within academic circles.[13]

Vienna's March revolution

News of the Paris Revolution and the spreading unrest in Baden and the Rhineland became official on 2 March and was greeted with enthusiasm by the academic community. With the end of Carnival on 8 March, students began to focus on the Paris uprising and organized a general debate for 12 March. The liberal lawyer Baron Alexander von Bach petitioned the Lower-Austrian Diet, requesting public accountability for state finances and support for the establishment of an imperial parliament. Students petitioned for complete press freedom, freedom of expression, the establishment of a militia and other basic rights. On the morning of the following day writers and academics joined some 400 students on a march to the seat of the Diet in order to emphasize the seriousness of their demands. They soon moved on to the *Hofburg*, seat of the Imperial Court. Meanwhile, outside the city walls, the workers began their uprising, attacking tax offices, police stations, as well as factories and new machinery. Hearing news of the march to the *Hofburg*, they began to move towards the inner city. Gas lamps were demolished and the escaping gas ignited to create a ring of fire around the city. Numerous speeches by leading demonstrators were taken up by the protesting crowds; all demanding Metternich's resignation, the expulsion of Jesuits, the formation of an armed Civil Guard and the establishment of a constitution.[14] The poet and journalist Herrmann Jellinek wrote: 'The March Revolution was the work of the people, of the "rabble" so despised by the bourgeoisie, the "riffraff" which the aristocracy defined as "animals": the March Revolution was the great achievement of the mass of the people.'[15]

The 'hawks' at the Imperial Court did not dare to employ the army of General Windischgrätz against the masses in uproar. Archduke Albrecht, still supporting Metternich, employed regular troops to clear the streets, supported by contingents of the newly formed National and Civil Guards. In the ensuing violence, forty-eight demonstrators were killed, a majority of them workers.[16] This caused further uproar: solidarity between students, craftsmen and the industrial proletariat gained in strength, to present a united front against Metternich. Under pressure from the city authorities, the army withdrew and a University-based Academic Legion was formed which, together with the Civil Guard, took control of the city, a development which threatened to alienate the proletariat from the students. Metternich's fall had by now become inevitable, even his closest allies turned against him. Faced with no alternative, Metternich resigned his position on 13 March, only minutes before the ultimatum issued by the Civil Guard expired. He left the city secretly the next day and went into exile in London.

Metternich's departure was greeted with jubilation, but led to widespread looting and rioting in the city outskirts, where the Civil Guard and the Academic Legion were employed to restore order. On 14 March a constitution was promised and a new government was established several days later, led by prime minister Karl Ludwig Ficquelmont with Baron Franz Xaver Pillersdorf as minister of the interior, both liberal opponents of Metternich. Things were, however, not quite as rosy as an American observer believed who was confident that 'Austria, from being the farthest in the rear, had, by a single step, taken the advance of all Germany in the path of freedom'.[17] The new government met with a good deal of opposition; by 4 May Ficquelmont was forced to resign, making way for the more accommodating Pillersdorf. Pillersdorf began work on the promised constitution, following the Belgian bi-cameral model, but delays and rumours of a reactionary backlash caused resentment and led to further disturbances. The people were represented by an Imperial Diet and a second chamber, the Senate, consisting of members of the imperial family, imperial nominees and the landed gentry, was intended to uphold their historic privileges in Austria and Bohemia, but not in Hungary and Italy.[18] The second, inherently reactionary chamber was anathema to those who believed in the sovereignty of the people and in Austria's closer alliance with Germany. News of German demands for a universal suffrage as the basis for the National Parliament in Frankfurt strengthened this opposition and promoted strongly pro-German sentiments, indicated by the display of the new red, gold and black German colours. The 'agreement clause', which bestowed special privileges on the emperor, including his inviolability, sole executive power and supreme command over the armed forces and remained unclear on a number of other constitutional details, such as the relationship between the central government and the provinces, gained a mixed response. The nobility and the more prosperous bourgeoisie approved of it; the Academic Legion, the Democratic Club and other radical associations rejected it. The stage was set for a second, more radical phase.

From the May revolution to the September crisis

Violent disturbances flared up again on 15 May, forcing the new government to give way to this 'pressure from the streets',[19] reinforced by an influx of the proletariat from the city outskirts. The second chamber was abolished and the revolution was now seen to have progressed from its 'liberal' phase in March to a 'democratic' phase. Such a pattern would seem the norm for most revolutions and certainly applied in the case of Paris. In Vienna, however, the mood was already changing, a shift which seemed symptomatic of its revolution.

While the liberals had been satisfied with a parliament which would simply check the emperor's absolute powers and participate in legislation, the democrats now pushed for universal suffrage and popular sovereignty. Against this background the court fled Vienna on 17 May and, without prior consultation with the Pillersdorf government, took up residence in Innsbruck. The news of the emperor's departure from Vienna caused some consternation and public opinion became more volatile. While the liberal *Wiener Zeitung* compared the emperor's 'departure' with the flight of Louis XVI, suggesting that it would hasten 'the day of the republic',[20] conservative and liberal forces feared that the survival of the empire was at stake and with it the city's position as the capital of a multi-lingual state. Civil servants, fearing for their position, anticipated the declaration of a republican Vienna, a term associated with anarchy, communism and mob rule. They denounced the workers as robbers, intent on abolishing private property, and they charged members of the Academic Legion as 'irresponsible agitators' for having led on the workers.[21] Petitions by citizens' groups, among them the National Guard, were dispatched to Innsbruck, begging the emperor to return. The *Wiener Zeitung* asked for the 'close cooperation of all well-intended people [to secure] persons and property, and the preservation of the constitutional throne'.[22] Such statements were also prompted by a virtual collapse of the banking system as customers withdrew their savings, threatening financial insolvency. A serious rift between the bourgeoisie, the Academic Legion and the proletariat in the industrial outskirts had arisen, with the power struggle between liberals and radicals finely balanced. Democrats were held responsible for the flight of the imperial court, the Academic Legion was dissolved, but re-established in the face of protest from students and workers. When matters reached a climax on 26 May, 160 barricades were constructed in the inner city and regular troops found themselves in armed conflict with students, workers and the National Guard. Fewer than 12,000 troops in the Vienna garrison faced nearly 40,000 student legionaries and national guardsmen, as well as thousands of workers streaming into the city to support them.[23]

   The democratic victory led to the formation of a Security Committee, consisting of members from a Citizens' Committee, the National Guard and
the Academic Legion. One of the new Committee's first demands was the
removal of all 'unnecessary military forces' from Vienna and the surrender
of Count Hayos, former Commander in Chief of the Vienna National Guard,
as a hostage to the students.[24] It also urgently attempted to persuade the
emperor to return to Vienna. A programme of public works was established
but, in failing to ameliorate existing social and economic problems, it fared
little better than its French model. Scores of radical newspapers emerged,
most prominent among them the *Wiener Katzenmusik* and the *Volksfreund*.
They published vitriolic attacks against the *camarilla* and the church and even
printed some articles critical of the monarchy. When their denunciations
targeted the wealthier members of the bourgeoisie, the fragile union between
the middle-class Viennese and the workers came under strain. As the
economic situation deteriorated and friction between the bourgeoisie and
the workers became more apparent, utopian socialist ideas began to gain
ground in certain quarters.[25] The twenty-thousand earth workers, among
them many women, protested against a wage reduction, the National and
Civil Guards interfered with bloody consequences. Vienna was not ready for
a genuine class struggle or for a republican resolution of its political problems. In fact, for the next few months, while the Security Committee was
virtually the only executive power, the city enjoyed relative calm. In June a
parliament was elected, but public support was lukewarm. The revolution
began to lose its momentum.
   While monarchist loyalty may account for the weak support for a republic,
it cannot explain the faltering support for the revolution. A closer analysis
of the political and economic situation may indicate the issues more directly
responsible for the decline in revolutionary fervour. Three such issues need
further clarification. Firstly, in establishing the Security Committee, the revolutionaries had achieved one of their major aims and with the government's virtual capitulation there was no clear consensus as to what should
happen next. Secondly, the coalition between the property-owning bourgeoisie and the proletariat was, in essence, unsustainable. The earth workers'
riots in the *Prater* during the summer of 1848, coupled with a sharp economic downturn, increased tension between both classes, especially once
parliamentary elections had returned a decisive majority of middle-class
representatives. The liberal Pillersdorf government resigned, making way
for a team with more monarchist leanings, headed by Count Johann Philip
von Wessenberg. The return of the Imperial Court to Vienna on 12 August
simply confirmed such tendencies. Nevertheless, the radical Silesian delegate
Hans Kudlich, speaking up for peasant interests, was successful in his demand
that 'from now on all servile relationships, together with all rights and

obligations coming therefrom, are abolished'.[26] Although the issue of the indemnification of landlords remained to be resolved, Kudlich's proposal had been largely accepted by September and, once their goal had been achieved, the peasants quickly abandoned the revolution. A further crucial element was thereby removed from the revolutionary equation.

The third and most decisive reason for the waning of the revolutionary drive was the nationality issue. Separatist national interests soon gained in importance over and above liberal aspirations, as every national group sought to secure for itself a position of power. The Austro-German minority within the empire were faced with the difficult decision of whether to enter a closer union with the rest of Germany, causing the collapse of the Habsburg Empire, or whether to stay within this empire, risking the dilution of their German cultural hegemony in the face of Slavonic and Hungarian demands for cultural and national emancipation. Their difficult relations with Germany were not improved when Prussia concluded the Peace of Malmö on 26 August; a move that indicated that power within the new Germany would lie with Prussia. The old rivalry between Austria and Prussia was rekindled and when the Basic Rights of the German people (declared on October 8 by the Frankfurt National Assembly) stated explicitly that 'no part of the German Reich must be united with non-German countries',[27] the dilemma facing the Austro-Germans was reinforced.

Alongside this inner-German conflict was the growth of a Pan-Slavonic movement which threatened to divert the revolutionary aims. Austro-Germans and Hungarians were fearful of a united Slavonic front, which raised the prospect of Russian influence in the Balkans. A Pan-Slavonic conference met in Prague in early June to consider a possible union of all the Slavonic peoples as a defence against their partition between Germans and Hungarians. Their manifesto demanded 'full equality of all nations, irrespective of their political power or size', and the conversion of the Habsburg Empire into 'a federation of nations all enjoying equal rights'.[28] When revolutionary disturbances erupted in Prague General Windischgrätz seized the opportunity to quell the unrest with a fierce bombardment of the city, crushing the rebellion and halting the aspirations of Slav nationalists. The Prague uprising presented the Vienna revolutionaries with a dilemma: satisfaction with the failure of the Czech insurrection was coloured by the fear that their own revolutionary ambitions might also be ended by such a military intervention. The latter fear was recognized by the earthworkers who had petitioned parliament, requesting unity with and equal treatment of all nationalities.[29]

Karl Marx, not always a prudent judge of the Viennese revolution, clearly recognized the counter-revolutionary potential that sprung from such Germanic nationalist feelings. Commenting on the defeat of the Prague uprising, he wrote: 'Gripped by revolutionary ferment, Germany seeks relief in a *war of restoration*, in a campaign for the consolidation of the old authority *against* which she has just revolted.' Only war against Russia would be justified, since this would shake off 'the claim of long, indolent slavery and make herself [Germany] free within her borders by bringing liberation to those outside'.[30] Even more dangerous for the survival of the Austrian Empire were the rivalries between Hungarians and Croats. In March, the principalities of Croatia, Dalmatia and Slovenia had chosen to remain under the Hungarian crown, provided they were granted virtual autonomy. Exploiting the hostility between Croatia and Hungary, and without any recourse to the government in Vienna, Emperor Ferdinand appointed Baron Josip Jelačić as Ban of Croatia, despite the impassioned protests of Hungarian leaders. By forging a pincer movement, firstly against Hungary and secondly against Vienna, Jelačić strengthened his links with the Habsburg dynasty, in particular with their most reactionary generals Radetzky and Windischgrätz. The nationality issue further weakened Vienna's revolutionary credentials, when many Austro-Germans sided with Radetzky against the revolutionary Italians,[31] leaving the city free only to enter a coalition with Hungary. However, even this alliance remained problematic because of the nationality issue. The radical and national liberal factions, though in a minority, favoured joint action, recognizing the need for an alliance with Hungary as a defence against Pan-Slavonic (and Russian) aspirations. With the conservative and moderate wings in Vienna opposed to such an alliance, the imperial authorities were, yet again, able to take advantage of a disunited opposition.

The Hungarian situation was only one factor in developments during the summer and autumn of 1848, which indicated a general resurgence of reactionary forces. The dismissal of the Pillersdorf government by the Security Committee, with Archduke John's support (8 July), initially suggested a strengthening of the democratic faction. The Wessenberg administration appeared to support the liberals; however, the ministers Bach and Schwarzer soon abandoned any democratic leanings in favour of a reactionary position. As a result of moderates forsaking the revolutionary cause, the June parliamentary elections returned a majority of middle-of-the-road liberals to power who stood for a united, constitutional monarchy and a strong state. Approximately 60 per cent of the parliamentarians belonged to the bourgeoisie, 25 per cent were peasants. With almost half of all deputies of Slav origin and mindful of Vienna's ambivalent attitude during the Prague uprising, few of them had any sympathy for the Viennese revolution.[32] Only the extreme left remained 'revolutionary', still seeking to reject all historic rights and privileges, though even they were in favour of retaining the monarchic principle. Most of the new ministers were conservative with professed loyalties to the monarchy and only a quarter had the backing of the Security Committee. Additional events provided further evidence that the revolutionary cause was in decline. Upon Ferdinand's return to Vienna on 12 August, rifts between a defiantly oppositional Academic Legion and the bourgeoisie erupted once more.

During the following weeks, tensions between the revolutionary minority and a counter-revolutionary majority increased. A radical address by a member of the Democratic Club further increased divisions between the Academic Legion and Security Committee on the one side and the Civil and National Guards on the other. Reduced to 45 per cent of its previous strength, even the National Guard began to lose support.[33] The continuing economic depression forced a government clamp-down on those elements which seemed to be exploiting the situation. The failure of the public works project, particularly disillusionment over the apparent inefficiency and laziness of the earth workers at the *Prater*, who were in no shape to perform the hard work demanded of them, further contributed to discontent and division within the revolutionary ranks. The resulting uproar necessitated the employment of the Civil and National Guards and on 23 August, pitched battles ensued between earth workers and the Guards. Although the Academic Legion refused to mobilize against the workers, by the evening of that day the workers were defeated. The Security Committee came under very heavy criticism for remaining neutral during these disturbances and felt obliged to dissolve itself two days later.

By now only the students and various lower-middle-class groups remained faithful to the revolution. These consisted of artisans, journeymen and small shopkeepers, whose economic position had deteriorated considerably in recent months and their campaign, supported prominently by women, came to a head in September. The government, though generally sympathetic to their plight, could do little to ameliorate their position. A self-help organization was set up, attracting more than 40,000 members, but it soon collapsed amid accusations of corruption. Victims of the debacle turned to the government for help, but gained little support, resulting in violent demonstrations on 12 and 13 September. Students and several units of the National Guard sympathized with the angry crowd, which began storming the ministry of the interior. When the arrival of regular troops aggravated the situation and led to large-scale rioting, only prudent action by parliament prevented serious bloodshed. Troops were ordered back to their garrisons and innocent victims of the collapsed organization were promised financial aid. Calm was restored and the forces of law and order regained their confidence. For the first time since the fall of Metternich, the government attempted to regain control of the press: several journalists were harassed, fined or even imprisoned.[34] The real losers were journeymen, artisans and traders who felt even more isolated from the majority of the Viennese. The Academic

Legion, too, had not emerged unscathed, antagonizing many moderate students by its sympathies with the workers.

The 'October revolution' and reactionary victory

The month of October saw the final act of the Vienna revolution. As political pressure increased, poor leadership and increasing divisions led to defeat. Although democratic forces in both Vienna and Hungary were prepared to unite in the fight against the reactionary upsurge, national priorities and mutual distrust hindered any progress towards the establishment of a strong coalition between both factions. With relations between students, the National Guard, the petit bourgeoisie and the proletariat strained, and in the absence of clearly defined political objectives, radical leaders among the students and within the democratic clubs could no longer rely on public support. Political in-fighting and corruption were rife, chaos and anarchy the natural consequence. Austro-Germans themselves were increasingly divided, some favouring a closer union with Germany and others remaining loyal to the 'black yellow' colours of the Habsburg dynasty, with the latter gaining ground among the bourgeoisie and substantial sections within the National Guard.

The actual 'October revolution' began when Count Theodor Baillet Latour, the minister of war, ordered some troops to be transferred from Vienna to Hungary to assist Jelačić's army in its campaign against the rebellious Magyars. The democrats, already furious at parliament's refusal to meet the Hungarian deputation which had arrived in Vienna to plead for support against Jelačić could not condone such a move. On 6 October the Academic Legion, supported by crowds of angry Viennese workers and the more radical elements of the National Guard prevented regular troops from leaving Vienna. During an exchange of fire several people were killed, including the general in charge of the operation.[35] Encouraged by their success, the revolutionaries marched on the ministry of war, intent on overthrowing the government. Prime minister Wessenberg and his minister of the interior, Bach, managed to escape, but the despised minister of war, Latour, was seized by the crowd and brutally murdered.[36] The crowd then stormed the armoury in an attempt to secure the city against military attack and declared a provisional government. The Imperial Court fled Vienna for a second time, seeking refuge in the Moravian city of Olmütz. Student radicals, the petit bourgeoisie and the proletariat now took control of Vienna. On 10 October they declared solidarity with Hungary, but still wary of a close alliance with the Magyars, hesitated to march against Jelačić. Responding to such violent action, the emperor declared war on Vienna. However, when his stern communication of 17 October was followed, two days later, by a conciliatory declaration promising to guarantee the liberal laws already granted, Ferdinand lost further credibility. Both sides now prepared for war. Vienna appointed a new Security Committee and appointed the poet, Messenhauser, Commander in Chief of the National Guard and the Polish revolutionary leader, Jósef Bern, head of all military operations. A mobile guard, largely consisting of the proletariat, became a third force in defence of the city. Despite all these efforts, the position of the revolutionaries was pretty hopeless. Their various factions and armed units were undisciplined, poorly led and badly equipped. The counter-revolutionaries, by comparison, relied on experienced generals and professional units. On 20 October General Windischgrätz informed Vienna, that he would liberate the city from 'a small, insolent faction that shrinks from no infamous action'.[37] He proceeded to encircle the city and, three days later, issued the ultimatum to surrender. Displaying an air of defiance, the revolutionary forces prepared for a siege, but within days shortages of food and water became serious and the general will to resist reached breaking point. The absence of the peasantry from the revolutionary cause proved a decisive drawback. On 28 October an artillery barrage signalled the beginning of the struggle for Vienna; advancing infantry over-ran strategically important outskirts, causing acute anxiety in the inner city. As negotiations for a speedy surrender began, news reached Vienna that Kossuth, at the head of 25,000 troops, was on his way to relieve the revolutionaries. Premature optimism interrupted the surrender negotiations but, by the evening of the next day, Kossuth's army was already in retreat and on 31 October the city was taken and the revolution was at an end.

Loss of life during the tempestuous period from March to October had been considerable; the imperial armies had lost fifty-six officers and 1,142 soldiers, the revolutionaries had suffered between 4,000 and 6,000 casualties,[38] amongst them many casual labourers and domestic servants. The military revenge was harsh; Jelačić's Croatian troops plundered the city and killed anyone offering resistance, but many revolutionaries managed to escape via Switzerland, Italy or Germany and emigrated to America. Windischgrätz dissolved the National Guard and the Academic Legion; Messenhauser was put in charge of his own execution. The most controversial act was the execution of Robert Blum who, together with Julius Fröbel, had arrived in Vienna on 13 October as delegates of the Frankfurt Assembly's democratic faction. While still in Frankfurt, Blum recognized that success in Vienna was vital for the revolutions elsewhere in Germany and Europe.[39] Elected an honorary member of the Academic Legion, he had taken part in the defence of the city. Blum's execution, sanctioned by the new prime minister, Prince Felix Schwarzenberg, and carried out on 9 November, caused shock waves and anger throughout Germany[40] and had direct consequences for the beginning of the counter-revolution in Berlin.

Prince Schwarzenberg's new government was reactionary by nature and, although adopting some of the reforms instituted during the revolution, Schwarzenberg made certain that they were enforced only after receiving the imperial seal of approval. Parliament was exiled to Kremsier and dissolved on 4 March 1849, when a new constitution, his own work, was announced, but never actually implemented. Ferdinand was persuaded to resign in favour of his eighteen-year-old nephew, Francis Joseph, who completely ignored the constitution and governed without an elected parliament until his death in 1916. After the fall of Vienna the imperial forces turned against Hungary where the revolution had the support of the lesser nobility, the petit bourgeoisie and the peasants. After initial Hungarian victories at Komorn and Ofen, the Magyars faced defeat when Tsar Nicholas I entered hostilities with an army of 130,000 men in support of the 80,000 strong Austrian army and a 35,000 strong Croat force. In the face of such overwhelming superiority the Hungarians were routed on 9 August 1849 at Temesvár. Kossuth escaped to Turkey and the victors imposed a strict military regime, ensuring that the last embers of Magyar national freedom were suppressed.

The revolution in Berlin

Until the revolution of 1848, Berlin was the second city within the German-speaking lands. Despite extensive rivalries between Austria and Prussia, Metternich's 'system', firmly established as the major force of reaction, kept the Prussian capital in a subordinate position right to the end of his rule. Events in the spring of 1848 affirmed Berlin's dependence on Vienna. Although news of the revolution in Paris reached both cities simultaneously, Berlin's citizens seemed to wait for a signal from the Austrian capital. It was only on hearing the news of revolution in Vienna that Berliners were stimulated into political action. The head of the Berlin police reported that citizens had felt humiliated that 'all around Prussia things are in motion' and a feeling of shame emerged that the Prussian capital exhibited 'only faithful affection and servile obedience',[41] so that 'when news arrived from Vienna, one felt uneasy that nothing was getting under way'.[42] Similarly, Prussia's final counter-revolutionary moves only came into force once the revolution in Vienna had been defeated, and this despite the fact that other monarchies were now looking towards Berlin for political leadership. Subsequent events brought about a subtle change of emphasis between Austria and Prussia, with Berlin gaining in importance at Vienna's expense.

Social and economic conditions in Berlin

Although Vienna was much larger and more cosmopolitan than Berlin, their social and economic structures were comparable. Berlin probably benefited from a slightly stronger industrial output while her bourgeoisie was weaker and more provincial. Population growth in Berlin was unrivalled on the continent; between 1800 and 1848 Berlin's population increased from 172,000 to 410,000, with every second person having moved to Berlin from the provinces.[43] Among the city's poorest people, 95 per cent were immigrants. Berlin's middle class amounted to only 5 per cent of her population, while over 80 per cent of her people belonged to an as yet ill-defined underclass. Within the small section of the bourgeoisie, industrialists and merchants made up only 0.6 per cent, while students constituted 0.7 per cent and minor civil servants and artisans 12 per cent.[44] Berlin had considerably fewer millionaires than most other European cities, the majority of them coming from banking. A relatively larger number of her bourgeoisie were pensioners and retired civil servants. They, together with the upper civil service, the nobility, officers and self-employed professional people formed a homogeneous group, united by their educational background and common interests. Academics, journalists and freelance writers were less well represented than in Vienna, but nevertheless formed a vocal group, impatient for change and more liberal policies.

The proletariat in its widest sense accounted for 85 per cent of all inhabitants. Within this ill-defined group 38 per cent were journeymen or skilled workers, 27 per cent unskilled workers or domestic servants and approximately 10 per cent belonged to the sub-proletariat. In contrast to the situation in Vienna, Berlin's workers were geographically more integrated into the city, thereby giving them less of an identity while mobilizing them more easily to political action. During the 1840s Berlin began to acquire a significant position in the field of mechanical engineering, being particularly renowned for steam locomotives.[45] Even prior to the actual revolution, reports indicate strong tensions between the 'proletariat' and the city administration, but all the various accounts seem to indicate that the demonstrators specifically excluded the king from their accusations, suggesting that he was not informed about their true plight. One newspaper described Berlin as a magnet which attracts the poor[46] and, by 1848, 30,000 of her poorest citizens received some kind of social benefit. Other estimates suggest that one hundred thousand people, a quarter of Berlin's population, lived at or below subsistence level, a high percentage among them the younger and single people.[47]

The artisans began to lose their group identity. Many master craftsmen had fallen on hard times, sinking to subsistence level; more than three quarters were exempt from any form of taxation, while others prospered as suppliers to the royal court. Early signs of a new class structure began to emerge: journeymen and industrial workers overcame their old divisions, since the former had lost their personal privileges in housing and food and were increasingly employed in big workshops or factories. The textile industry was still in a dominant position, employing approximately 7,000 workers, whereas mechanical engineering accounted for no more than 4,500 workers. However, here as elsewhere, textile workers suffered mass redundancies and Berlin counted more tailors among her citizens than potential customers.

Despite the treacherous calm of the first days of March, news of the Paris revolution made a deep impact on Berlin citizens. Already during the last days of February people gathered on the streets and in coffee houses, crowded into public libraries, eager to consult foreign newspapers. Lectures and public readings were organized on such topical subjects as the building of barricades. From 6 March, public gatherings took place at *Unter den Zelten* in the region of the *Tiergarten*, beyond the jurisdiction of the Berlin police. In an attempt to defuse the growing tension, the police had advised the ministry of the interior to tolerate these gatherings and the Prussian government initially followed a strategy of appeasing Berliners with vague promises of a relaxation of its anti-democratic laws, but without entering into binding obligations. On 14 March, the king agreed to call a meeting of the *Vereinigte Landtag* for 27 April and, as unrest increased, the meeting was brought forward to 2 April. Despite this move and a promise to relax existing press laws, the public mood remained volatile. The king's move was seen as belonging to a bygone 'absolutist patriarchal' era while a closer response to actually existing public demands was requested.[48]

In order to understand the official Prussian reaction to developments in Berlin, a brief profile of King Frederick William is necessary, a figure who stands in stark contrast to the hapless Emperor Ferdinand. The king's character had been formed by childhood experiences, among them Napoleon's occupation of Prussia and the Wars of Liberation. As a result, he became a sworn enemy of 'the ideas of 1789', of liberalism and constitutional democracy and was instead obsessed with medieval romantic concepts of monarchic rule by divine right. He believed in a decentralized corporate society and dreamt of the revival of the Holy Roman Empire, within a modernized concept, based on national, patriotic forces.[49] In general, however, his outlook was by no means entirely old-fashioned. He was keenly interested in technological innovation, had a love of architecture and became patron of Germany's most famous architect, Karl Friedrich Schinkel. He also promoted the natural sciences and became acquainted with the explorer Alexander von Humboldt. Many of the king's political advisors, however, were of a neo-pietist, illiberal background, amongst them Leopold von Gerlach and

Ernst Wilhelm Hengstenberg, who strengthened the king's views on divine rights. The king's closest confidant between 1824 and 1850 was the Hungarian catholic, Joseph Maria von Radowitz, who was strongly influenced by the anti-democratic views of the constitutional historian Ludwig von Haller.[50] Although very volatile and given to periods of sentimentality, Frederick William had a fairly sharp intellect and was politically more astute than most of his fellow monarchs. He abhorred violence and was shaken by the bloodshed that accompanied the revolution. His interest in and commitment to the national issue was genuine but, true to his monarchic principles, he was strictly opposed to any constitutional settlement that might impinge on his divine rights.

Supporting this regime was the protestant church, another bastion of reaction which had been centrally involved with the Prussian state ever since its inception in the sixteenth century. Under the influence of the theologian Hengstenberg, founder of the influential *Evangelische Kirchenzeitung*, the protestant church became the hub of conservatism, illiberalism and anti-Semitism. It considered Judaism as the seat of socialism, declaring it the 'natural opposition to Christian princes and their states'.[51] Following the Lutheran tradition of an alliance of throne and altar, the *Kirchenzeitung* proclaimed that opposition to authority was disobedience against God.[52] When the balance swung back to the counter-revolution, the protestants made no secret of their support for the reactionary Brandenburg government and for the role of the Prussian military under General Wrangel.

The 'March revolution'

As the political climate in Berlin became more tense, neither side seemed capable of producing a decisive leader prepared to take resolute political action, a particular problem for the revolutionary side. Their main target was the oppressive military presence in Berlin, especially when guards were reinforced in the vicinity of strategic locations. While ostensibly the most daring offence against public order consisted of smoking in public places,[53] several incidents between 13 and 16 March ended in bloodshed when demonstrators provoked reactionary officers of the guard to violent retaliation.[54] The city council appointed special stewards to be responsible for keeping the peace and to replace soldiers; students, too, kept order. This scheme failed, partly because of animosity from the 'proletariat' and the lower middle classes and partly because regular troops continued to intervene, with bloody consequences. As news of Metternich's removal caused further excitement and jubilation amongst the masses, consternation grew in government circles. Radowitz sought to calm matters by advising the king to dismiss unpopular government ministers, to promise press freedom and to make some constitutional concessions.[55] The king hesitated, reflecting divisions amongst his advisers, and eventually responded with a complex and contradictory resolution. Radowitz and some key ministers (Canitz, Bodelschwing) advised moderation, while the crown prince and most generals favoured a decisive military response.[56] At this time the opposition had not yet formulated a revolutionary, or even a political, programme, and the fact that many demonstrators wore cockades displaying the national colours, will illustrate this: ill-defined national aspirations had the priority over genuine material and constitutional demands.

The climax of the revolution was reached on 18 March, and the course of events is well known: a council delegation went to the royal palace, supported by tens of thousands of people. A majority of their demands were granted, amongst them press freedom, an immediate meeting of the *Landtag* as well as minor government changes. The king also promised his support for the reform of the German Confederation. The granting of these concessions met with general approval, though some groups, especially journeymen and workers, were unhappy at their failure to gain a ministry of public works.[57] The reinforcement of particular sentry posts to block a passageway through the castle gates led one section of the crowd to demand the removal of military forces. This demand, though expressed by a minority, was not just a reaction to the military violence of the previous days but had as its political agenda the request for a civil king to entrust himself to a civil guard and disavow the military regime.[58] As some troop contingents advanced in order to clear the square in front of the castle, two ill-fated shots were fired, the signal for a general tumult.

Many events of that day have become part of a general myth and have entered several historical accounts. While it is quite likely that the two shots went off unintentionally, the troop reinforcement was certainly planned. It is also beyond question that the royal concessions, given under duress, did not go far enough and left demonstrators in little doubt that they would be rescinded, should the balance of power swing back to the king.[59] From the afternoon of 18 March until well into the next day Berlin experienced heavy fighting between regular troops and revolutionaries. Church bells rang out as hundreds of barricades were set up and fighting raged against a background of cannon fire, rifle shots and the shouts and screams of the opposing sides. The troops and their officers gave no quarter, the most vicious being soldiers from East Elbian regiments. The animosity between Berlin and its provinces was given full rein, and differences between conservative Borussian (Prussian) and liberal or democratic national German sentiments came to the fore. At this stage of the revolution, before social issues caused a rift, solidarity between workers and the bourgeoisie still seemed intact. In little over twenty-four hours over 900 people had been killed, severely injured or imprisoned, with most fatalities incurred by the revolutionaries, and countless eye-witness accounts testifying to the barbarity of the military assault.[60] The vast majority of the 900 victims were civilians, less than 100 officers and regular soldiers had been killed, demonstrating the one-sidedness of the conflict. Most civilian fatalities occurred among the lower middle classes and the proletariat, suggesting that 'as far as its social participants were concerned (but not its political contents) it [the Berlin March Revolution] can be described as a quasi-proletarian revolution',[61] since at least 90 per cent of revolutionaries were of the lower social strata. Groups heavily involved were tailors, blacksmiths, joiners and tradesmen, and, among the lower middle strata, teachers and railway officials.[62] Though women constituted only a small percentage of the fatalities, their participation during the fighting was high, especially from the lower strata.

An assessment of the role of the military remains somewhat contentious. The conventional view is that the king reacted under considerable emotional duress, that the command to withdraw the troops after two days of fighting was unclear and that the military could easily have restored order. Other historians suggest that 'discipline was crumbling'[63] and that the Paris example had illustrated that a military solution was not advisable. Most contemporary historians tend to view events in a different light: whilst the troops were victorious at first, the balance of power began to change, almost by the hour, raising doubts among officers that the military could suppress the fighting throughout the city.[64] The Prussian army, famous for its discipline and fighting spirit, had failed to conduct itself properly and subsequent criticism of its role had led to wide-spread demoralization throughout the ranks.[65] The retreating troops had to endure scenes of humiliation, especially in the less prosperous parts of the city, where they were harangued, abused and insulted.[66] Furthermore, the political climate did not favour a military solution. The king, still harbouring ambitions for a national role in Germany, could not afford to be seen as a brutal oppressor. In the light of rumours that, at the height of the fighting, the crown prince had issued the order to shoot at the defenceless citizens,[67] he became the chief target of the crowd's hatred and was forced into exile to England.[68]

Public mourning for the victims and their burial became highly politicized, symbolic acts. At several processions, revolutionaries carried the bodies of those who had been killed by the troops, bringing them into the city centre towards the royal palace. The king was forced to appear before the crowd and remove his military cap in honour of the men and women who had been killed by his soldiers. His homage to the dead became a symbolic expression of consent to a revolutionary change: his gesture had ushered in the constitutional monarchy. The king's power, hitherto based on military authority, had changed to one based on the sovereignty of the people:

The army in Prussia was not only the weapon of reaction as in the Habsburg Empire or the Tsar's domains, but rather the actual substance of the state, the soul of the monarchy, the basis of its legitimacy as well as its popularity, that which distinguished the Prussian community from all other states. A Hohenzoller without an army was not just a citizen king, but only a shadow of a king, and the question of what power then ruled in the state had to be decided first.[69]

Following the pattern of Vienna, the Berlin masses did not question the legitimacy of their king, they simply wished to free him from 'bad advisors', and from the hated army and its officers. The revolution at this stage, had become a battle between the citizens and the king's army, with other considerations taking a lower priority. The majority of officers associated with the landed gentry; they had nothing but contempt for townsmen and the lower classes. The apparent success of the revolution was illustrated by the king's act of humiliation: adorned with the national colours, he rode at the head of a procession, through the streets of Berlin. By honouring the national colours and by his proclamation, indicating his willingness to support the national issue and immerse Prussia into a united Germany, the king encouraged democratic and constitutional expectations. His other statements indicated, however, that he was not prepared to base his government on the will of the people, but only on the consent of his fellow princes; he was only prepared to act with their consent as *primus inter pares*.[70]

The funeral of the March victims, notwithstanding its symbolic significance, contained some aspects of a political farce, and also revealed incipient signs of the early counter-revolution. On 21 March the city council decided on a joint funeral for the dead of both sides, hailing revolutionaries and soldiers alike as 'brothers of the same fatherland'.[71] Troops and civilians were to march together in a further gesture of peace and reconciliation. However, this plan failed because of the army's veto, revealing a near anarchic situation. Nearly 200,000 people took part in the procession or lined the streets, including delegations from many German cities and from Poland and Italy, involved in their own freedom struggles. As a result of public pressure, about eighty freedom fighters, mostly Poles imprisoned by the Prussian state, were released. When the procession reached the palace, the king and his ministers stepped out on to the balcony, baring their heads beneath a German flag. The symbolism of this action was clear enough: the king, accustomed to accepting the homage of his troops from such a position, was now forced to honour the victims of his army's actions.[72] The protestant state church, true to its Lutheran anti-revolutionary tradition, employed the king's gesture of apparent forgiveness, to proclaim 'peace, unity and reconciliation'.[73] It also stirred national feelings by warning against foreign (French) troublemakers and by appealing to the national spirit of 1807 and 1815. All efforts to bring about political change were condemned. With democrats insisting on a fitting memorial for the dead and with government circles playing down the historical significance of the occasion, subsequent controversies over the nature and accessibility of the cemetery continued for well over fifty years.[74]

A period of consolidation?

It soon became obvious that the revolution was running out of steam. Although some of the more prosperous bourgeoisie began moving out of Berlin to the much 'safer' Potsdam, the general public seemed content with what had been achieved so far. A new government had been appointed by the king, formed by the Rhenish liberals Camphausen and Hansemann, but there were well-founded doubts as to whether they wanted to continue the revolution. The *Neue Rheinische Zeitung* commented satirically:

> The 'attitude of the people' consisted in being so busy enthusiastically 'facing history itself' when it should have been making history . . . the people never got round to preventing the Ministers from conjuring away one part after the other of the freedom it had won.[75]

A Civil Guard was established, the inevitable consequence of the army's withdrawal. In contrast to Vienna and right from its inception, Berlin's Civil Guard was conceived of as a primarily royalist organization, politically opposed to the revolution. Its members saw themselves as a substitute for regular troops, protecting those strategic parts of the city from which the regular units had been withdrawn. Though poorly equipped and considerably less disciplined than regular troops, they recruited almost exclusively from the wealthier middle strata. During its initial stages, civil servants were 'encouraged' to join the guard, in order to instil a royalist Prussian ethos within its ranks. Fluctuating from 15,000 to 30,000 men, the Guard was put under the command of the Chief of Police, Julius von Minutoli. Their reactionary nature at this stage of their development may explain their opposition to the all-German national issue. From mid April, however, the Guard's political stance began to change: middle-class citizens and civil servants who could no longer afford the time to serve, were replaced by the 'flying corps', a semi-autonomous group of students and workers. They were supported by many metal workers under the stewardship of August Borsig, Berlin's leading metal manufacturer, as well as by industrialists, bankers and manufacturers within the newly founded *Handelsverein*.[76]

Although hatred against the over-riding military presence had ignited the revolution, by the end of March a majority of the middle classes, but also many metal workers and the *Handelsverein* were in favour of a controlled return of the troops. They were obviously fearful of increasing instability and further damage to the economy. Only democratic forces among students and journalists opposed such a move, insisting that the army must first be 'democratized'.[77] The first contingent of soldiers re-entered the city on 30 March, and by July some 11,000 soldiers had returned to Berlin. This remilitarization of the city caused resentment among members of the Civil Guard and the democratic clubs, who reminded the king that the troops had to swear a loyalty oath to the constitution. The king ignored the emerging tensions and informed his advisors that only the army could successfully defeat the revolution.[78] Various arguments over voting rights, the new constitutional assembly and elections to the city council and to the Prussian and German parliaments gave an early indication of a shift away from a power base of workers and the lower social strata towards the upper middle classes and a more moderate, anti-revolutionary agenda. Reflecting this shift, key positions within the Camphausen administration went to reactionary monarchists. Such moves prompted Karl Marx and Bruno Bauer to declare that the government was attempting to shield the monarchy from the effects of the revolution by acting as a lightning conductor.[79] The recall of the *Vereinigte Landtag*, seen as a rebuff to demands for a democratic parliament, met with considerable opposition. Many of its representatives sought to disregard the revolution, while others – including the young Otto von Bismarck – began to hatch out plans for a counter-revolution. Nevertheless, its guidelines were surprisingly liberal. All men over the age of twenty-four, who had been resident for at least six months and were not dependent on social benefits, were to be enfranchised. Elections were to follow the indirect principle, via electors who would, in turn, elect the members of parliament. The king, supported by the Camphausen cabinet, favoured elections based on the corporate principle, but he was forced to concede, following protests from the Political Club and the Berlin council.

Two incidents, arising from the debate over the electoral system, indicate how the concerns of the revolutionary working man had lost out to those of the bourgeoisie: on 20 April a demonstration against the proposed indirect election system was unsuccessful, vetoed by the Civil Guard. The following day, the socialist democrat Adolf Schlöffel made a speech, attacking the Camphausen government; he was promptly arrested and sentenced to six months' imprisonment. A succession of legal cases against journalists signalled how controversial issues were no longer being decided by public debate, but referred to the courts. Further evidence was provided by the three elections in May 1848, for the Berlin council, the Prussian parliament and for the nomination of Prussian delegates to the Frankfurt National Assembly. The new council consisted of a majority of middle-class citizens, mostly artisans and tradesmen; the Frankfurt delegates included a similar percentage of middle-class members, but this time representing academics and civil servants. The Prussian Assembly was made up of a similar majority of both wings of the middle classes, rising to almost two-thirds in 1849.[80] Three distinctive political divisions had begun to emerge: a constitutional–liberal faction, a conservative–royalist group and a democratic wing, as yet not clearly defined.

Despite the fact that the Berlin proletariat had failed to produce a prominent leader during the March upheavals, this situation changed on 11 April, with the establishment of the Central Committee of Workers under the leadership of Stephan Born. The Committee represented twenty-eight professions, but excluded factory owners and independent master craftsmen.[81] It became the nucleus of the Federation of Workers, established in September 1848 in Leipzig, which is frequently considered to be the foundation of the German trade union movement. The Committee encouraged a variety of social and political activities, such as special workshops and medical care for workers. It also took the lead among other workers' associations, which at that time were mainly concerned with educational issues. Berlin followed Paris and Vienna in organizing work schemes for the unskilled and unemployed; its most important project provided employment for earth workers, known as the *Rehberger*, after a district in Berlin. Like their counterparts in Paris and Vienna, these workers suffered from a reputation for laziness and insubordination, accusations which should be placed in context. With unemployment reaching alarming proportions, neither city council nor government could master the situation. Berlin's first employment office had opened as early as 9 March and by late summer the figure for earth workers had reached 8,000. They were employed to build roads, railways and canals, but some of their work seemed completely pointless, so that their commitment to the project suffered. Most of these poorly paid *Rehbergers* were not accustomed to heavy physical labour: 41 per cent of the work force had been textile workers, 30 per cent day labourers. They constituted a fluctuating work force with little initial solidarity among members. They were usually older than the average labourer, since officials employed a system of positive discrimination in favour of married men.[82] Soon recognizing their political power, they saw themselves as the force to continue the revolution. Their wages were barely above starvation level and when a system of piecework was introduced, together with a system of compulsory insurance against future unemployment disguised as a means to educate them and instil in them the virtues of thriftiness, their patience came to an end. They turned their anger against machines and National Guard troops as well as police constables who were employed to subdue them.

Political developments took another crucial turn on news of the decision of Crown Prince William to return to Berlin from his exile in London.

By late April the king was already making plans for his brother's return, supported by the Camphausen government.[83] On 12 May, news of the prince's intention was condemned by virtually all of Berlin's political factions who insisted that his presence would constitute a threat to law and order and that only the newly elected Constitutional Assembly could take a decision on the prince's return. Several delegations made representations to Camphausen and a 10,000 strong demonstration advanced on the prime minister's residence. Some 30,000 demonstrators threatened to storm the prince's palace, a move deflected only when the building was declared a national property. Demonstrations continued for two more days, but when they failed to make any impact, interest subsided. The only concession gained was that the prince's return was postponed by several days, ensuring that his arrival would not coincide with parliament's inaugural session. The Berlin masses had demonstrated a willingness to oppose the forces of the counter-revolution, but with no charismatic political leader emerging, they had failed to gain ground. The monarchy and other reactionary forces, particularly those from the provinces, consequently strengthened their position while the army was re-asserting its authority, now that its unofficial leader had returned to Berlin.

A second revolutionary phase?

With anti-revolutionary factions regrouping, the revolutionaries lacked a clear political programme. The middle classes believed that the 'March achievements' had settled the most pressing constitutional issues, whereas the workers felt their material requests for improved living conditions had been ignored. The *Neue Rheinische Zeitung* regretted such lack of action, deploring that the Assembly 'was without judgement'.[84] Events in June were soon to underline their divisions, divisions already evident during the ceremonial procession on 4 June in honour of the victims of the March revolution. Of the approximately 200,000 people who joined the march to the cemetery at *Friedrichshain*, the vast majority were workers, journeymen or working women; representatives of the upper-middle strata were conspicuously absent. The memorial celebration itself illustrated the revolution's lack of vision and of a political programme,[85] though the symbolic significance of the sacrifice of the March victims must not be overlooked. This was demonstrated on 8 June when, following the prince's address to the Constitutional Assembly, Julius Berends, co-founder of the democratic *Volksklub*, gave a speech reminding the assembly that they owed their very existence to the martyrs of 18 and 19 March. At the same time, the democratic paper *Die Locomotive* commented: 'The constitutional National Assembly is ashamed of its origins just like a badly brought up son does not respect his father.'[86] Angry protests outside the assembly marked a general feeling that the king and 'his' government were planning the counter-revolution. Such suspicion was not without substance since, by re-establishing his relationship with the military, the king had broken a solemn promise. Furthermore, the working classes were refused entry to the ranks of the Civil Guard on the pretext that there was a shortage of weapons, thereby denying the revolutionaries their demand for a general arming of the people. When rumours began to circulate that the armoury was to be removed from Berlin, matters came to a head: on 14 June crowds of people, mostly workers, stormed the armoury. Resistance by the guard was ineffective since many of its members now sided with the revolutionaries. It looked as if the 'March events' would be repeated, but some important differences cannot be ignored. By now the royal house had fallen into disrepute and the masses were inspired by republican feelings. The workers' change of mood expressed itself in the many red flags, whereas the 'German' colours were increasingly associated with the bourgeoisie. Socialist sentiments were clearly expressed in demands for the right to work. As a rift developed between workers and the bourgeoisie, most conservative and liberal papers condemned the storming of the armoury. Important changes also affected the character of the Civil Guard. Recruitment to the Guard had long been in decline, with many of its wealthier members absenting themselves from their duties, to be replaced by new recruits from among the lower-middle strata. Tension between the Guard and the council increased, and the former, possibly following their comrades in Vienna, declared their independence from the council. In general, the Civil Guard had become much more assertive than was the case in March, at last finding their own role on the side of the revolution. The *Bürgerwehrklub* (Club of the Civil Guard), founded in April as an apolitical pressure group to represent guard members, was replaced in September by the Democratic Civil Guards' Association, a politically active, democratic organization. Such a change echoed the guard's response to counter-revolutionary pressures and an attempt to assimilate them into the regular troops under royal command. The head of the Berlin police, Minutoli, in an effort to challenge the Guard's role, recommended the establishment of a Berlin constabulary, following London's example, where such a police force had successfully suppressed the Chartists. During June a 2,000 strong force, drawn mainly from among artisans who had trained as conscripts in the regular army was set up, soon to gain the hatred and contempt of Berlin citizens. Other developments, too, were signalling a showdown with reactionary forces: the right to free assembly was restricted, police harassed political clubs and animosity between Berlin and her provinces increased even further.

Political clubs and associations

Such tensions and the growing distrust of Berlin's citizens as to the king's true aims only served to activate political life in the city. On 23 March the Political Club was formed, later renamed the Democratic Club which became Germany's largest political association. It aimed to achieve national sovereignty, based on democratic principles and initially considered itself to be in alliance with the Camphausen Ministry. Among its demands were direct voting rights for the election of the Prussian parliament, direct taxation, press freedom, a jury system, the separation of state and church, the abolition of all privileges and a reorganization of the army into a militia. Although these demands were primarily of a constitutional nature, many workers joined up and other associations soon followed. The *Volksverein*, more of a debating society than an association, lacked a clear political mandate. It had a huge following among the lower social strata, recruiting up to 20,000 members.[87] The *Volksklub*, an association favoured by journeymen and workers, mainly addressed social issues, while the Constitutional Club, popular among civil servants, academics and the more enlightened middle classes, represented liberal views and supported the Camphausen administration. It usually failed to take a stand on the crucial issues of the time and soon split up into smaller factions, further losing credibility. In general, and regardless of the shift in favour of counter-revolutionary forces, the various Berlin clubs and assemblies displayed an astonishing degree of democratic awareness, which could hold its own in any comparison with political culture elsewhere.

The conservatives, though numerically always in the minority, were politically skilful in employing their newly founded infamous *Kreuzzeitung*; they established two important counter-revolutionary factions: the Patriotic Club and the Prussia Association. Middle-class circles, particularly academics and civil servants, supported them. The Association for King and Fatherland, founded in late June, recruited strongly from among aristocrats, Junkers and members of the *camarilla*, among them Otto von Bismarck and the influential Gerlach brothers. By exploiting Prussia's 'glorious history' during the wars of liberation, these factions fostered strong anti-French and anti-revolutionary sentiments.[88] The decline of the liberal Constitutional Club was yet another sign of the increasing polarization of political views during the summer of 1848.

The most interesting developments occurred within democratic circles. The large public gatherings of the spring had given way to organized and disciplined political assemblies. Age and social background distinguished membership of the various democratic clubs. Many of their leaders had an academic background, but not usually tied to a specific profession or civil office. The Democratic Club was the largest, but the Linden Club was more interesting as far as its constitution and organization were concerned. It held its meetings in the centre of Berlin and came into its own in the autumn of 1848, once the constabulary had been formed and public gatherings required a police licence. The Linden Club never sought such a licence but its members carried on meeting at the customary places, waiting for the constabulary to disperse them. No sooner did this happen than they would regroup a few hundred yards away to continue their cat and mouse game with the constabulary. At their gatherings their most charismatic leader, 'Linden Müller' discussed contemporary events, especially German national and republican issues, always spicing his speeches with sharp humour, intent on ridiculing the forces of law and order. The Republican Club was formed on the initiative of Professor Rudolf Virchow, a famous surgeon at the Berlin *Charitée*, and a number of other eminent academics, eager to develop a democratic and socialist political culture, were invited to join.[89] The *Sozialverein*, also a product of the summer of 1848, cultivated a particularly populist atmosphere. Its leader was Friedrich Wilhelm Held, a controversial demagogue and founder of the popular journal *Die Locomotive*, whose fiery speeches attracted the proletariat and whose social concern for the underprivileged guaranteed him a huge following. Finally, the *Bezirksvereine* (district associations) were of a very different, more practical and humanitarian nature. They took on the task of promoting political education and general social welfare, organizing help for the unemployed and lending money to struggling small businesses. In general, public life in Berlin exhibited a pluralist, politically committed mindset; political aims were well defined and a variety of often highly organized forms of political activity were employed.

The final phase

Concurrent with the political culture generated by clubs and associations, the army, also experienced some interesting developments as it proved unable to remain immune to the struggle between the forces of revolution and reaction. The garrison town of Potsdam, now the king's residence, witnessed a revolt in the ranks and a fraternization of soldiers and citizens, which culminated in an assault on a number of reactionary officers. Such an incident was unprecedented in the annals of Prussia's highly disciplined army. As its effects spread to other army units in Berlin, the king was moved to nominate the reactionary General von Wrangel as Commander in Chief of all units east of the Elbe. The king's decision led to fierce arguments in the Assembly, where the role of the army in general was under discussion, especially the question of its legally binding loyalty to the constitution, rather than to the king, with parliament insisting that all officers must maintain a distance from reactionary activities.[90] This issue was seen to be of crucial significance for two reasons: firstly, the militaristic nature of Prussia, together with the image and tradition of the Prussian army, based on absolute loyalty to the monarch, had been a major factor which had provoked the revolutionary events of March. Secondly, the Paris revolution recently put down by military force, had ended in a blood bath.

As the struggle moved into its final phase, the revolution now supported only by the proletariat and some intellectuals, activists began to resort to increasingly radical measures. On 12 October, the earth workers at Köpenick, provoked by a bourgeois press, revolted against their inhuman working conditions. In an attempt to restore order, the Civil Guard was responsible for the death and injury of several workers. The constabulary, called upon as reinforcement, caused even greater bloodshed. In the immediate aftermath of the violence, a repeat of the emotional March demonstrations was planned. The bodies of the workers were brought to the royal palace and a public funeral, together with financial compensation was demanded. This time, however, the government did not yield to such pressures: the funeral ceremony attracted mass support, even members of the Civil Guard joining the procession, but the king and his government ministers remained absent. At about the same time the Second German Democratic Congress took place in Berlin and the first signs of disunity amongst workers became apparent. The majority of delegates were republican, but they could not reach agreement as to whether the new political order should be centrist or federal. The social issue was even more contentious; a strong radical wing supported a communist agenda, advocating the abolition of all privileges, grassroots democracy and a general arming of the proletariat. Declarations of solidarity with the Viennese revolutionaries, dispatched by the end of October, further served to illustrate a lack of political realism. Their hope that other German states might offer armed assistance to the Viennese was naïve to say the least and their petition to the Berlin Assembly, demanding such support, was unsurprisingly rejected. As angry crowds besieged the Assembly, manhandling some delegates, the Civil Guard was forced to intervene. A report of fatalities provided the reactionary minister of the interior with the pretext to summon up further regular troop contingents.

Once the revolution in Vienna had been defeated, counter-revolutionary forces in Berlin seized their opportunity. As the dynastic families of Austria and Prussia pledged moral support to each other, Frederick William IV recovered his nerve and revoked all the promises given in the spring. The counter-revolution in Prussia now became associated with two names, both profoundly undemocratic, aristocratic and hostile towards the civilizing ideas of freedom and democracy: Count Brandenburg, illegitimate son of Frederick William II and former commander of the Sixth Army Corps in Breslau, and General von Wrangel who had aided Russian troops in their suppression of Polish freedom in 1831. Both men could rely on the *camarilla*, in particular on the Gerlach brothers. All shared a belief in the Prussian military tradition and, with no sympathy for human rights or national aspirations, they were prepared to dissolve the Assembly. Although parliament had by now lost much of its support, its delegates reacted with courage and dignity. When Count Brandenburg was nominated as the new prime minister on 2 November, the Assembly dispatched a delegation to the king in Potsdam. They were received in a rude and condescending manner and the king declined to enter into negotiations. A royal decree commanded parliament to leave Berlin, in order to be 'unmolested by criminal demonstrators'.[91] The Assembly ignored this order, insisting on its constitutional rights versus the crown. It pronounced its passive resistance on 10 November, the very day when Wrangel moved large troop contingents into Berlin. The next day the Civil Guard was disbanded and martial law imposed. One by one the political clubs were closed and prominent newspapers such as the *Locomotive* were prohibited. At its last official session on 15 November, the Assembly decided to refuse taxation rights to the new government. Wrangel's troops moved in and closed the Assembly's official meeting place. For a short period the remaining 227 delegates met in various public places, but were soon dispersed by the military.

There are several reasons for the failure of the revolution at this crucial moment. The threat posed by Wrangel's soldiers certainly discouraged any effective opposition.[92] The working classes had become disillusioned with parliamentary democracy, finding parliament largely unsympathetic towards their social needs. The most serious reason was probably related to the general political situation: the revolutions in Paris and Vienna had failed, the Baden Republic been crushed, the national cause in Schleswig–Holstein defeated and there was a persistent fear of Russian intervention. In view of all these setbacks, it is perhaps not surprising that Berliners capitulated.

In a paradoxical way, the defeat of the revolution in November 1848 did not immediately negate the achievements of March. The imposed new constitution of 5 December included a series of liberal objectives: franchise for all (male) Prussians, inviolability of property and residence rights, a jury system, the abolition of the death penalty, religious and academic freedom, freedom of assembly and of the press, free elementary education, together with other basic rights of a modern democratic state.[93] These liberties, however, did not apply to the citizens of Berlin which remained under martial law, nor did they extend to the military. Furthermore, the king was no longer answerable to parliament where the second chamber guaranteed an element of conservatism. Elections early in 1849, however, resulted in a victory for the democratic parties in Berlin and other cities: 67 per cent of the Berlin electors represented democratic or left-of-centre parties. Continuing political tensions led the king to dissolve parliament in April, a decision which caused large-scale demonstrations in Berlin, but the momentum for a last revolutionary stance had been lost. The *Dreiklassenwahlrecht* (three class franchise), introduced by the government in May 1849, changed the political balance overnight. New voting rights were related to personal taxation bands, the secret ballot was rescinded, allowing the intimidation of voters in vulnerable positions. The results were spectacular. A comparison of the May elections with those in January indicates that the democratic vote in Berlin was reduced from 67 per cent to 0.8 per cent,[94] only four democratic candidates were elected. A new Chief of Police virtually abolished press freedom and the right of assembly and even the courts, which for some time managed to preserve existing laws, soon gave in to state pressure. All these measures proved particularly detrimental to the lower classes: municipal democracy, too, had become a victim of the reaction. The new franchise was also related to income, reducing the electorate to 17 per cent of the male population. Such measures turned the clock back by half a century, wiping out all the progress achieved since the Stein reform programme of 1808.

A comparison of the revolutions in Vienna and Berlin

Anyone comparing the revolutions in the two major German capitals will be struck by the similarity of events, of problems, failures and achievements. The extent to which Paris was the model for both cities, despite the differences in size, social and industrial development and political makeup, also becomes obvious. The revolutionaries in all three cities were successful in overthrowing their respective governments, though Parisians alone succeeded in actually overthrowing their system of government and replacing a monarchy with a republic. It is generally considered, however, that the Prussian crown was never in serious danger, whereas the Habsburg dynasty genuinely faced extinction, if only for one or two brief periods. While Berlin saw no rebellious armies, nor full-scale battles,[95] her 'proletariat' appeared stronger in its republican sentiments. This assumption gains further credence from the fact that student involvement in Berlin was minimal and that the workers had to form their own organizations. Workers also had little sympathy for the liberal government and the concept of 'agreement', a consensus between king and parliament which might possibly secure 'freedom to read', but not the 'freedom to feed'.[96]

While such differences in aspiration indicate a good deal about the force and political maturity of the respective revolutionaries, we must also consider the other side and examine the role played by the monarchies in the three cities. In France where a dynastic continuity had already been lost, Louis Philippe was closely associated with the Guizot government, representing the interests of a wealthy bourgeoisie. In Vienna by contrast, the weak emperor, whose subjects remembered fondly the reforms introduced by his forebears Joseph II and Maria Theresia, was relatively popular. Furthermore, the Habsburg dynasty was seen to be the mortar binding the Austrian Empire together. The actual irritant was Metternich, and with his fall the chief focus of popular anger was removed. Berlin, too, had a volatile monarch, and identified strongly with the Hohenzollern dynasty, treasuring the traditions of Frederick the Great and the memory of the wars of liberation in 1812. Metternich was to the Viennese what the Prussian army was to Berliners, symbolized in the figure of the crown prince. After an apparent rift with the king, the crown prince's exile to London brought him into the sphere of other figures of public hatred, Louis Philippe and Metternich. Once troops had been removed from Berlin and the king had made his wide-ranging, popular concessions, the revolution seemed to falter. Indeed, one of the major weaknesses of the Berlin revolution was its lack of clearly defined political and social objectives. With the 'March events', the success of the revolution seemed all but assured. Further incidents could do little more than revive the same issues, almost re-enacting the scenes of 18 and 19 March. The revolution in Vienna involved greater potential for progression, quite possibly because of a wider scope for manoeuvre, both on the part of revolutionaries and their opponents. A relatively wise and moderate approach on the part of Habsburg and Hohenzollern preserved both dynasties and promised wide-ranging reforms. In addition, both cities were restricted in their revolutionary energies by the nationality issue, compelling them not only to look warily towards Frankfurt, but also to regard each other jealously, conscious of their long-standing rivalry over German supremacy. Revolutionaries in Vienna seemed to pay more heed to Frankfurt than did their friends in Berlin, partly because the new imperial regent, Archduke John, was the emperor's youngest brother, but more significantly, because the Viennese were keenly aware of their minority position within the Habsburg Empire. Their national sentiments played an integral part in their revolutionary programme, drawing them more closely to the still elusive German fatherland. Berliners were more confident in this respect, as they began to sense that their city would emerge as Germany's new capital:[97] Prussia had taken the initiative in the Schleswig–Holstein conflict, the Prussian king had proclaimed himself a German leader. Both cities feared outside intervention, notably from Russia and France, but Vienna was more vulnerable, involved in the Habsburg conflict with France over Italy and fearing Russian intervention in support of the Slav minorities.

As far as the political aims and social impact of the revolutions were concerned, Vienna probably took the lead over Berlin. Its revolution not only resulted in a much greater loss of life, it also gained stronger support from intellectuals, students and the proletariat. Berlin had nothing to equal Vienna's Academic Legions; Berlin's university teachers were more concerned with university reform than with revolution.[98] Berlin's students either remained aloof or chose to become integrated within one of the many political clubs. At the same time, Berlin's young people were heavily involved. Less concerned about national issues, they succeeded in breaking down class barriers by participating in a large variety of political associations. Any such observation, however, remains problematic. In both cities the revolutions suffered from a progressive bifurcation between a liberal and moderate bourgeoisie, increasingly responsive to counter-revolutionary promises of economic recovery and anxious for the return of the *status quo ante*, and a proletariat growing ever-more desperate and frustrated and seeking more radical and extreme solutions. This development was symbolized most clearly by the change in the colours of the flags on display. The German national colours, predominant in the spring of 1848, were gradually replaced, either by the traditional Austrian or Prussian colours in the case of the bourgeoisie, or by the red flags favoured by the proletariat, expressing their desire for a resolution of socio-economic rather than constitutional matters.

The next chapter will examine the role of the National Assembly in Frankfurt and its attempt to serve as a focal point for the establishment of a German nation state. Our discussions will return to Vienna and Berlin for, once the decision was made to opt for a lesser Germany, Berlin inevitably emerged as Frankfurt's rival at a time when faith in parliamentary democracy had been shaken and new demands for *Realpolitik* were rife.

Notes

1 Ludwig Börne: 'Austria is the European China, a mature but stagnant state. She drives her strong roots well beyond her own territory underneath the soil of other states. . . .' 'Über Österreich und Preußen' [1818], in *Sämtliche Schriften*, I. and P. Rippmann eds, vol. 1 (Düsseldorf, 1964) p. 635. Cf. also the Austrian refugee Karl Postl, known by the pseudonym of Charles Sealsfield, who published his *Austria as it is* and Count Anton Auersperg, writing under his pen name Anastasius Grün, who published his *Spaziergänge eines Wiener Poeten* (Strolls of a Viennese Poet) in 1831.

2 Victor von Andrian – Werbung, *Österreich und dessen Zukunft*, 3rd edn, part I (Hamburg, 1843), quoted from R. John Rath, *The Viennese Revolution of 1848* (New York, 1969), p. 21.

3 Cf. H. Rieder, *Die Völker läuten Sturm. Die europäische Revolution 1848/49* (Gernsbach, 1997), p. 106.

4 P. Molisch, 'Die Wiener akademische Legion und ihr Anteil an den Verfassungs-kämpfen des Jahres 1848', *Archiv für österreichische Geschichte*, 110 (1926), p. 16.

5 W. Häusler, *Von der Massenarmut zur Arbeiterbewegung. Demokratie und soziale Frage in der Wiener Revolution von 1848* (Munich, 1979), p. 175.

6 W. Häusler, 'Wien', in Christof Dipper and Ulrich Speck eds, *1848. Revolution in Deutschland* (Frankfurt/M. and Leipzig, 1998), p. 100.

7 W. H. Stiles, *Austria in 1848–49: A History of the Late Political Movements in Vienna, Milan, Venice and Prague; with a Full Account of the Revolution in Hungary*, vol. 1 (New York, 1852), p. 102.

8 Häusler, *Von der Massenarmut*, p. 155.

9 E. Bauernfeld, *Aus Alt- und Neu-Wien, Deutsche Hausbücherei 87* (Vienna, 1923), p. 215.

10 Häusler, *Von der Massenarmut*, p. 180.

11 L. A. Frankl, *Die Universität. Erstes censurfreies Blatt aus der Josef Stöckholzer von Hirschfeld'schen Buchdruckerei* (Wien, 15 March 1848), No. II/83. Quoted from Rath, *Viennese Revolution*, p. 30.

12 Häusler, *Von der Massenarmut*, p. 208.

13 Maximilian Bach, *Geschichte der Wiener Revolution im Jahre 1848* (Vienna, 1898), pp. 12–23. Full text of Kossuth's speech in J. A. Helfert, *Geschichte der Österreichischen* Revolution, vol. 1 (Freiburg, 1907), pp. 241ff.

14 Bach, *Geschichte*, pp. 201f.

15 H. Jellinek, 'Kritische Thesen über die Verfassungsurkunde vom 25. April für das Kaisertum Österreich', *Kritischer Sprechsaal*, 2 (1848), pp. 25–8. Quoted in Häusler, *Von der Massenarmut*, pp. 221f. Jellinek's assessment of the situation is sharply countered by that of W. H. Stiles who observed that 'the numerous *proletaria*, or rabble, in and around the city ... together with the thousands of idle and criminal beings [became] easy converts to the Communist principles'. Stiles, *Austria in 1848–49*, vol. 1, p. 117.

16 Häusler, *Von der Massenarmut*, p. 149.

17 W. H. Stiles, *Austria in 1848–49*, vol. 1. p. 112.

18 The text of the Constitution is reprinted in J. A. Freiherr von Helfert, *Geschichte der Österreichischen Revolution*, vol. 1 (Freiburg, 1907), pp. 499–504.

19 F. Kaiser, *Ein Wiener Volksdichter erlebt die Revolution*, F. Hadamowsky ed. (Vienna, 1948), p. 58.

20 *Wiener Zeitung*, 18 May 1848. Cf. also F. Stamprech, *Die älteste Tageszeitung der Welt. Werden und Entwicklung der "Wiener Zeitung"'* (Vienna, 1974), p. 203.

21 *Wiener Zeitung* 145 (25 May 1848), p. 719.

22 *Wiener Zeitung*, Beilage (18 May 1848), no. 2, p. 18.

23 Rath, *Viennese Revolution*, p. 211.

24 Ibid.

25 Cf. K. Marx and F. Engels, *Germany: Revolution and Counter-Revolution* (vol. 13 of Marxist Library: Works of Marxism–Leninism) (New York, 1933), p. 70.

26 Quoted in Rath, *Viennese Revolution*, p. 315.

27 Cf. also unofficial discussions with Gagern in Heinrich Laube's memoirs, in H. Fenske ed., *Quellen zur deutschen Revolution 1848–1849* (Darmstadt, 1996), pp. 174–9. Journalists in the *Wiener Zeitung* from 23 to 25 March had already been incensed by the Prussian king's attempt to take the leading role in a future German nation state.

28 Quoted in Rath, *Viennese Revolution*, p. 255.

29 Häusler, 'Wien', p. 105.

30 K. Marx and F. Engels, *Collected Works*, M. Dobb *et al.* eds, vol. 7 (London, 1977), p. 212.

31 Cf. Grillparzer, *Feldmarschall Radetzky*, praises the general as the strong leader towards union, declaring that he and his fellow citizens 'aus Torheit und aus Eitelkeit sind wir in uns zerfallen', in Franz Grillparzer, *Sämtliche Werke*, A. Sauer ed., vol. 1 *Gedichte* (Vienna, 1932), pp. 230f. Cf. also *Radetzky* in *Gedichte*, vol. 3, 1, p. 200.

32 Rath, *Viennese Revolution*, p. 277.

33 Ibid., p. 289.

34 Cf. J. A. Freiherr von Helfert, *Die Wiener Journalistik im Jahre 1848* (Vienna, 1877), pp. 166–75.

35 Rieder, *Die Völker*, p. 204.

36 For a good report on Latour's murder cf. Bach, *Geschichte*, pp. 704ff; also the somewhat biased account by Stiles, *Austria in 1848–49*, vol. 2, pp. 99–102.

37 Rath, *Viennese Revolution*, p. 348.

38 Häusler, 'Wien', p. 107.

39 Letter to his wife, 20 October 1848, in R. Blum, *Briefe und Dokumente*, S. Schmidt ed. (Leipzig, 1981), p. 480.

40 Cf. Ferdinand Freiligrath's poem *Blum* in *Freiligraths Werke in einem Band*, W. Ilberg ed. 3rd edn (Berlin and Weimar, 1976), pp. 133–5.

41 K. Gutzkow, *Unter dem schwarzen Bären. Erlebtes 1811–1848* (Berlin, 1971), p. 531.

42 Theodor Fontane, *Von zwanzig bis dreißig, Sämtliche Werke, Aufsätze, Kritiken, Erinnerungen*, vol. 4 (Munich, 1973), p. 489.

43 R. Hachtmann, *Berlin 1848. Eine Politik- und Gesellschaftsgeschichte der Revolution* (Bonn, 1997), p. 69.

44 Ibid., p. 71, see in particular the statistical table.

45 R. Hachtmann, 'Berlin', in Dipper und Speck eds, *1848. Revolution*.

46 *Augsburger Allgemeine Zeitung*, 9 March 1847.

47 Cf. Hachtmann, *Berlin 1848*, pp. 80f.

48 Fontane, *Von zwanzig bis dreißig*, pp. 487f.

49 Cf. D. B. Barclay, 'Friedrich Wilhelm IV, König von Preußen: Gottesgnadentum in einem revolutionären Zeitalter', in S. Freitag ed., *Die Achtundvierziger. Lebensbilder aus der deutschen Revolution 1848/49* (Munich, 1998), pp. 290ff.

50 R. Hachtmann, 'Joseph Maria von Radowitz: Ein in preußischem Boden verwurzelter deutscher Staatsmann', in Freitag ed., *Die Achtundvierziger*, p. 279.

51 *Evangelische Kirchenzeitung*, 43 (1848), col. 225f.

52 A Thiel, 'Die Evangelische Kirche und die Revolution', *Evangelische Kirchenzeitung*, 31–33 (17–22 April, 1848), col. 278–312, in part. col. 289.

53 Hachtmann, *Berlin 1848*, p. 151.

54 Fontane, *Von zwanzig bis dreißig*, p. 489.

55 'Immediatbericht Radowitz' to King Frederick William IV, Frankfurt, 24 May 1848, in Fenske ed., *Quellen*, pp. 97–100.

56 K. L. von Prittwitz, *Berlin 1848: das Erinnerungswerk des Generalleutnants Karl Ludwig von Prittwitz und andere Quellen zur Berliner Märzrevolution und zur Geschichte Preußens um die Mitte des 19. Jahrhunderts*, G. Heinrich ed. (Berlin, 1985), pp. 49–53.

57 Hachtmann, *Berlin 1848*, p. 155.

58 R. Stadelmann, *Social and Political History of the German 1848 Revolution*, trans. by James G. Chastain (Athens, OH, 1975), p. 58.

59 Fontane, *Von zwanzig bis dreißig*, p. 503.
60 For details of social background and biography of the victims, cf. Hachtmann, *Berlin 1848*, pp. 173f.
61 Hachtmann, *Berlin 1848*, p. 178.
62 Cf. statistical table in Hachtmann, *Berlin 1848*, p. 180.
63 Stadelmann, *Social and Political History*, p. 61.
64 Leopold von Gerlach, *Denkwürdigkeiten aus dem Leben Leopold von Gerlachs, Generals der Infanterie und General-Adjudanten König Friedrich Wilhelms IV. Nach seinen Aufzeichnungen herausgegeben von seiner Tochter*, vol. 1 (Berlin, 1891), p. 138.
65 Cf. several statements by officers and politicians, quoted in Hachtmann, *Berlin 1848*, p. 198.
66 Stadelmann, *Social and Political History*, p. 63.
67 Cf. the presentation of events by General von Prittwitz, *Berlin, 1848*, p. 139.
68 For a detailed account of events as seen from the prince and his environment cf. Jessen ed., *Die deutsche Revolution*, pp. 92–6.
69 Stadelmann, *Social and Political History*, pp. 58f.
70 Frederick William's speech of 22 March 1848, quoted in Hachtmann, *Berlin 1848*, p. 210. Cf. also his letter to Dahlmann of 3 May 1848, in Fenske ed., *Quellen*, pp. 92f.
71 For a detailed account cf. Hachtmann, *Berlin 1848*, p. 214.
72 For an eye witness account, cf. Bettina von Arnim, *Werke und Briefe*, vol. 5, pp. 407f.
73 Hachtmann, *Berlin 1848*, p. 217.
74 H. Czihak, 'Der Kampf um die Ausgestaltung des Friedhofs der Märzgefallenen im Berliner Friedrichshain', in W. Schmidt ed., *Demokratie, Liberalismus und Konterrevolution. Studien zur deutschen Revolution von 1848/49* (Berlin, 1998), pp. 549–63.
75 *Neue Rheinische Zeitung*, 16 June 1848, in Marx and Engels, *Collected Works*, vol. 7, p. 79.
76 Hachtmann, *Berlin 1848*, p. 359.
77 Ibid., p. 266. Cf. also Gustav Julius in *Berliner Zeitungshalle*, 30 March 1848.
78 K. Haenchen ed., *Revolutionsbriefe 1848. Ungedrucktes aus dem Nachlaß König Friedrich Wilhelm IV. von Preußen* (Leipzig, 1930), p. 65.
79 *Neue Rheinische Zeitung*, 16 December 1848, in Marx and Engels, *Collected Works*, vol. 8 (London, 1977), p. 163. Cf. also Bruno Bauer, *Die bürgerliche Revolution in Deutschland seit dem Anfange der deutsch-katholischen Bewegung* (Berlin, 1849), pp. 255f.
80 Calculated as 56 per cent and based on a statistical survey in Hachtmann, *Berlin 1848*, p. 301.
81 Stephan Born, *Erinnerungen eines Achtundvierzigers*, 3rd edn (Leipzig, 1898), p. 65.
82 Hachtmann, *Berlin 1848*, pp. 445–9.
83 Cf. *Neue Rheinische Zeitung*, 9 June 1848, in Marx and Engels, *Collected Works*, vol. 7, pp. 66f.
84 *Neue Rheinische Zeitung*, 14 June 1848, in Marx and Engels, *Collected Works*, vol. 7, p. 86.
85 A good account is given by Fanny Lewald, *A Year of Revolutions. Fanny Lewald's Recollections of 1848*, H. B. Lewis trans. and ed. (Providence, Oxford, 1997), pp. 101–4.

86 *Locomotive*, 13 June 1848, in Hachtmann, *Berlin 1848*, p. 562.

87 Hachtmann, *Berlin 1848*, p. 278.

88 For a detailed account cf. ibid., pp. 614f.

89 Ibid., p. 626.

90 Ibid., pp. 706f.

91 Ibid., p. 747.

92 Wrangel commanded an army of approx. 80,000 men to use against Berlin revolutionaries. Cf. Hachtmann, *Berlin 1848*, p. 761.

93 'Verfassungsurkunde für den preußischen Staat', in W. Grab ed., *Die Revolution von 1848/49. Eine Dokumentation* (Stuttgart, 1998), pp. 155–72.

94 Calculated from figures in Hachtmann, *Berlin 1848*, p. 806.

95 Cf. J. J. Sheehan, *German History 1770–1866* (Oxford, 1989), p. 702.

96 C. Tilli *et al.* eds, *Century*, p. 221. Cf. also *Neue Rheinische Zeitung*, 14 June 1848, in Marx and Engels, *Collected Works*, vol. 7, p. 74: 'The united reactionary parties began their fight against democracy by *calling the revolution in question*. . . . The United Diet convoked before the revolution was now actually convened by the Government, in order *post festum* to fabricate a legal transition from absolutism to the Constitution.'

97 Hachtmann, 'Berlin', p. 97.

98 Hachtmann, *Berlin 1848*, p. 360.

Chapter 5

The move towards parliamentary democracy

Introduction

Previous chapters have sought to determine the extent to which a democratic political culture was able to develop before 1848; it was evident that the support of an intellectual elite was vital for such a development. However, the actual revolutions in Berlin and even more so in Vienna appear to have involved a much wider and more diverse public participation. The emergence of many different clubs and associations, attracting men and women from many varied walks of life, represented a wide spectrum of society. It became apparent that their various political aims were clearly defined, and embraced an awareness of constitutional issues and social problems. These political aims, as drawn up at the various 'party' gatherings, found their popular counterpart among street activists and this interaction was to become a chief agent of revolutionary energies which provided the impetus for revolutionary progress.

This chapter will attempt to explore and supplement these observations. It will return to events in the Third Germany, in order to examine to what extent the establishment of political associations there had an impact on the different factions which eventually took their seats in the National Assembly in Frankfurt. As this analysis will revolve around two major areas of discussion, the extra-parliamentary political activities and the establishment of 'national' parliaments, a number of specific problems should be borne in mind.

1. Since the 1848 revolutions it has been widely held that the Frankfurt National Assembly consisted largely of professors, who failed to represent the many different, often radical, political groups and the established views of public political opinion.[1] Though not a parliament of professors, it had a significant over-representation of academics and civil servants, allowing scant opportunity for representation from the crafts, from trade and industry or from agriculture. This chapter will examine the extent to which this imbalance between parliamentarians and public opinion, as generated in clubs and associations, may have weakened the new parliament.

112

2. Many interpretations of the 'German' revolution seem to base their findings too heavily on West European or American patterns of liberal democracy. The debate stimulated in recent years by D. Blackbourn and G. Eley, on the nature of liberalism in Germany, has accentuated the notion of a 'failed bourgeois revolution' as being responsible for the failure to establish a modern democratic culture in Germany.[2] Whilst their criticism of Ralf Dahrendorf's rather defensive approach to Germany's political culture is certainly overdue, especially with regard to his claim that the absence of a liberal polity can be held responsible for the late development of a modern Germany,[3] they seem to have underestimated the relevance of some other German 'peculiarities'. There is the peculiarly German concept of a people's sovereignty (*Volkssouveränität*), a concept indebted to aspects of Western Enlightenment, while steeped in German Romantic tradition. Some of the leading representatives of the Frankfurt Assembly, notably Ludwig Uhland, Jacob Grimm and Ernst Moritz Arndt, were enthusiastic proponents of such romantically conceived German traditions. In general, it must be recognized that the liberal tendency was only one of many different perspectives which influenced the course of events. Alongside the liberals, Otto Dann lists a conservative, a catholic and a democratic movement,[4] to which can be added the women's movement and the workers' initiatives. Another factor, easily overlooked in this context, is the complication that the German revolutions, in common with Italy and many Eastern European countries, also involved the objective of national unification, an objective which was to compete with liberal and democratic agendas, particularly where national minorities were concerned.

3. An analysis of the many political clubs and associations reveals the danger of employing concepts such as class in an attempt to unify and categorize the different social components of the revolutions. Such attempts impose structures borrowed from Western democracies on a German scenario, where there was neither a cohesive middle-class movement nor a definable working-class structure. It may indeed be better to refer to the professional orientation of individuals and to avoid a consistent use of class concepts, since German society at that stage was very much in transition.[5]

4. An analysis of the social roots of the revolutions can also easily fall victim to exaggerated charges of exclusivity or inclusion. This is particularly the case when discussing the roles of women and Jews, where there is still a popular tendency to overemphasize their contribution, thereby denying them a broader social base. Both Jews and women had their own important and charismatic representatives, who had a major impact on the course of the revolutions. However, this impact was seldom the result of either a Jewish or feminist background, neither category being sufficiently emancipated to

113

play a decisive role in events at that time. Furthermore, any group identity can be defined either inclusively from within the group or in an exclusive sense from outside, in an attempt to ostracize or discriminate against them. This was particularly true in the case of the Jewish community.[6] Long established in banking and respected within their orthodox communities, a majority of older and established Jews were suspicious of any revolutionary activity, in contrast to a younger, emancipated Jewish element within the intelligentsia, who were ardent revolutionaries, demanding equal rights and identifying themselves with the democratic aims of the revolution. An interesting example, combining the Jewish and feminist role, is Fanny Lewald. Endowed with an astute sense of the limited achievements that could be expected in the Germany of her time, and from her viewpoint as a liberal and emancipated Jew, she supported the revolutions in both France and Germany along broad constitutional and political lines.[7] She was more restrained on feminist issues. Her observation on a delegation of women from the Democratic Club, marching down a Berlin street, was pertinent: 'No matter how much one recognizes the intellectual equality of women, their personal presence in a crowd is alien to the German character. Such appearances should therefore not be called for intentionally, because they do not gain anything for the real elevation of the status of women or for the people, and much can be lost.'[8]

5. Many accounts of the revolutions have, in the past, been restricted by an exclusively historical perspective, allowing insufficient scope for the discussion of social, cultural, political and economic issues. Noteworthy exceptions are the works of Langewiesche, Gall and Sperber. Equally valuable are individual case studies, based on specific cities or regions, especially where they have adopted an interdisciplinary approach, such as those of Carola Lipp, who is indebted to the discipline of Empirical Culture Studies.[9] In many other instances, observations made on the 1848 revolutions stand entirely within their historical discipline or are confined within their own specific time scale, allowing no opportunity for any form of comparative study. This is particularly regrettable in instances where specific issues are concerned, such as the implementation of local or regional politics within a federal context or the execution of day-to-day policies in local clubs or associations.

Extra-parliamentary political activities and their interaction with the National Assembly

Chapter 3 has indicated how a political culture was able to establish itself during the Pre-March period, based on sound and often intimate knowledge of political events at home and abroad. In turn, the desire to participate in the process of political decision making gradually increased. The rapid establishment of political clubs and associations before and during 1848 is proof of such a political will. In the former free city of Esslingen, for instance, a town of 13,000 inhabitants, nineteen associations existed before 1848, with another fifteen societies being founded during the revolution.[10] Although the titles of many of these clubs suggest that they were non-political in nature, it has been shown that the various gymnasts' societies, choral groups and reading clubs owed much of their popularity to a lively interest in local and national politics. The reclusive bookworms of the *Biedermeier* had gradually become more outgoing; they had turned from a 'culture-debating public to a culture-consuming public'.[11]

Robert Blum's *Redeübungsverein* (Rhetorical Society) was founded in 1845 in Leipzig, in an effort to unite the disparate forces of opposition.[12] Although described as the precursor of a political party,[13] it offered only a limited political programme, expressing some general views on popular sovereignty and the common good.[14] Manfred Botzenhart, examining early examples of such political associations in Germany, has concluded that these initial examples of popular representation embraced the concept of national sovereignty, in opposition to autocratic governments. Most individual factions addressed only a very narrow range of interests, often in conflict with the common good of the people.[15] Their views can be traced back to the Freiburg constitutionalist von Rotteck, but they are also present in Hegel's philosophy. In the entry in the *Staatslexikon*, Rotteck singles out democratic parties as being unique in expressing 'general human interests', in contrast to bodies of state absolutism, the churches and the bourgeoisie whose particularist interests must be rejected.[16] Such populist human-interest views have profoundly influenced Germany's political culture up to and into the twentieth century, and it is therefore of prime importance to recognize that the revolutions posed a challenge to such a political agenda. All the various voluntary associations were based on an organized union of people with similar views, a majority taking their lead from the popular gatherings at Offenburg and Heppenheim. In their wake came the development of the first political parties, based on the democratic or liberal programmes adopted there.

The tensions between the radical democrats surrounding Hecker and Struve and the liberal constitutionalists surrounding Bassermann and Mathy resulted initially in a voluntary retreat by the radicals, in the general interest of unity. The liberals were sceptical of the aims of any revolutionary movement, fearful of the spread of a French-style revolution on to German soil.[17] The question of moderation, the exclusion of social concerns in favour of liberal political principles, began to open up a division between a moderate, constitutional 'liberal' majority and a radical left-wing minority, which focused on social and economic demands, along the lines of those expressed by their Parisian comrades.[18] Following the establishment of the Pre-Parliament, the foundation of the Democratic Central Committee has been described as 'the first attempt at forming a political party'.[19] Siemann relates the formation of five political groups to five impulses generated by the revolutions: the early political protests of spring 1848, the negotiations of the Frankfurt National Assembly, the period of the emerging counter-revolution in the autumn of 1848, regional elections in the winter and the dissolution of the National Assembly in the spring and summer of 1849.[20] Without a detailed discussion of whether such a clear division, moving broadly from the political left to a centre-right position, can actually be established, it seems beyond doubt that the more radical, republican and democratic groups were the first to gain a clearly defined political profile. Their effective exclusion from the parliamentary forum meant that they were obliged to formulate and put across their opposition views clearly, giving themselves the kind of profile which we associate with a genuine political party.

Any examination of the establishment of political parties during the revolutions must consider both the extra-parliamentarian clubs and associations and the various factions which formed within the Frankfurt National Assembly. Stadelmann's discussion of the emergence of political parties does not give sufficient weight to this interrelationship between the parliamentary process and organized public opinion 'at street level'. He seems to over-emphasize the latter, failing to recognize that to this day political parties depend on both forms of political activity in order to justify their existence.[21] Stadelmann's opinion may have been influenced by the somewhat fluid meaning which the term *Partei* had acquired in Germany. During the Pre-March period, the general pattern of political activity involved taking sides and, in some cases, abandoning the lofty position of aestheticism, usually in favour of a broadly left of centre opposition to the existing government. In 1842, prior to the emergence of actual political parties, a literary dispute between Ferdinand Freiligrath and Georg Herwegh provoked the latter to pen the following:

> *Partei, Partei!* Who should not wish to side
> With it, the mother of all victories!
> How could a poet shun such word,
> A word that gave us all that's splendid?
> Be honest like a man: for or against?
> The battle cry is slavery or freedom? . . .[22]

In the wake of the public gatherings in Baden in the spring of 1848, the meaning of the term *Partei* became more specific. With the fall of Metternich and the success of the 'March Demands' came the freedom to express political opinions, making it possible to define specific political views more precisely and to afford them an organizational status through which they could be expressed.

The earlier phase of the revolutions during spring and early summer of 1848 revealed specific problems, associated with the attempt to define particular political views and to present them within an organizational framework. Two factors will illustrate these difficulties: firstly, a peculiar over-representation of intellectuals, particularly among democrats and liberals, who dominated established politics at the expense of the grass-roots worker and craftsmen activists; secondly, an exaggerated emphasis on national sovereignty, a German version of the more rational and enlightened *volonté générale* which can be traced back to early Pre-March days. The champions of such a concept of national sovereignty or, in its more German terminology, 'sovereignty of the people' tended to align themselves with the democratic camp, with parliamentary democracy, based on a republican model or, at the very least, with the principle of an elected monarch.[23] They were soon immersed in the nationality debate and inclined towards the option of a 'Greater German' solution, which included the German-speaking population of the Habsburg Empire. In addition, they tended to move to the left of the political spectrum, not only becoming opposed to any form of constitutional monarchy, but also favouring the abolition of a privileged nobility.[24] They desired the establishment of a general militia and sought the abolition of a standing professional army, loyal to the monarch.[25] In this they were influenced by the French notion of patriotism, and also by the Germanic tradition of the freedom to bear arms (*Wehrhaftigkeit*), revived during the Romantic period and reaffirmed during the Wars of Liberation. As a consequence, they sought to enfranchise every free man, irrespective of social or economic status.[26] With the departure of Struve and Hecker from the parliamentary forum, the democrats were in a minority position at Frankfurt. In order to strengthen their camp they were keen to form political alliances and to present a clear and well-developed political programme. In June 1848 they organized the first Congress of German Republican Democrats in the hope of establishing some centralized support for their policies. By November that year, when the counter-revolution seemed poised to gain the upper hand, the Central March Association was founded, uniting all democratic factions in a last attempt to sustain the revolution. At the same time the more republican wing of the Frankfurt Assembly sought to undermine and discredit the parliament, even contemplating the formation of a counter-parliament. Their interpretation of national sovereignty was closer to that of the Paris revolution, in that their programmes covered social and economic issues, especially the right to

117

work, the demand for a progressive income tax and a closer link between parliamentarians and the grass roots. A particularly effective result of their political activity was the establishment of the *Vaterlandsverein* in Leipzig (28 March 1848), with forty-three branches and a membership of almost 12,000 within the first few weeks. This association will demonstrate that political parties could operate effectively outside parliament, and in several such extra-parliamentary associations prominent left-Hegelian intellectuals, who would not have wished to sit in the Frankfurt parliament, took a leading role. At the first Congress of Democrats in Frankfurt (June 1848) Julius Fröbel, pedagogue and political theorist, the philosopher Ludwig Feuerbach and the poet Ferdinand Freiligrath joined the Frankfurt parliamentarian Andreas Gottschalk to discuss the political situation; they also established links with the Silesian farmers, one of the very few instances where the farming population was involved.[27] The Congress demonstratively moved its headquarters to Berlin, indicating its preference for revolutionary Berlin over liberal Frankfurt. Fröbel, who had recent experience of the Swiss revolution, was fascinated by the political concept of dissolving liberalism into 'democratism', as suggested by the philosopher Arnold Ruge,[28] who defined liberalism as sympathy with democracy 'in intention'.[29]

Many parliamentarians in Frankfurt who were enthusiastic supporters of the idea of national sovereignty were averse to joining any political faction. Their romantic standpoint demanded a direct link with the people, a view which would today be associated with the concept of direct democracy. Almost one third of the Paul's Church delegates did not profess any political affiliation.[30] The romantic poet Ludwig Uhland was such a 'wild' delegate. Elected at the age of sixty-one by nearly 90 per cent of his Tübingen-Rottenburg constituency, this eminent author of popular ballads and historical dramas never joined a club or political faction. The first professor of German literature at Tübingen University, from where he had been expelled for his opposition to the Württemberg government, he was famous for his stubbornly uncompromising stance. His passionate belief in the sovereignty of the people usually led him to cast his vote with the radical left. He shared their opposition to a hereditary monarch, the retention of the aristocracy and to a German nation state which excluded the German-speaking parts of Austria. Uhland's own populist romantic views on sovereignty prevented him from understanding social issues; rejecting all modern political concepts he adhered to the undifferentiated notion of *Volk*.[31]

The liberals formed the largest group in the Frankfurt parliament. While holding to the principal ideas of the Enlightenment, they did not wholly share the democrats' belief in national sovereignty. As practising politicians during the Pre-March period, mostly associated with regional opposition movements, their politics were more pragmatic and their general outlook more bourgeois, based on the support of the urban middle-class associations which had developed prior to the revolution. They opposed the old concept of a corporate order[32] and saw the granting of the 'March Demands' – press-freedom, the freedom to assemble and to form associations – as their ultimate achievement. Fearing more extreme objectives, they had no wish for the revolution to continue but sought to consolidate the new *status quo*. Content with the establishment of a constitutional monarchy and a federal system of national unification, they favoured a hereditary monarchy,[33] opting at an early stage for Berlin and Prussian hegemony over the greater-Germany solution, under Austrian rule. In rejecting Struve's application to declare the Pre-Parliament a permanent body until such time that a national parliament had been established, liberals actually voted for the pre-revolutionary Federal Diet, thereby transforming the revolution into an evolution.[34] Fanny Lewald observed ironically, how in liberal circles the word 'revolution' had become unpopular and how the new Prussian prime-minister, Camphausen, avoided it altogether, speaking instead of an 'occur-rence', 'although Mr Camphausen and his colleagues should regard this revolution as their *mother*'.[35]

Heinrich von Gagern serves as a good example of such liberal politicians. Coming from a dynasty of diplomats and generals, his father had enjoyed the friendship of Freiherr von Stein and he himself had negotiated with Talleyrand. His brother, a Dutch general, was killed while fighting Hecker's revolution in Baden. Gagern had been a delegate to the Hesse–Darmstadt parliament and in March 1848, while attending the Heidelberg Assembly, he was appointed minister of the interior. He also played a leading role in the Pre-Parliament, being instrumental in defeating the crucial Struve-Hecker membership application. Although decisive in arranging the election of the Habsburg Archduke John as regent of Germany, he always favoured national unification under Prussian hegemony and pursued this policy even subsequent to the collapse of the National Assembly.[36] Many liberals, less influenced by Western traditions of public spiritedness and the promotion of individual rights, had their political origins in 'the old moralistic Spirit of Protestantism' denounced by Ruge as 'empty good will'.[37] Predominantly middle class and urban, they were often associated with conservative circles.[38] The liberal citizens' action groups (*Bürgervereine*), whose politically active members were academics and civil servants, and the occasional business-man, tended to be rather loosely organized, usually operating only at local level. From September 1848 onwards, in response to the development of democratic central organizations, the liberals established their national associations, with strongholds in northern and central Germany, and to a certain extent also in the southwest.[39]

While the major players in the 1848 parliaments were the democrats and liberals, other stakeholders also occupied the political scene. Strongly wedded to the emancipatory principles of the Enlightenment and to revolution were the workers' associations, who eagerly assimilated the theories and philosophies of Saint Simonism, Owen's co-operative experiments, the Chartist movement and Marxism. Their activities originated in the secret associations of the Pre-March period, such as the *Bund der Gerechten* and the *Bund der Geächteten*. They encouraged projects based on Louis Blanc's labour organizations, especially in the industrialized areas of the Rhineland, Saxony and Berlin, and cultivated close contacts with the gymnastic societies, with reading clubs and similar associations fostering emancipatory and educational aims.[40] Karl Winkelblech was a leading activist in the early stages of the movement, postulating equality between masters and journeymen, but in some respects still wedded to the antiquated system of guilds.[41] In the spring of 1849, Winkelblech was succeeded by Stephan Born, whose Workers Confederation was much better organized and could be seen as an embryonic trade union. By pronouncing that the only meaningful division was that between capital and labour, Born abolished divisions based on status alone.[42] He succeeded in organizing an all-German network of organizations which, though on fraternal terms with the democrats, distanced itself from the National Assembly and, later, the nationality issue. Born rallied behind the red flag – symbol of emancipation and socialist fraternity – rather than the German tricolour.[43]

While the search for a solution to the social issues of the day was their over-riding concern, workers' associations on the whole rejected the more radical alternatives of anarchy and revolution. The tailor-journeyman Wilhelm Weitling was the exception. Addressing an audience in Paris, he declared: 'In my opinion a socialist democracy can only be achieved once we have resolved the social question according to communist principles, but the immediate need is anarchy, revolution, dictatorship.'[44] Committed democrats, such as Blum, Gottschalk and Fröbel, kept their distance form such anarchist movements, still pinning their hopes on parliament. By the spring of 1849, workers' associations, however, had become increasingly disenchanted with the parliamentarians' efforts, turning instead towards social self-help organizations and co-operatives, and some early form of trade union activity was established, notably by printers in Mainz and cigar workers in Leipzig. The communists, led by Marx and Engels, had only a marginal influence on workers' associations, being deemed too intellectual and preoccupied with theory.[45] Similar observations apply to the influence of other radicals of the Left-Hegelian school; they, too, were seen as steeped in theoretical argument and unable to offer practical solutions.[46]

Two other quasi-political factions, both opposed to the political legacy of the Enlightenment, are of interest in this context. Catholicism had played an important part in Pre-March politics, particularly in the Rhineland, where the dominant catholic population found itself under the control of protestant Prussia. The election of Pope Pius IX (1846) was greeted with enthusiasm[47] and much was expected from his liberal reforms and from developments in Switzerland, where catholicism had become a crucial political force during the *Sonderbund* war. Political catholicism in Germany had its roots in southern and western Germany, in the German Romantic movement and in the influential Silesian nobility.[48] It began as a conservative ideology, strongly opposed to the spirit of the French Revolution and supportive of the monarchy and of a corporate state. Felix Prince Lichnowsky, a prominent Prussian catholic and delegate to the National Assembly supported the extreme right wing. However, by 1848 the catholic position had shifted, not least as a result of the dispute with Prussia over mixed marriages. An important power behind the movement was the Freiburg theologian and popular preacher Franz Joseph Buss. Following the March revolutions, he took advantage of the new liberal environment to argue for the independence of the catholic church from the state, for the freedom to establish religious orders, especially the Jesuit order which had been prohibited in some states, and for the free election of bishops.[49] However, such policies, although appearing to be liberal, were in fact opposed to any radical, free-thinking tendencies, as indicated by this statement from the Archbishop of Cologne: 'We will not say freedom of instruction for all, rather freedom of instruction for the church.'[50] Such statements led to clashes between catholics and liberals, especially on education issues, where liberals demanded freedom from church interference.[51] Most influential among catholics were the Pius Societies, founded in March 1848 in Mainz, from where they spread across south and west Germany, supported by local priests in small towns and rural communities.[52] By October Baden alone accounted for 400 societies with 100,000 members.[53] At their general assembly in Mainz, often referred to as the first all-German Catholic Diet, they established the 'spiritual parliament of the catholic people'.[54] The Pius Societies maintained only a loose association with the National Assembly, supporting liberals in their desire for a constitutional monarchy but opposing them over the 'smaller Germany' issue and the separation of education from church influence.[55] They were successful in reinstating the Jesuit order and in gaining an input into educational policy and, in general, their impact was anti-democratic and illiberal. Prominent catholics, such as Buss, Döllinger, Ketteler and Radowitz, supported the extreme right *Café Milani* faction, while others, such as the Reichensperger brothers, sided with the centrist *Casino* faction.[56] Though linked with the Pius Society, the Vincentius Society devoted itself more to social issues and stayed aloof from politics, as did the Kolping Society whose welfare programme is still in existence today.

The conservative associations, by their very nature, remained hostile to the revolution and at first played no part in public debates. However, when the March revolutions seemed about to threaten the established social and political order, they took the opportunity to exploit anti-modernist tendencies among peasants, craftsmen, civil servants and the nobility. Prussia and Bavaria became strongholds of conservatism, seeking to reverse the March achievements and to re-establish the corporate state. They rejected any form of constitutional monarchy and stalled the process of national unification. Ernst Ludwig Gerlach, a member of the Prussian *camarilla*, founded the *Kreuzzeitung*, their first political newspaper. He also founded the Society for King and Fatherland, with links to the reactionary Prussian and Patriotic Societies. As the revolutions in Vienna and Berlin began to weaken, the conservatives gained in strength, pandering to reactionary, petit bourgeois aspirations by advocating such policies as rent increases or further trade protection measures.[57] They also favoured an alliance between throne and (protestant) altar and supported the army.

The establishment of the Frankfurt National Assembly

It would appear that in the spring and summer of 1848 the political public was broadly divided into democrats and liberals. Although both modernist and wedded to the principles of the Enlightenment, the liberal 'pragmatic' solution increasingly adopted an anti-revolutionary stance. We shall now examine the extent to which the Frankfurt National Assembly nurtured such anti-revolutionary sentiments and whether, to paraphrase Danton, it was this parliament which devoured the revolution.

In attempting to resolve the question we must return once more to the earliest revolutionary programme at Offenburg and its related protest movements in the southwest. This democratic Offenburg programme contained all the demands, which were later to find expression in the Basic Rights, drawn up by the National Assembly, but it also contained many more radical proposals which did not find their way into the Basic Rights. It demanded a progressive income tax, a more equitable division between capital and labour, army allegiance to the constitution rather than to the monarch and weapons for all free men.[58] The liberal Heppenheim assembly, organized only a month later, struck a rather different note. More conciliatory in tone towards the established order, it emphasized the importance of free market forces and sought national unification through the existing customs' union. The next city on the road to Frankfurt was Heidelberg, where fifty-one liberal and democratic delegates met to discuss their plans for a German National

Assembly. Among the liberals were Bassermann, Gagern, Gervinus, Mathy, Römer, Soiron and Welcker, while the leading democrat representatives included Brentano, Hecker, Itzstein and Struve. A vast majority of delegates came from the southwest; with no legal or constitutional authority, they were simply motivated by their own political will and the strength of their political views.[59] The assembly at Heidelberg already displayed deep divisions, with democrats demanding the formation of a German republic with a constitution fashioned after the North American model, while liberals, by contrast, opted for a constitutional monarchy, based on the British system. An unsatisfactory compromise was reached on 19 March, when Hecker proposed a conciliatory resolution, deferring a decision on the type of government – whether republican or constitutional monarchist – for resolution by an all-German parliament in Frankfurt.[60] Hecker had in essence capitulated to the presence of a strong faction of March Ministers, who were seen as 'the answer of the princes against the revolutionary movement'[61] and whose influence interrupted the revolutionary process, thereby undermining the basis on which they had been brought into office.[62] At Heidelberg the task of the National Assembly was already being defined in such a manner that it contained an anti-revolutionary overtone, suggesting that it should 'surround the entire German fatherland and the thrones with this strong protective wall.'[63] The Frankfurt Diet's subsequent conciliatory and supportive declaration reinforced the Confederation belief that the revolution could now be contained. The Diet immediately accepted the proposed national colours, supported the nomination of the Committee of Seventeen and rescinded all Metternich's restrictive legislation.[64] A series of further agreements between democrats and liberals avoided an immediate conflict: individual governments were to decide on their own election procedures for the national government, and a Pre-Parliament was to be installed, consisting of delegates from every German state, according to rules laid down by a Committee of Seven. The 'constitutional' approach, as implemented by the German Diet, was one-sided, lacking any revolutionary counter-weight. The Committee of Seven, though moderate, consisted of March Ministers and associated delegates.

By the end of March, the following bodies assembled at Frankfurt: the Federal Diet, still consisting of delegates from pre-revolutionary days, the Committee of Seventeen, in essence a sub-committee of the Federal Diet charged with reforming the Federation and the 574 delegates of the Pre-Parliament, with a strong base in the southwest and only two representatives from Austria. Nominated by the Committee of Seven, the Pre-Parliament consisted of delegates from the new state parliaments and of members pre-eminent within public life, such as Robert Blum. The only body not institutionally linked to the old regime, it sat from 31 March to 3 April, but had no legal standing. In practice, it was the only institution capable of maintaining a revolutionary momentum, though the fact that several of its members functioned in a dual capacity, serving one or two further bodies as well, hindered its revolutionary potential. A certain rivalry could be observed, especially between the Pre-Parliament and the other associations and it was clear that the democrats, though strongly represented in the Pre-Parliament, were afraid that they might be outmanoeuvred by the forces of moderation. The Pre-Parliament concerned itself with four different issues:

1. It attempted to formulate its role in relation to the actual aims of the revolution. This and related issues came to a head when Struve introduced a motion designed to give the Pre-Parliament enough permanence to enable it to see the National Assembly established; it would also have made it the sole legal authority, thereby advancing the revolution a step further.
2. Struve also pleaded for a constitution based on the federal, North American model and for an elected president. He also favoured the abolition of both the civil service and a standing army, the latter to be replaced by a militia.
3. The proposal for national elections to a future parliament was generally supported, but with the proviso that only men of independent means were entitled to vote, a clause which had not been debated and seemed to have appeared from nowhere.
4. Radical democrats demanded that the existing Federal Diet be 'cleansed' of reactionary members. Struve's republican proposal was deferred, a final decision being left to the National Parliament. This deferral was essentially a rejection, amounting to the defeat of radical democracy. In the meantime, the proposal regarding the Diet was diluted, with the liberal Bassermann suggesting a compromise solution which effectively retained the *status quo*. Demonstrating their disgust with such a compromise, the radical democratic faction of Struve and Hecker left the Pre-Parliament, reducing the moderate wing around Blum, Jacoby and von Itzstein to a minority group. This division of the left had crucial repercussions, most notably giving rise to the accusation that the moderate democrats were content to abandon the revolution in favour of an evolution. By not supporting the radicals, they effectively undermined the establishment of a rival parliament.[65]

Agreement was achieved on the territories to which the National Assembly would be answerable. It exceeded the borders of the old Federation to include West and East Prussia, Schleswig, the 'German' parts of Austria, including Bohemia and Moravia, but not the Polish provinces. These would be returned to some new future Polish state. Elections would be free, secret and direct, with each delegate representing some 50,000 constituents.

As a result of the decision to abolish the Pre-Parliament, a further compromise was agreed: a Committee of Fifty was to be elected from within its ranks to advise the Federal Diet prior to the selection of a National Assembly. It strengthened the numerical representation of the Austrian constituencies, but retained its otherwise liberal moderate outlook. The constitutional liberals and the moderate democrats gained virtually equal representation, while Struve and Hecker failed to get elected. In essence, the Committee continued the work of the 'March Ministries' but failed to tackle any of the pressing social issues. It advocated the right to German citizenship, general military service, open access to political office at local and national level, an independent legal code based on the jury system, a fairer taxation law and academic freedom.

The constitutional committees

The majority of the chief participants in these constitutional committees were members of the *Bürgertum*, a term which defies precise translation, since it corresponds neither to the English 'middle classes' nor to the French 'bourgeoisie'. Its members were neither entrepreneurial nor defined by a particular class, but were best identified by the high standard of their education with its strong, neo-classical, humanist ethos. A large proportion of German *Bürger* were employed as civil servants, many of them teaching in schools and universities or working as advocates in the numerous state or city administrations. However, it would be misleading to emphasize the occupational significance of this group at the expense of the cohesiveness of their general way of life. While the number of actual academics in Germany was still very small, though notably higher than in Britain and France,[66] a large number of educated citizens enjoyed the benefits of a cultural environment. Lothar Gall's definition 'classless society of *Bürger*',[67] does go some way towards describing a society which was not defined by wealth or social status, profession or corporate identity, but largely by its own particular environment and neo-humanist education. Such a *Bürger* enjoyed an urban, small-town existence, with the cultural opportunities presented by the proximity of a princely court, still in the pre-industrial pattern and identifiable by its liberal values and aspirations. These *Bürger* citizens would not take to the barricades or favour the complete overthrow of a political order on whose employment they depended and whose cultural *milieu* they enjoyed. So great was the cultural dominance of the *Bürger*, that even 'proletarian' democrats such as Blum or socialists such as Born tended to overestimate the importance of education in order to reach this esteemed level, as is evident from their promotion of workers' education. An example of this aspiration to achieve equality with the status of *Bürger* can be found in the

125

statute of the Stuttgart Workers' Association, which advocated 'striving for the general and moral education of all workers, in order to enable them by every lawful means to attain the full enjoyment of all civil rights, as well as to the highest representation and promotion of their material and intellectual interests'.[68]

While most parliaments, now as then, consist of a large number of public employees who can more easily be freed from their normal occupation, while retaining a certain degree of job security, the situation in the Germany of 1848 was extreme. This was particularly true in the case of civil servants with a legal background. The importance of the Freiburg and Heidelberg law schools, together with the contribution of jurists, such as von Rotteck, von Itzstein and their various disciples, has already been discussed. Even the radicals Hecker and Struve and poets or scholars like Uhland had a legal training. Ralf Dahrendorf, in analysing the twentieth century, observed that the study of law tends to reinforce an etatist tradition,[69] that jurists have often been part of an elite within the German party system and that they have contributed significantly, not only to the shaping of the German *Rechtsstaat*, but also to Germany's political tradition, founded on an exaggerated conformity to the rule of law:

> As civil servants belong to the state of Hegelian phantasy and Wilhelminian reality, lawyers are the 'general estate' securing the rule of law. . . . The general estate, being committed to neutrality, cannot take sides in political matters, so it remains untainted by the struggles of civil society. This means, however, that such an estate is always dependent on masters who give it directives; if we look at it as a social reality rather than a fiction of metaphysics, the general estate is invariably a service class. It is really subject to the demand of unquestioned obedience that the theorists of authoritarian tradition would like to prescribe for us all.[70]

It was this legal background which was largely responsible for the triumph of constitutional over revolutionary energies, especially in the more liberal regions of the southwest, the cradle of the revolution.

The over-representation of academics, particularly among democrats and liberals accounts for a strange bifurcation within the revolutionary movement. The activists, whose public gatherings, demonstrations and barricades constituted the moving force at street level, did not find their counterparts among the elected delegates who acted as their representatives within parliaments and newly developing political parties.[71] The newly enfranchised electorate chose to be represented by notable public figures, often academics with impressive titles, rather than by members from within their own circles. Although at least 75 per cent of men were enfranchised, the social and professional composition of the Frankfurt parliament was considerably more 'bourgeois' than parliamentary assemblies abroad. Of the Assembly's 812 delegates, 75 per cent had a university education, 54 per cent were civil servants, only 18 per cent were tradesmen or businessmen, less than 6 per cent were farmers or landowners, only 0.5 per cent were craftsmen and an even smaller proportion came from industry. More than 13 per cent of delegates had a legal training and nearly 12 per cent were professors at a university or *Gymnasium*. Wolfram Siemann concludes: 'in terms of profession, the National Assembly was a parliament of civil servants, judged by its education it was a parliament of academics with a predominance of judges'.[72] However, it is misguided to criticize the Assembly for an academic and 'bourgeois' imbalance[73] without recognizing the degree to which it was indebted to the German concept of *Bildung*, to an ideal of education which was in itself liberal, as illustrated by the many Pre-March rallies.[74] Several of the Assembly's most eminent members had suffered political persecution during the Pre-March period, as seen in the example of Professor Dahlmann, one of the 'Göttingen Seven'. Now, as an Assembly delegate, he seemed to enjoy a more cordial relationship with the establishment. In a letter, relating to matters of the highest constitutional and political importance, the Prussian king 'pours out his heart'[75] to him. Dahlmann himself, writing to a friend, is critical of the parliamentary left and expresses the hope that reforms can prevent the revolution.[76]

Another important delegate to the National Assembly whose career will illustrate the *Bürger*'s liberal dilemma was Friedrich Daniel Bassermann. Born into an entrepreneurial business environment in Mannheim, Bassermann was educated in the neo-classical, Humboldtian spirit. At Heidelberg University, he studied for the state examination in science, a subject necessary to establish himself in business, but also read history and philosophy. Under the guidance of his father, he joined several of Mannheim's prestigious societies, associated with the arts, music and the natural sciences. In 1835 he became a founder member of the Casino Association, a society devoted to cultural and general civic issues, which by 1848 would form the nucleus of the National Assembly's right-of-centre liberal party. Bassermann's political career developed out of these general cultural and civic interests. Elected to the city council at the age of twenty-seven, his concern for civic rights and responsibilities brought him into the circle of Adam von Itzstein, the political sponsor of Friedrich Hecker. On his election to the Baden parliament in 1841, Bassermann sold his business and devoted himself exclusively to politics, becoming a vehement critic of the old Baden government and promoting Baden's accession to the Customs' Union, generally following Adam Smith's philosophy of free enterprise. Favouring issues associated with commercial freedom to matters of social justice, he found himself at an early stage in opposition to radical democrats such as Struve and Hecker. Bassermann surrounded himself with other moderate liberals to pursue a 'smaller Germany' course based on the existing Customs' Union, with the goal of a Germany under the Prussian constitutional monarch. He was also one of the initiators of the liberal Heppenheim programme and became vice-president of the Committee of Seventeen, serving simultaneously in the Pre-Parliament where he defeated Hecker's proposal to expel reactionary delegates from the Frankfurt Diet. After the demise of the Pre-Parliament, he was elected to the Committee of Fifty and subsequently to the National Assembly, where he became chair of the committee charged with forming the National Constitution. He met the Prussian king on several occasions, but failed to persuade him to become leader of the new democratic Germany. During his time as delegate, Bassermann broke with almost all the values espoused by the Heppenheim programme and declared: 'If I could achieve Germany's unity and future greatness by temporarily forfeiting all rights to freedom, I would be the first to submit myself to a dictatorship.'[77] During the revolution's end phase he aligned himself with von Radowitz, one of Frederick William's most ardent supporters and in May 1849, fearing a clash with Prussia, he resigned his seat in the National Assembly. In 1850 he returned to Mannheim, now under Prussian occupation and, disappointed by the failure to achieve German unity, abandoned politics and committed suicide in July 1855.

This relatively detailed account of one of the leading liberal figures of the National Assembly serves as an example of the many parliamentarians who viewed the situation differently from those pursuing even the more moderate aims of the revolution. Hecker and other committed democrats must have become increasingly frustrated in their efforts to salvage any of their aims.[78] Divisions between the parliamentarians in Frankfurt and street activists in Baden, Vienna or Berlin became all too obvious. Returning from Berlin in November 1848, Bassermann is alleged to have described the revolutionaries as 'dark and depraved characters'[79] roaming the streets of the city, a statement which serves to indicate how worlds separated the members of the Assembly from the activists in Vienna and Berlin. In contrast to these delegates, the correspondent of the liberal *Augsburger Allgemeine Zeitung* reported with astonishment that Berlin demonstrators, Bassermann's 'dark and depraved characters', had not taken advantage of their victory to steal any property, as they were anxious to uphold their reputation for honesty and morality.[80] It is also generally acknowledged that meetings of journeymen and workers strictly observed the rules and regulations of their own associations in all matters of debate and procedure and that minutes and financial accounts were painstakingly recorded.[81]

Occasionally, however, matters got out of hand. Tensions developed between catholics and protestants and between workers and craftsmen. The majority of street activists were young and enthusiastic, giving vent to their protests in caterwauling (*Katzenmusik*) and other usually minor street disturbances and confrontations with the local police. Within these circles the concept of democracy was still rather loosely understood, but certain symbols, such as the German tricolour, together with patriotic songs and other tokens associated with the democratic cause were respected and cultivated. Habermas' observation that the concept of a public mind in the mid nineteenth century was too narrowly defined by liberal and bourgeois criteria, so that any conflict of interest could be obliterated and nullified by the 'general interest' or channelled into bureaucratic control mechanisms, comes to mind.[82]

As the movement towards parliamentary democracy gathered momentum, the choice of Frankfurt as the seat of a German National Assembly became a foregone conclusion. Frankfurt had long been the undeclared capital of the Holy Roman Empire and was the home of the German Confederation and its Diet. It therefore seemed the obvious venue for the new gathering where a constitution was to be designed and a parliament would exercise its legal powers. The choice of Frankfurt also reconciled romantic nostalgia with political astuteness, since a city of only 60,000 inhabitants was considered less of a risk than either of the two major capitals, where street violence and social unrest posed more of a threat. At Frankfurt, revolutionary ardour would be channelled into constitutional reform, an abstract, conceptual form of democracy, divorced from street violence and other radical exertions by the 'people'.

The Frankfurt region, however, was not without its share of revolutionary unrest. Its neighbouring cities, in particular Mainz and Darmstadt, but also Wiesbaden and Hanau experienced demonstrations and disturbances, involving craftsmen and peasants. Most of these incidents were of a local nature and could be contained. Frankfurt, as a major administrative centre, was home to many academics and civil servants who supported liberal demands for basic rights and greater individual freedom. The city was also within easy travelling distance of the liberal strongholds in the southwest and in the Hesse–Darmstadt–Nassau regions.[83] Here, liberal demands for a declaration of basic rights and personal freedoms could easily merge with national desires for a unified German nation state.

Frankfurt – Vienna – Berlin: three contenders for the nation's capital

A comparison of the Frankfurt National Assembly with the parliaments in Vienna and Berlin will elicit two interesting factors.

1. Any brief or superficial glance at the three assemblies would bewilder the uninitiated observer, especially if the German terminology is considered, suggesting rivalry or lack of co-operation rather than a common

revolutionary strategy. The new Vienna parliament, established more than two months later than its Frankfurt counterpart, called itself *Reichstag*. It claimed to represent patriotic interests and defined its territory as that of the Austrian Empire, which was 'absolutely dependent on the intimate union [*Anschluß*] with the great German motherland'.[84] As if to underline this 'intimate union' with Germany, the *Reichstag* was opened by the newly elected German Regent, in the absence of the Austrian Emperor. Territorial definitions, however, were further obscured by the fact that Hungary and Austria's north-Italian provinces were not represented in this parliament. With the German delegates in a minority among the 383 members, with Poles, Rumanians, Ruthenians and Czechs forming a majority, it remained unclear as to whom this parliament sought to represent. A similarly confusing picture emerges when one examines the Berlin parliament. On 1 May the citizens of Prussia voted both for a German and for a Prussian 'national' Assembly. The Prussian National Assembly in Berlin had its inaugural meeting four days later than the German National Assembly in Frankfurt. Even for the more educated voters, it must have been confusing to elect delegates to two different national assemblies simultaneously. A closer inspection would indicate that 94,000 men were entitled to vote for the German National Assembly as compared to 115,000 men for its Prussian counterpart. Several thousand Prussians, mostly citizens from Polish or East Prussian territories, were obviously not entitled to vote for the German assembly. The confusion over these two 'national' parliaments not only reflects a general confusion within revolutionary circles, but also reveals an element of obfuscation attributable to the Prussian king. His royal edict of 18 March recognized that the German Confederation had become an anachronism, acknowledging also the need for action in the light of 'the Viennese events'.[85] In his edict, the king insisted that he was speaking not only to Prussia, but 'God willing' also to an 'intimately united' German people. This phrase anticipates his famous declaration three days later, addressed 'to my people and to the German nation'. He declares his readiness to lead Germany out of the danger caused by revolution and warfare 'through the intimate union of German princes and peoples'.[86] Whatever the role or influence of elected representatives or monarchs within these parliaments, their names and claims to national sovereignty would seem to suggest that the old rivalries for German hegemony between Prussia and Austria were still very much alive. For his part, the Prussian monarch could hope to gain political advantage from such constitutional confusion, and Prussian negotiations with Bavaria, Saxony and other states of the Third Germany would seem to strengthen this assumption.[87]

2. A comparison of the three parliaments with regard to their political allignments is also of interest. It is undisputed that both the Viennese and

the Berlin parliamentarians were 'further to the left' than those at Frankfurt. To suggest that this simply reflects 'a different potential of candidate'[88] does not provide a sufficient explanation. The fact that both Berlin and Vienna elected representatives who did not belong to the 'classless society of *Bürger*' serves as an important corrective to earlier observations, which claimed that the bourgeois and academic element was always over-represented in parliamentary assemblies. Of the 395 delegates in Berlin, 47 per cent were civil servants and jurists formed 23 per cent of this group. In contrast to Frankfurt, the farming community accounted for 18 per cent of members, industry for 10 per cent and even craftsmen for 5 per cent. Figures for Vienna show a similar deviation from the Frankfurt Assembly, with 25 per cent representing the farming community. In the Berlin National Assembly factions left of centre formed a majority of 53 per cent.

The assessment of the Frankfurt parliament in this chapter has come up with a rather negative picture, giving the impression that its parliamentarians had betrayed the principles of the revolution, almost to the point of collusion with reactionary governments. The next chapter will examine the actual working patterns and political achievements of the National Assembly, especially in as far as its attempt at creating a national German forum was concerned; a slightly more positive picture will emerge.

Notes

1 Georg Herwegh, *Werke in einem Band*, H.-G. Werner ed. 3rd edn (Berlin and Weimar, 1977), pp. 163f.

2 David Blackbourn and Geoff Eley, *The Peculiarities of German History. Bourgeois Society and Politics in Nineteenth-Century Germany* (Oxford University Press, 1984), chapter 2, in part. pp. 54–9.

3 Ralf Dahrendorf, *Society and Democracy in Germany* (New York, 1969), chapter 13.

4 Otto Dann, *Nation und Nationalismus in Deutschland 1770–1990* (Munich, 1993), pp. 117f.

5 Wolfram Siemann, *The German Revolution of 1848–49*, trans. by Christiane Banerji (London, 1998), p. 121.

6 Arno Herzig, 'Die Juden', in C. Dipper and U. Speck eds, *1848. Revolution in Deutschland* (Frankfurt/M. and Leipzig, 1998), pp. 286, 292.

7 A. Ballin Lewis ed., *A Year of Revolutions. Fanny Lewald's Recollections of 1848* (Providence and Oxford, 1997), pp. 59f.

8 Ibid., pp. 102f.

9 W. Kaschuba and C. Lipp, *1848 – Provinz und Revolution. Kultureller Wandel und soziale Bewegung im Königreich Württemberg* (Tübingen, 1979); C. Lipp, 'Aktivismus und politische Abstinenz. Der Einfluß kommunalpolitischer Erfahrung und lebensweltlicher Strukturen auf die politische Partizipation in der Revolution 1848/49', in Christian Jansen and Thomas Mergel eds, *Die Revolutionen von 1848/49, Erfahrung, Verarbeitung, Deutung* (Göttingen, 1998), pp. 97–127.

10 W. Häusler, 'Wien', in Dipper and Speck eds, *1848 Revolution*, p. 100.

11 J. Habermas, *The Structural Transformation of the Public Sphere. An Inquiry into a Category of Bourgeois Society*, trans. by T. Burger (Cambridge, MA, 1989), pp. 159–75.

12 T. Maentel, 'Robert Blum: Ich sterbe für die Freiheit, möge das Vaterland meiner eingedenk sein!', in Sabine Freitag ed., *Die Achtundvierziger. Lebensbilder aus der deutschen Revolution 1848/49* (Munich, 1998), p. 139.

13 Manfred Botzenhart, *Deutscher Parlamentarismus in der Revolutionszeit 1848–1850* (Düsseldorf, 1977), p. 319.

14 Maentel, 'Robert Blum', p. 136.

15 Botzenhart, *Deutscher Parlamentarismus*, p. 315.

16 Carl von Rotteck and Carl Welcker eds, Das Staatslexikon, Enzyklopädie der Sämmtlichen Staatswissenschaften für alle Stände. 2nd edn, vol. 4 'Faction' (Altona 1845), pp. 576ff.

17 Lothar Gall, *Bürgertum in Deutschland* (Berlin, 1989), p. 292.

18 Siemann, *German Revolution*, pp. 90f.

19 Botzenhart, *Deutscher Parlamentarismus*, p. 320.

20 Siemann, *German Revolution*, pp. 56f.

21 R. Stadelmann, *Social and Political History of the German 1848 Revolution*, trans. by James G. Chastain (Athens, OH, 1975), p. 96.

22 Herwegh, *Werke*, pp. 113f; cf. also D. Langewiesche, 'Die Anfänge der deutschen Parteien. Partei, Fraktion und Verein in der Revolution von 1848/49', *Geschichte und Gesellschaft*, 4 (1978), pp. 326f.

23 U. Speck, 'Das Parlament', in Dipper and Speck eds, *1848 Revolution*, p. 205.

24 H. Reif, 'Der Adel', in Dipper and Speck eds, *1848 Revolution*, pp. 222f.

25 Gall, *Bürgertum in Deutschland*, p. 296.

26 Ibid., p. 304.

27 Siemann, *German Revolution*, pp. 96f.

28 R. Koch, 'Julius Fröbel: Demokratie und Staat', in Freitag ed., *Die Achtundvierziger*, p. 150.

29 W. Breckman, 'Diagnosing the "German Misery". Radicalism and the Problem of National Character, 1830 to 1848', in David E. Barclay and Eric D. Weitz eds, *Between Reform and Revolution. German Socialism and Communism from 1840 to 1990* (New York and Oxford, 1998), p. 44.

30 Speck, 'Das Parlament', p. 205.

31 D. Langewiesche, 'Ludwig Uhland: Der Ruhm des Scheiterns', in Freitag ed., *Die 48iger*, p. 21.

32 Langewiesche, 'Die Anfänge', p. 327.

33 Ibid., p. 341.

34 Ernst Rudolf Huber, *Deutsche Verfassungsgeschichte seit 1789*, 3rd edn, vol. 2 (Stuttgart, 1988), p. 602.

35 Ballin Lewis ed., *A Year of Revolutions*, p. 100.

36 W. Klötzer, 'Heinrich Freiherr von Gagern, Präsident der Frankfurter Nationalversammlung', in Freitag ed., *Die Achtundvierziger*, pp. 130f.

37 Breckman, 'Diagnosing the "German Misery"', p. 44.

38 M. Wettengel, 'Frankfurt und die Rhein-Main-Region', in Dipper and Speck eds, *1848 Revolution*, p. 146.

39 Siemann, *German Revolution*, pp. 99–102.

40 H. Zwahr, 'Städtische Unterschichten', in Dipper and Speck eds, *1848 Revolution*, pp. 248ff.

41 Siemann, *German Revolution*, pp. 89f.
42 Ibid., p. 91.
43 Zwahr, 'Städtische Unterschichten', p. 255.
44 Ibid., p. 257.
45 Siemann, *German Revolution*, p. 92; Thomas Nipperdey, *Deutsche Geschichte 1800– 1866: Bürgertum und starker Staat*, 6th edn (Munich, 1987), pp. 621f.
46 Breckman, 'Diagnosing the "German Misery"', pp. 44–7.
47 Günther Heydemann, *Konstitution gegen Revolution. Die britische Deutschland- und Italienpolitik 1815–1848* (Göttingen, Zurich, 1995), pp. 288f.
48 Huber, *Verfassungsgeschichte*, vol. 2, pp. 358ff.
49 Stadelmann, *Social and Political History*, p. 99.
50 Ibid.
51 Siemann, *German Revolution*, pp. 101–3.
52 Wettengel, 'Frankfurt und', p. 147.
53 Siemann, *German Revolution*, p. 103.
54 Huber, *Verfassungsgeschichte*, vol. 2, p. 703.
55 Ibid.
56 Nipperdey, *Deutsche Geschichte*, p. 611.
57 Siemann, *German Revolution*, pp. 106f.
58 'Das Offenburger Programm der südwestdeutschen Demokraten', in Walter Grab ed., *Die Revolution von 1848/49. Eine Dokumentation* (Stuttgart, 1998), pp. 25f.
59 Huber, *Verfassungsgeschichte*, vol. 2, p. 593.
60 Franz X. Vollmer, *Offenburg 1848/49. Ereignisse und Lebensbilder aus einem Zentrum der badischen Revolution* (Karlsruhe, 1997), p. 88.
61 Siemann, *German Revolution*, p. 72.
62 Langewiesche, 'Die Anfänge', p. 349.
63 Siemann, *German Revolution*, pp. 75f.
64 Huber, *Verfassungsgeschichte*, vol. 1, p. 330 and vol. 2, p. 595.
65 Huber, *Verfassungsgeschichte*, vol. 2, p. 603.
66 F. Lenger, 'Das Bürgertum', in Dipper and Speck eds, *1848 Revolution*, p. 237.
67 Ibid., p. 239.
68 Quoted from M. Hundt, 'Zur Frühgeschichte der revolutionären Arbeiterbewegung in Stuttgart', *Jahrbuch für Geschichte*, 7 (1972), p. 299.
69 Kurt Sontheimer, *Grundzüge des politischen Systems der Bundesrepublik Deutschland*, 5th edn (Munich, 1976), p. 86.
70 Dahrendorf, *Society and Democracy*, p. 221.
71 Lenger, 'Das Bürgertum', p. 235.
72 Siemann, *German Revolution*, p. 122.
73 Nipperdey, *Deutsche Geschichte*, p. 610.
74 J. J. Müller, 'Die ersten Germanistentage', in Jörg Jochen Müller ed., *Germanistik und deutsche Nation 1806–1848. Zur Konstitution bürgerlichen Bewußtseins* (Stuttgart, 2000), pp. 316ff.
75 Letter by Frederick William IV to Dahlmann, 3 May 1848, quoted from Hans Fenske ed., *Quellen zur deutschen Revolution 1848–1849* (Darmstadt, 1996), p. 93.
76 Letter by Droysen to Arendt, 9 June 1848, in Fenske ed., *Quellen*, p. 105.
77 L. Gall, 'Friedrich Daniel Bassermann: Sei dein eigner Herr und Knecht, das ist des Mittelstandes Recht', in Freitag ed., *Die Achtundvierziger*, p. 110.
78 Cf. letter by Hecker to Emma Herwegh, 11 June 1848, in Marcel Herwegh ed., *Briefe von und an Georg Herwegh 1848* (Paris, Leipzig and Munich, 1896), pp. 249f.

79 Gall, 'Friedrich Daniel Bassermann', p. 107.
80 Zwahr, 'Städtische Unterschichten', p. 248.
81 Ibid., p. 254.
82 Habermas, *Structural Transformation*, pp. 129f.
83 Wettengel, 'Frankfurt und', pp. 130ff.
84 'Programm des zentralen Wahlkomitees für den österreichischen Reichstag', in W. Grab ed., *Die Revolution*, von 1848/49. Eine Dokumentation (Stuttgart, 1998), p. 91.
85 'Patent König Friedrich Wilhelms IV, in Fenske ed., *Quellen*, pp. 77f.
86 Proklamation des Königs von Preußen, 21 March 1848, in Grab ed., *Die Revolution*, p. 46.
87 Immediatbericht Bernstorffs an König Friedrich Wilhelm IV, 18 March 1848, in Fenske ed., *Quellen*, p. 79.
88 Nipperdey, *Deutsche Geschichte*, p. 610.

Chapter 6

The Frankfurt National Assembly and international reverberations

The establishment of parliamentary business

On 18 May 1848, 380 elected representatives from the various German states assembled in the Imperial Hall of the Frankfurt *Römer* to choose the father of their new house, his deputy and various officials. The elections over, members moved in solemn procession to the nearby Paul's Church where they began their work on formulating a German democratic constitution and on the task of establishing a central government.[1] Their aim was no less than to contribute to the 'happiness of world history' through an assembly 'the like of which Germany has never seen before'.[2] In view of such ambitions which were clearly beyond the reach of the delegates, the Assembly became the butt of much adverse criticism and some scathing satire. Karl Marx was one of its most merciless critics, deploring the slow pace at which it came into being, a full ten weeks after the outbreak of revolution in Germany. Once instituted, a further eight weeks were to elapse before a provisional government took office. Marx castigated the elected representatives as yesterday's men:

> an Assembly composed in its majority of liberal attorneys and *doctrinaire* professors, an Assembly which, while it pretended to embody the very essence of German intellect and science, was in reality nothing but a stage where old and worn-out political characters exhibited their ludicrousness and their impotence of thought, as well as action, before the eyes of all Germany. This Assembly . . . was, from the very first day of its existence, more frightened of the least popular movement than of all the reactionary plots of all the German Governments put together.[3]

Marx's criticism has entered the historical canon to become accepted wisdom. However, once it is understood that the elected Assembly had little inclination to further the revolution, wishing instead to channel its energies into the constitutional waters of a democratic *Rechtsstaat*, the work of the Assembly should be re-assessed from a less hostile perspective.

The elections to this first all-German parliament highlighted the problems that had to be overcome in order to eliminate the many irregularities and inconsistencies which had emerged during the process of its inception. Individual constituencies were of unequal size, electoral registers were outdated and election procedures varied from state to state. Candidates' eligibility was often disputed and weeks passed until some delegates eventually reached Frankfurt.[4] Czech candidates boycotted the Assembly while Polish and Italian members took their seats, but had little interest in the creation of a German nation state. Of the 649 members who eventually constituted the Assembly, few were acquainted with each other and it took some time for a working climate to be established. Nevertheless, it would be an exaggeration to suggest that each member formed his own party.[5] Specific political groupings began to emerge while parliamentary procedures still had to be devolved. By the end of May the French model of an elected president with a clearly devised order for plenary debates and voting procedures was adopted. Individual committees were set up where motions were prepared for plenary debates.[6] Of the seventeen standing committees and ten temporary ones in operation, the two most influential ones were the constitutional and economic committees.

Before discussing how the different political parties coalesced within the Assembly, a brief description of the salient features of the Paul's Church will be relevant. Completed in 1833, this protestant church with its neoclassical rotunda, was, apart from the cathedral, the largest building in Frankfurt, affording space for 500 delegates and gallery accommodation for 2,000 spectators. Its refurbished interior provided a raised seat for the president, where the altar had previously stood.[7] Opposite the president's chair was the rostrum from which members addressed the Assembly. The building was by no means ideal for parliamentary business: having virtually no committee rooms and, with little space between the benches for delegates to move about, communication between sessions was restricted. The galleries, on the other hand, offered too much room for spectators, providing the opportunity to monopolize delegates or to encourage popular rhetoric at the expense of political substance. Delegates on the left tended to respond readily to the gallery, probably in accordance with their interpretation of Rousseau's concept of popular sovereignty, while moderate and right-wing delegates adhered to Burkean principles of representative democracy, viewing contributions from the public galleries as a hindrance to parliamentary business.

These architectural constraints made the need for order and efficiency all the more urgent. The opening speech by the father of the house had already ended in noisy chaos,[8] but matters improved with the election of Heinrich von Gagern as President of the Assembly. Elected on 19 May with a 77 per cent majority, he strove to improve the efficiency of parliamentary procedure and emerged as an unchallenged and eminently respected authority in parliament.[9] Standing orders were introduced with delegates divided into fifteen sections, with the aim of streamlining parliamentary business by effectively pre-selecting speakers and those delegates who would serve on parliamentary committees. However, since individual members were allocated to sections by drawing lots, they formed no common bond. As a result, their influence declined so that, in time, clearly distinguishable political parties superseded them. This development also arose from the problematic structure of the Paul's Church. Gagern therefore advocated the establishment of political groups under individual leaders.[10] The lack of committee rooms and other amenities resulted in the formation of different political groups, many of them short lived and of little significance,[11] gathering in inns and clubs in the city.

The emergence of political factions within the Assembly

Although the terminology of left and right was already in common use, adopting the convention established by the Chamber of Deputies during the 1789 French Revolution, its application to the Frankfurt parliament can give rise to misunderstandings. This is especially the case when we consider that the Assembly, in its early stages, had no executive power to respond to, so that there was no distinction between parties in government and others in opposition. Furthermore, it will emerge that the conventional associations of 'right' with 'nationalist' and 'left' with 'internationalist' did not always apply. As an indication of parliamentary division, Veit Valentin's classification of four parties, is still useful.[13] According to him, the far right wished to conserve the power of the princes and was therefore inherently hostile to parliamentary democracy. The far left sought to eliminate monarchic power, relying entirely on the sovereignty of the people and, in the last resort, on a republic and a centralized nation state. The centre right party advocated some form of constitutional monarchy, broadly following accepted practice in existing March governments, while the centre-left wished to submit the princes to the will of parliament, advocating a more radical variation of the constitutional principle. In general, the left was opposed to the *Vereinbarungsprinzip* (collaboration between parliament and the crowns) and to the concept of a second chamber or upper house of nobility. They saw these principles as detrimental to the pursuit of national self-determination, aware that the Diet had originally insisted that the Assembly should be restricted to revising the old constitution of the Confederation, thereby denying the Assembly its full autonomy.[14]

The *Donnersberg* faction represented the extreme left position inside the Assembly. It was strictly democratic with about twenty members, including the prominent left-wing Hegelians Arnold Ruge and Julius Fröbel and the Baden delegate Lorenz Brentano. Their manifesto stipulated direct elections, the establishment of a one-chamber parliament, an executive committee elected by and responsible to this parliament and a president as head of a nation state.[15] It rejected any notion of the *Vereinbarungsprinzip* and opposed the prospect of military action against Germany's neighbours. The possibility of a second revolution and the creation of a counter-parliament were never ruled out. The position of the right, as represented by *Café Milani*, amounted to the exact opposite to that of the *Donnersberg* faction, and need not be spelt out here.

Nationwide political parties had not yet developed; clear regional differences were still the rule. More than half the members of *Café Milani* came from Prussia, with no representation from the southwest, in contrast to the *Casino Club* which recruited a majority of its members from southwest Germany. Liberals from the Third Germany found their home in the *Württemberger Hof*. Other differences reflected various social and professional backgrounds. While parties of the right contained a majority of higher civil servants, university professors, judges and country gentry, parties on the left tended to represent freelance journalists and intellectuals, as well as low-ranking civil servants and members from the lower middle classes.[16] A frequently observed difference between the parliaments in Vienna or Berlin and the Frankfurt Assembly was its high number of *Honorationen*. Almost every third member in the Frankfurt parliament was nationally or locally eminent, an individual of some social or professional standing.[17] With the establishment of political parties, these *Honorationen* often became integrated within party politics and, although prominent within their party groupings, were subject to party discipline. Other notable individuals such as Ludwig Uhland, who chose to rely on his national reputation and refused to be affiliated to a specific faction, failed to make a real impact in the Assembly. Whatever their individual, social or regional peculiarities, most delegates were obliged to conform to the formalities of the political process. Within a few weeks 'parties' had developed, practising the kind of political procedures associated with modern parliamentary business.

> From then on factions determined the course of business, turned important subjects of debate into 'party affairs', imposed discipline in votes, formed coalitions, limited the number of random decisions, steered the plenary debates and influenced the public with their own publications. Factions operated as mediators for pressure groups and for extra-parliamentary political associations; they received impetus from outside and in turn provided impetus to the public.[18]

The establishment of a central government

It has already been observed that the National Assembly found itself in an anomalous position, in so far as its intrinsic function was ill-defined. The formation of a central government therefore became a vital objective for its survival. The individual states, however, though now represented by liberal governments, still wished to preserve their own particularist power. Conservative factions within the Assembly, in particular *Café Milani* and *Landsberg*, also objected to conferring a distinctive function to the Assembly. They wanted a temporary parliament, concentrating on formulating a constitution; all executive functions should be determined once this constitution was approved. In their opinion, 'the National Assembly exercises constitutional control only over the business of the *Reich* ministry, it does not interfere in executive matters'.[19] The moderate and extreme left parties, basing their demands on their understanding of and commitment to popular sovereignty, specifically supported an executive power which was responsible to the Assembly. Matters came to a head on 19 May, when Franz Raveaux, a member of the democratic left, tried to force a decision on the superiority of the Frankfurt over the Prussian national assembly.[20] His party colleague Venedy, alluding to the famous promise by the Prussian king that Prussia would be absorbed within Germany, focused the debate on the Assembly's all-important national rule, suggesting that 'all that matters in this debate is the question whether we are the *Reichstag* or whether this role falls to the Berlin Assembly, whether Prussia is to become German or Germany Prussian'.[21] Both resolutions were intended to force parliament into a decision on the issue of establishing its primacy over individual state governments and the Federal Diet. Raveaux eventually managed to engineer a compromise solution which recognized the need for a provisional executive power. The supremacy of the Frankfurt National Assembly *vis-à-vis* individual state parliaments was secured by a resolution which stated: 'The German National Assembly . . . declares that all regulations of individual German parliaments which are not in agreement with its yet to be determined constitution will be considered valid only with reference to the latter [the Frankfurt Constitution], regardless of their current validity.'[22]

This decision freed the Assembly for a debate on the format of the new central government.[23] In April, Carl Theodor Welcker, a Baden delegate to the Federal Diet, had already suggested a triumvirate directory, on the French model of 1795, engendering considerable debate as to who should form the triumvirate. Disagreements continued and a majority favoured the participation of the Prussian and Austrian monarchs. The left opposed such a policy, preferring an executive committee formed from among Assembly delegates. The main issue was 'whether the new authority would be directly responsible to parliament, or whether it should be "irresponsible", with responsible ministers'.[24] Heated debates continued until 24 June, threatening the Assembly's very survival.[25] At this critical juncture the impasse was ended by the intervention of President von Gagern. He recognized that it was imperative to establish an executive power, which would inevitably lead to the abolition of the Federal Diet. However, he also saw the need for some conciliatory gesture towards the individual princes. Describing his solution as 'a bold stroke', he declared: 'We ourselves must create the provisional central power', and proposed Archduke John as head of the new executive and regent of Germany, 'not because, but although he is a prince'.[26] Despite involving concessions from all sides, Gagern's compromise proposal was well received since it was capable of uniting substantial majorities, both inside the House and within the various state governments. The election of an Austrian prince satisfied those parties advocating a greater Germany, without causing any affront to Prussia, since Frederick William was at this stage not opposed to Austrian supremacy, as long as an aristocrat was at the helm of the new Germany.[27] This initiative pleased the champions of popular sovereignty, while the provision that the regent would not be responsible to the Assembly appeased royalists. Unitarians who were opposed to a directorship supported the single leadership principle, and the person of the archduke was, to a certain extent, even acceptable to republicans. The youngest brother of the last German Emperor Francis II, Archduke John, was an acknowledged opponent of Metternich, had married the daughter of an Austrian postmaster and had moved out of court circles to live in the Tyrol mountains. Among intellectuals of most political persuasions he was a figure of fun. Heine referred to him as 'landless John' and Herwegh portrayed him as some kind of fake redeemer. The Austrian writers Anastasius Grün and Bertold Auerbach were highly critical, questioning his qualities of political leadership.[28]

The decision that the new central government was not responsible to the Assembly proved to be of little practical consequence. The archduke was far too weak to pursue his own initiatives, and, more importantly, the central government found no significant support outside the Assembly. With the exception of the last, rather unrepresentative, government, the first three administrations relied on parliamentary support and – within their own make-up – reflected the Assembly's balance of power. The abolition of the Federal Diet, boldly proclaimed by the Assembly on 28 June, remained in essence a compromise, since the individual states' representatives still had to be consulted by the central authority.[29] In an attempt to forestall the humiliation of abolition, the Diet opted to suspend its own activities forthwith, transferring its rights to the regent and thereby allowing for the possibility of its reinstatement. This move also supported the *Vereinbarungsprinzip* by implicitly maintaining the influence of individual sovereigns over all decisions of the regent and thereby serving to undermine the standing of the National Assembly.[30] Even ceremonial formalities afforded precedence to the Diet, almost elevating it to the position of a second chamber. After his visit to the National Assembly, the regent went to the Diet where he accepted, in the name of the German governments, the exercise of his legal responsibilities.

The various provisional governments achieved little and in fairly rapid succession were overwhelmed by excessive national pressures. The von Leiningen cabinet (July–September) reflected the Assembly's centre-right outlook and favoured a greater Germany solution. It established six major ministries, covering foreign affairs, the interior, finance, justice, trade and war. The memorandum, which it dispatched to the individual German governments, was exceedingly conciliatory, expressing a desire for full co-operation with individual heads of state.[31] The minister of war, a former Prussian general, communicated with state governments, to ask for their support in military matters. Only the smaller states agreed to this request while Austria, Prussia, Bavaria and Hanover refused to comply. The cabinet of von Schmerling (September–December) continued the policies of its predecessor with few changes of personnel, to be succeeded by von Gagern's administration (December–May) which, except for its support of a 'smaller Germany' solution, followed a similar political line. It is significant that all three governments fell over issues relating to the question of German nationality: the Prussian peace with Denmark in the Schleswig–Holstein conflict, the defeat of the Vienna revolution and subsequent rejection of a 'greater Germany' and the refusal of the imperial crown by Frederick William IV.

The central government was no more successful in its bid for international recognition. Only the United States, Sweden, the Netherlands, Belgium, Switzerland, Sardinia, Naples and Greece established diplomatic relations with the new German state. Britain, where Queen Victoria was a half sister to Prince von Leiningen, had indicated some initial sympathy for the Leiningen government.[32] With regard to the Assembly's foreign policy, and in particular its left-of-centre delegates, international peace and conciliation were of uppermost importance. They particularly sought the active support of the French republic and advocated peace or at least neutrality towards all foreign states except reactionary Russia. While the protection of the honour and legal sovereignty of Germany was its noblest aim, parliament promised that Germany would not 'hinder any foreign state in the pursuit of its inner affairs'. This principle was amended by Ruge, demanding Europe-wide disarmament and an international peace congress.[33] These noble principles changed when the war against Denmark broke out; this generated an increasingly anti-German public campaign in Britain and France. The refusal of the French Republic to enter into diplomatic relations with the central government was based on fear of an *Empire Germanique*, outweighing any sympathies for the revolutionary and liberal-democratic tendencies espoused in Germany.

The failure to acquire a credible diplomatic status in the international sphere had internal repercussions which emphasized the weakness of the

Frankfurt Assembly. An offficial of the Prussian foreign office revealed the complexities which hampered the central government in much of its activity. Frankfurt's lack of common sense and moderation is seen as the chief hindrance: a diplomat from the provisional central government might not carry much weight in Paris, London or St Petersburg, but could, at the same time, weaken the position of his Prussian or Austrian colleagues. More co-operation and a general slow-down in the move towards centralization were advised. Prussia could easily represent the *Reich* 'for Prussia's policy will be no different from that of the *Reich*, and a conflict could therefore not arise. Prussia could then bring to bear all her power, together with her true might and her established influence, to Germany's advantage'.[34] This advice might indeed have been well meant, but its straightforward claim of overall representation pointed in no uncertain way to the delineation of a future Germany under Prussian leadership. Its pragmatic nature failed to pay due attention to the aspirations of those who embraced liberal and democratic principles and whose priority was to establish parliamentary democracy in Germany. It also offers an interpretation along the lines of the *Vereinbarungsprinzip*, suggesting that the new Germany was simply a continuation of the old Confederation, thereby denying the very essence of the revolution and its principle of popular sovereignty.

The drawing up of Basic Rights

The formulation of basic rights was one of the first issues tackled by the National Assembly. It has often been stated that to address this issue first was a tactical error, taking up valuable time which should have been spent on urgent matters of substance, such as executive powers.[35] While such criticism is legitimate, it nevertheless fails to recognize the symbolic significance of this new code of laws. Throughout the Pre-March period and earlier, German citizens had suffered from the restrictions imposed by their various internal security systems. The March demands, which had been so recently conceded, required a legal basis. Furthermore – and these views rarely appear in historical debates – progress on matters of fundamental and universal importance was to parliament's advantage, providing it with a popular mandate to demand an executive power and to proceed in its efforts to unify Germany, at least in constitutional and legal terms. The newly created government could carry out its executive functions, confident of the Assembly's backing. Its legal framework constituted 'a vigorous blow against German particularism . . . a strong obliterating stroke through the German territorial absolutism of the past'.[36] The draft itself was completed in less than six weeks and 'accurately reflected the central concern of all *Vormärz* oppositional currents, moderate and radical, with this subject'.[37]

The Assembly's concern with basic rights aimed to consolidate the revolutionary successes of the spring and early summer of 1848. Its most important and most enduring legacy stems from its concern with the fundamental ideas of the philosophy of the Enlightenment, which it sought to reconcile with German thought and culture, in particular with the cultural inheritance of Weimar classicism and with aspects of the Romantic movement. It was this successful fusion of ideas which guaranteed its lasting influence, for without it neither the Weimar, nor the Federal Republic could have emerged.

In their deliberations on the basic rights, the American Constitution was of particular importance to German democrats. Some delegates had produced books on such subjects as American voting rights and the work of Thomas Jefferson, and the famous *Staatslexikon* by von Rotteck and Welcker contained excellent contributions on the American Constitution. A number of specific clauses, such as the relationship between federal and state law, aspects of international law and the conduct of war and peace, were modelled on the American Constitution.[37] The English constitutional example was also eagerly discussed, with opinions tending to be influenced by the works of conservative philosophers, such as Burke, liberal historians, such as Macaulay, and the liberal economist, Adam Smith. Like-minded liberal delegates within the Frankfurt parliament quoted their works sympathetically. In left-wing circles, however, Adam Smith's policy of free trade caused some concern, a surge in pauperism and the rise of a disadvantaged proletariat being associated with such policies. By contrast, the Chartists' struggle and Richard Cobden's reforms received a very favourable reception. As far as French legal principles were concerned, aspects of the *Code Napoléon* were still respected, especially its concept of citizenship and civil marriage. The political philosopher Montesquieu and his formula of the division of power were often quoted, as was Rousseau's concept of representative democracy. Representatives of the centre right in contrast favoured Mirabeau's idea of a constitutional monarchy.

However, it was not just Western European and American political philosophy that influenced the work of Frankfurt delegates. Their rhetorical fervour was also fired by Schiller's verse, by Goethe's 'philosophy of action', by Kant and the German romantic philosophers Fichte and Hegel. In short, many of the ideas and inspirations of the writers and philosophers discussed in chapter 1 were appropriated, illustrating an urbanity, an impressive knowledge of international affairs and a general erudition, to which so many speeches in the Assembly bear witness. Unfortunately, these same delegates lacked a personal understanding of the social problems confronting the population at large and failed to grasp their implications, with the result that, as one representative remarked, there was 'little trust for the learned men of the *Paulskirche*, who are viewed as too theoretical and moderate'.[38]

The eminent professor of history and constitutional law, Friedrich Christoph Dahlmann, was the major force behind the Constitutional Committee, and it was his draft of the basic rights which provided the ground for all future debates. The Constitutional Committee itself consisted largely of *Casino* liberals, with a majority of academics, but it also included Blum and Wiegand from the left-wing *Deutsche Hof*. The final version contained twelve articles of forty-eight clauses. Many of its provisions corresponded with modern Western ideas of citizenship, including *habeas corpus*, the various individual freedoms espoused in March, including the abolition of all remaining feudal dues and the creation of independent courts. Reading these basic rights today, it is not too difficult to single out a number of articles which are striking in their progressive nature: the abolition of capital punishment (para. 135), the abolition of aristocratic privilege (para. 137), equality in appointment to public office (para. 137), complete religious freedom (para. 145), state supervision of schooling (para. 153), free basic education (para. 157), an equitable tax system (para. 173), public nature of parliamentary sessions, both in Frankfurt and in the various state parliaments (para. 187), state protection extended to every German citizen abroad (para. 189).[39] The content of some clauses caused major controversy in the Assembly, especially the apparently straightforward phrase 'every German'. For a country with no clearly defined borders and containing so many different nationalities within its Austrian and Prussian territories, the phrase remained somewhat ambiguous.

Schleswig–Holstein and the issue of a German nation state

Within the context of the European revolutions of 1848, four major themes emerged: the concept of a liberal constitution, the notion of a democratic republic, an emancipatory form of socialism and the concept of a German nation state. While the German revolutions achieved some, albeit modest, success in addressing the first two themes, they failed to resolve the problem of the nation state or to provide a solution to burning social issues. Both these themes were to haunt Germany well beyond the nineteenth century. Of the two, the nationality issue was seen as the more pressing one, not only because of romantic notions of a culturally united fatherland, but also since the last remnants of its particularist medieval feudalism had to be discarded in order to expedite a rapid process of industrialization.

For some considerable time the discrepancies between linguistic and cultural borders, on the one hand, and those of the state and economy, on the other, had occupied much of Germany's cultural elite. Herder's concept of *Volk*, Fichte's plan of a national education scheme, the romantic notion that language and culture define a nation's borders rather than historical conventions,[40] all played their part in the development of a German national identity, threatening to separate Germany from her Western traditions. The development of European nationalism can be traced back to two different concepts.[41] The first-type of nationalism, a subjective-political form with its roots in the Enlightenment, had found expression in the French Revolution of 1789. Based on a particular understanding of patriotism, it developed into an essential element in the definition of citizenship. As a democratic form of nationalism, it is founded on the sovereignty of the people and does not depend on ethnic or even linguistic considerations. Defoe's *True-born Englishman* presents a good example of this type of nationalism, where, in this case 'Englishness', is defined as 'personal virtue'.[42] The second type of nationalism, defined as objective-cultural, is associated with the Romantic movement, particularly that of Germany and Eastern Europe. It is 'objective' in the sense that it denies the individual any choice in the matter. Language and culture define each individual, possibly even supported by ethnographic considerations.[43] This kind of nationalism was represented in the Assembly by romantic delegates, such as Jacob Grimm and Uhland, and by a generation of writers who had come to fame during the war of liberation, represented by Arndt and Jahn.

The two types of nationalism are, however, by no means mutually exclusive. Men who had fought in these wars were now joined by a younger, politically more astute generation, amongst them Johann Gustav Droysen, one of Germany's most influential historians and political scientists. Droysen managed to embrace both kinds of nationalism, even merging them with the German love of ancient Greece, as illustrated in his writings on Alexander the Great and on Hellenism.[44] Droysen's two great icons were Freiherr von Stein and Wilhelm von Humboldt, and he exemplified a generation which saw the Hellenistic spirit reflected in German nationalism. In addition, and largely outside the Assembly, a more radical, revolutionary, francophile nationalism found expression in Freiligrath's poetry, in the views of left-wing Hegelians like Ruge and in revolutionary statements by Hecker and Struve. This camp developed a political agenda, which was on a collision course with that represented by the delegates in Frankfurt. Three problems in particular were to test the Assembly's attitude to the nationality issue: the Schleswig–Holstein conflict, the question of national minorities in Posen, Bohemia and elsewhere and the problematic union with Austria.

Previous chapters have already referred to the Confederation's conflict with Denmark and the problem will be discussed here only in so far as it impacted on the National Assembly. In March 1848, a German nationalist movement, imbued with the all-pervasive European revolutionary sentiment and responding to the Danish crown's provocative attempt to incorporate Schleswig into the Danish state, seized the initiative and formed a provisional government. On 24 March revolutionary nationalists, among them many academics, moved on the fortress of Rendsburg, forcing its surrender. In May Prussian troops crossed the Danish border and, having recognized the new revolutionary Schleswig government, the German Diet effectively elevated the conflict into a war to be supported by the Confederation. This situation was inherited by the new provisional central government, which declared it a national war. Troop contingents from northern German states, reinforced by volunteers from all over Germany, were despatched to aid the Prussian troops. The German troops successfully repelled the Danish advance, almost driving them out of the Jutland peninsula, but the Danish navy was supreme at sea and blockaded the entire German coastline, causing serious damage to northern Germany's shipping industry and trade. In response to this action, German nationalists demanded the formation of a German navy and donations towards this project were received by the Assembly from the whole of Germany.[45] German–Danish hostilities soon brought about diplomatic intervention from Britain and Russia, ultimately forcing Prussia to withdraw her troops from Schleswig and to conclude her own armistice with Denmark at Malmö on 26 August.

Some historians tend to exaggerate this international pressure on Prussia, thereby playing down the motives of the Prussian king.[46] Frederick William was keen to appease his monarchic relatives in Russia and Britain. He also welcomed the return of General von Wrangel, hoping to employ his troops against Berlin renegades.[47] The King's tactical deliberations, as well as subsequent events, clearly indicate that Schleswig–Holstein was no longer seen as worthy of support, but had instead become a pivotal element in the success or failure of the revolution. The conflict brought existing political alignments into disorder. Grimm envisaged the whole of Jutland as belonging to the 'Germanic tribes' of which 'not one single sod of earth could ever be abandoned'[48] and Dahlmann bridged the divide between romantics and liberals by insisting that 'Germany's national honour' had been offended, suggesting that free corps 'from all parts of Germany should assist these heroes of the fatherland'.[49] Democratic and left-of-centre delegates also abandoned their pacifist and cosmopolitan stance. A closer analysis of their contributions to the debate indicates, however, that they were not normally moved by nationalist concerns. For them, the conflict provided a last chance to regain the initiative, to liberate the revolution from the Frankfurt compromise. They were concerned with the role of the central government, which had remained entirely passive during the negotiations and had not been acknowledged by the parties at war. Blum suggested mockingly that the emissary of the central government 'went to Berlin, where he was scarcely listened to; he went to Schleswig–Holstein, where once more he stood entirely behind the scenes like some young person who has smuggled himself into the theatre, not wishing to be noticed'.[50] For Blum and his friends the issue had become part of Germany's internal revolutionary struggle. One *Donnersberg* delegate saw similarities between the German struggle for Schleswig, the Italian campaign for national unification and the Polish demand for national independence.[51]

The revolutionary cause faced defeat in all three cases and delegates argued that they should resign their mandates and form an opposition against the National Assembly. Such views anticipated the 'second revolution' of the autumn of 1848. Another delegate of the moderate left criticized ratification of the armistice since, in the event of a European war, Russian, French and English intervention would 'lead to a German national rising such as world history may perhaps not yet have seen . . . which might, incidentally, easily also like an avalanche make the thirty-four German thrones and much else reel before it'.[52] As news emerged on the 16 September that the Assembly had accepted the armistice, Frankfurt experienced widespread unrest. At a public meeting, protesters castigated those who had supported the armistice as 'traitors of the German people, and of German freedom and honour'.[53] Barricades were erected and tension mounted; the minister of foreign affairs was assaulted and two prominent right-wing Prussian delegates, Prince Lichnowsky and General von Auerswald were murdered. The storming of the Assembly was averted only when the central government sought military assistance from the federal fortress at Mainz and by September the Frankfurt rebellion was defeated.[54]

Conflicting nationality issues

The Frankfurt disturbances led to the onset of a second wave of revolutions: frustrated by the defeat of the revolutionary cause in the Frankfurt Assembly, Struve initiated a second uprising in Baden; other disturbances erupted in the Rhineland and the Palatinate. Although recognizing the unlawful and hopeless nature of the uprising, the united left declared that 'nobody should be so blinded by partisan passion, as not to see that the feeling for Germany's endangered honour, freedom and unity has provoked [the uprising] and has driven to their deaths, men who would rather have died joyfully confronting the foreign enemy than in this struggle against their brothers'.[55]

Counter-revolutionary measures imposed by the central government must be seen in the context of the Europe-wide reactionary movement of the autumn of 1848. Any prospect of a successful national uprising and a renewal of revolutionary energies had been lost, the political and military initiative had been seized by counter-revolutionary forces, especially in Prussia and Austria. It is against this background that the Frankfurt 'September events' have been interpreted as a turning point, as the sign of a revolution in crisis.[56]

The Assembly's approach to the other nationality issues provided a contrast to the Schleswig–Holstein conflict. It has been argued that Frankfurt politicians were somewhat inconsistent in their attitudes to the nationality issue in that imperialist or chauvinist tendencies afforded priority to German over other national claims.[57] The situation on Germany's western borders was even more complicated, largely as the result of autocratic traditions, allowing for the transfer of whole provinces from one monarch to another, regardless of public opinion. The German-speaking Duchy of Limburg, for instance, had been placed under Dutch control. The Assembly's refusal to rule on this matter was criticized by the left and centre-left as lacking in political courage. An additional aspect, which may account for some of these inconsistencies, concerns the definition of the term 'nation state'. Throughout Europe, a nation was frequently defined by the objective cultural type of nationalism, by cultural achievements, by the importance attributed to its language and literature, and these criteria were used for the definition of national sovereignty.[58] Such an interpretation would explain why Polish and Italian nationalism were afforded more weight than Czech nationalism in Bohemia, where the cultural hegemony was German. Other nationality issues were complicated by the fact that they also involved revolutionary uprisings, often against one of the German states. This was the case in Posen and in South Tyrol, where the whole province had belonged to the German Confederation as part of the Habsburg Empire.

The situation in Posen, which had been awarded to Prussia at the Congress of Vienna, was most interesting; it provides a mirror image to the Schleswig–Holstein conflict. Posen contained a large German minority but was never part of the Confederation. German liberals and democrats had always voted for Polish autonomy – the *Hambach* festival was fired by the Polish struggle for independence – and during the March revolutions Polish demands for the restoration of their nation state were endorsed by the Pre-Parliament. By the summer of 1848 however, when the Assembly debated the Posen issue, a majority of delegates followed Prussia's lead in voting for a division of the province.[59] This incident deserves closer examination, since it illustrates the unwholesome invidious nature of German nationalism. Whereas the Schleswig–Holstein debate had largely been confined to patriotic statements or romantic dreams, the debate about Posen engendered nationalist and even racist sentiments. Arndt spoke of the cultural superiority of Germans over Poles, accusing 'the Polish of the primordial sin of untidiness, lack of patriotism, even treason against their fatherland' and accused pro-Polish speakers of being 'rogues and fools' who were prepared to surrender 'to the Polacks half the Prussian monarchy'.[60]

The main speaker, Wilhelm Jordan, presented a more complicated argument. Frequently accused of rampant racism,[61] a closer examination would indicate that a new form of *Realpolitik* overrode his racism, based on the conviction that the end will justify the means. Jordan, who had begun his parliamentary career as a left-wing radical, supported a 'healthy national egoism', based on the rule of might rather than right, while deriding the pro-Polish party for its 'cosmopolitan liberalism'.[62] He dismissed an 'exaggerated feeling of justice', based on humanism and maintained that 'our right is different, it is the right of the strong, the right of the conqueror'.[63] Alluding to the German colonization since the twelfth century, he claimed that Prussia had educated Poles 'towards decency and humanity, in as far as this was possible for such opposing elements'.[64] And yet, there is another aspect in Jordan's argument, which brings him closer to Herder's concept of nationhood. His main attack is reserved for the Polish aristocracy which had sold short the peasantry. Polish tenants had benefited from Prussia's economy and when Prussia had liberated them, the aristocracy had started its 'nationalist' fight against Prussia.[65] Jordan's arguments are more dangerous than those of Arndt since they are based on the concept of *pleonexia*, unrestrained egoism, anticipating the imperialistic and fascist tendencies of later generations. 'Hissing' and 'loud protest' from the left accompanied Jordan's speech, while the right acclaimed his sentiments.

Even Ruge who in May had still defined 'German' as synonymous with justice, freedom and brotherhood[66] was not completely free from the new sentiments proclaimed by Jordan. While recognizing national sovereignty 'in the enlightened sense of the eighteenth century', he felt that Poland had been empowered by a 'higher civilization', implanted into it by 'German industriousness and German education'. These forces would enable Germany and Poland jointly to export this freedom to the east, 'beyond the borders of Poland and Russia'.[67] In pleading for an international conference in order to renegotiate the Polish question, Ruge hoped to gain the support of the liberals. However, the liberals had also been affected by the new nationalist *Realpolitik*. When Ruge's speech proclaimed that 'we, who desire the implementation of the peoples' new rights, who want the freedom of the European nations, we must wish that the tyrants of the Italians, . . . that the Radetzky's are defeated', the Assembly erupted tumultuously. Its president von Gagern, calling Ruge to order, commented that a desire for the defeat of a German army amounted to national treason. The Assembly's reversal of the Pre-Parliament's decision led to public protest by the *Donnersberg* faction, calling it 'an outrageous disaster which estranges us from the hearts of our Polish brothers'.[68] Even today, the injustices against Poland have not been universally acknowledged; a leading German historian pronounced the dispute 'an inevitable confrontation of nationalities and nationalism', a 'legitimate' but 'tragic' conflict.[69] The attitude to Posen indicated once more the extent to which the democratically elected Assembly was becoming an instrument of the counter-revolution.

The participation of the Assembly delegation in the Cologne Cathedral festivities of August 1848 further illustrate this state of affairs.[70] In 1841 King Frederick William had initiated an association charged with the task of completing Cologne Cathedral. This enterprise channelled national sentiments in a romantic-conservative direction, ridiculed by Heine as a return to the 'dark ages'.[71] The celebrations were intended as a festival of reconciliation, bringing together the imperial regent, the Prussian king and the Assembly delegates. In reality, however, the king took the place of honour, demonstrating royal privilege over the democratically elected delegates, with Prussian military representatives outnumbering the parliamentary delegation. Gagern seemed unaware of the reactionary associations which such imagery provoked. The Cologne Festival indicates clearly the extent to which nationalist sentiment was allowed to over-ride democratic principles, how antiquated notions, supported by 'romantic professors', dominated modern, revolutionary aspirations for self-determination. This was the intellectual climate in which the new Germany had to make a decision on its future relationship with Austria, this rambling archaic conglomeration of many peoples, which had thus far failed to address the nationality issue.

While drafting the new German constitution, delegates in Frankfurt had to reconcile the liberal and democratic elements of the basic rights with other concerns, such as a definition of who constituted a German and where to draw the borders of the new Germany. Article 1 stated bluntly: 'The German *Reich* consists of the territories of the previous German Confederation.'[72] The necessity for further clarification turned the whole matter into 'a question for Austria'.[73] The next paragraphs, while consistent with democratic views on popular sovereignty, were deemed to threaten the survival of Austria: 'if any German land shares the same head of state with a non-German land, he must reside either in his German land or must by constitutional means appoint an administration which consists solely of Germans'.[74] The wide-ranging discussion on this issue can only be summarized here. Economic and cultural considerations suggested a greater Germany solution, while the nationality issue favoured the constitutional draft. Alarmed by pan-Slavonic and Magyar nationalist movements, the majority of Austrian delegates together with southern German delegates and catholics pleaded for the inclusive, 'greater Germany' solution. Even delegates on the left, when faced with the alternative of Prussian domination, opted for the 'greater Germany' solution as the lesser evil. After the fall of the von Schmerling's pro-Austrian cabinet and the defeat of the Vienna Revolution, Austria herself provided the answer. The execution of Blum indicated that the new Schwarzenberg administration sought a break with Frankfurt. Confirmation came on 27 November: Austria would seek to strengthen her own central administration, building on the strength of her many nationalities, but would honour her commitments to the German Confederation. The Austrian Confederation, with its forty million people of diverse nationalities, threatened to dominate the new Germany of thirty million people. Schwarzenberg's policy amounted to a complete counter-revolution, attempting to dismantle the political gains of March and ignoring the constitutional and democratic achievements of the National Assembly. This left the Assembly with no option but to adopt the smaller Germany solution.

Gagern, although never fully aware of the modern nationality issue, initiated the progression towards a Germany without Austria, but was careful not to offend Austrian interests. Gathering a group of influential writers and delegates around him, he began to move the smaller Germany faction towards northern German values. These represented a Germany with Martin Luther at its core, with Frederick the Great, Luther's heir, as its national hero, sustained by the neo-classical tradition of Weimar and crowned by the victory of the Wars of Liberation. Since Austria could not be drawn into the German federal state, 'a wider federation with Austria had to be established'.[75] This proposed 'wider federation' anticipated the German–Austrian alliance of 1879, but it also heralded a tragic outcome, both for the National Assembly and ultimately for Austria. It was not possible to accommodate 'either the final achievement of a federal state, which meets the inmost need of the German nation and which finalizes the national movement of 1848, with the exclusion of Austria or, inclusion of Austria in the same manner as with every other German state and then no federal state, no German state'.[76] The exclusion of Austria was a severe blow for the Assembly; from now on it would continue in all but name. Parties began to lose their identities. The moderate factions started to split along regional or religious lines, the *Pariser Hof*, a new splinter group, adopting a programme which excluded all enemies of Prussia, all catholics and all those who fraternized with the left.[77] The left, demoralized in the aftermath of Blum's execution and the defeat of the Vienna revolution, reluctantly adopted the 'smaller Germany' solution, but only after Gagern had compensated them with additional safeguards against a monarchical head of state and with a German national parliament elected by universal manhood suffrage. All that remained for the parliamentarians was to complete their work on the constitution; they had ceased to have an impact on the further course of the revolution.

An assessment of the National Assembly

The work of the National Assembly consisted of two major tasks, the establishment of a set of democratic basic rights and the creation of a federal German state. Both tasks were linked through the drawing up of the

151

constitŭtion. As this project progressed, the nationality issue gained in importance. The Schleswig–Holstein conflict, inherited from the German Confederation, forced parliament to take a decision at a time when it was not yet fully constituted. The armistice of Malmö was considered a defeat and rekindled the revolutionary flame, which the Assembly had previously subdued in favour of a conciliatory approach to the old monarchical states. The Assembly, already weakened by its failure to gain the political initiative in Schleswig–Holstein, allowed itself to be wrong-footed again over the Posen issue, resulting in the pursuit of a German expansionist policy at the expense of the principle of self-determination. The problems associated with the creation of a greater Germany permitted a focus on the nationality issue to the detriment of everything else. The opponents of national self-determination in Austria, who had previously defeated the national democratic movements in Bohemia and Italy, gained the upper hand and the German national movement now abandoned Austria. The Assembly, fighting instead for its own survival by concentrating on the shaping of a German nation under Prussian hegemony, lost its more radical factions, who, disillusioned with the Assembly, pursued their aim of a second revolution.

The failure of the Paul's Church experiment has been much discussed, gaining centre-ground at the expense of other revolutionary aspirations. Some historians saw the failure to achieve a nation state paradoxically grounded in the advanced state of the German national revolution.[78] This interpretation is misleading because of its one-sided national outlook; it relates the strength of a national feeling to those apostles of nationalism, like Arndt and Jahn, who had diverted the idea entirely towards an 'objective cultural nationalism' which, by its very nature, sacrificed the enlightened idea of self-determination. By combining the notion of national sovereignty with historically 'given' cultural and linguistic confines, the concept of personal freedom was subsumed to the demands of the nation state.[79] This new nationalism, developed during the first half of the nineteenth century, was far removed from the nation state of Wieland, Herder and Fichte: it demanded exclusivity and failed to appreciate the national rights and individualities of its neighbours. This emerging new German nationalism was all the more dangerous for having failed in its democratic political mission. Its embracing of the romantic national myth of a German uprising in 1813 obfuscated the original purpose of the revolution, namely self-determination, economic progress and political emancipation from a princely and bureaucratic despotism. At the same time, the new national movement began to divide along the lines of existing social strata. Its mythical romantic form was appropriated by the educated middle classes, excluding or bypassing the artisans and the working class, minority religious groups and all those who found themselves outside the northern German cultural sphere.

In dealing with the 1848 revolutions, studies of German nationalism tend to ignore subsequent Austrian developments. While any attempt to construe an Austrian nationalism would be plainly self-contradictory, it is nevertheless possible to trace at least some elements which might represent a form of 'subjective nationalism', comparable to the American model. Despite Austria's reactionary development after 1849, an Austrian identity clearly emerged, which held together the conglomeration of ethnic groups for another fifty years. Franz Grillparzer saw the danger of the new 'objective' form of nationalism, as it developed in the 'lesser Germany' and in Austria's Slav provinces, warning of a descent from humanism, towards nationalism and a final degeneration into bestiality.[80] Grillparzer's vision of Austria was based on a pre-revolutionary, but enlightened, concept of humanity, incorporating the principles of tolerance and moderation. A good example of this vision is expressed in von Horneck's panegyric in his tragedy *King Ottokar*. Love for one's homeland is dearer than love for a nation; love of a particular tradition involves acceptance of tolerance and a harmonious co-existence with other peace-loving nations. In his memoirs Grillparzer favoured a 'smaller Germany' solution which would allow Austria to develop into a liberal *Rechtsstaat*.[81] Though this perspective was untimely, it was by no means entirely conservative or reactionary; and his idea of an Austrian identity is closer to our generation, which functions within multinational confederations and is more aware of global issues.[82] Significantly, Arnold Ruge, approaching the subject matter from an extreme left position, reached a similar conclusion: his nation state, too, was based on historic rights, on peoples' self-determination and on international treaties.

Notes

1 Ulrich Speck, 'Das Parlament', in C. Dipper and U. Speck eds, *1848, Revolution in Deutschland* (Frankfurt/M. and Leipzig, 1998), p. 197.

2 F. Wigard ed., *Stenographischer Bericht über die Verhandlungen der deutschen constitutierenden Nationalversammlung zu Frankfurt am Main*, vol. 1 (Frankfurt/M., 1848), p. 4.

3 Karl Marx and Frederick Engels, *Collected Works*, vol. 11 (London, 1979), pp. 40f.

4 For a good account of these measures see Frank Eyck, *The Frankfurt Parliament 1848–1849* (London, 1968), pp. 59–61.

5 Veit Valentin, *Die erste deutsche Nationalversammlung. Eine geschichtliche Studie über die Paulskirche* (Munich and Berlin, 1919) p. 27, provides an excellent account.

6 Wigard ed., *Stenographischer Bericht*, vol. 1, 18 May 1848, pp. 163–5.

7 Cf. Robert Heller's account in Hans Jessen ed., *Die deutsche Revolution 1848/49 in Augenzeugenberichten*, 2nd edn (Düsseldorf, 1968), p. 133.

8 Theodor Paur's account in Jessen ed. *Die deutsche Revolution*, p. 134, and Ludwig Bamberger, *Erinnerungen*, P. Nathan ed. (Berlin, 1899), p. 88.

9 Valentin, *Erste deutsche Nationalversammlung*, pp. 13f.

10 Cf. Manfred Botzenhart, *Deutscher Parlamentarismus in der Revolutionszeit: 1848–1850* (Düsseldorf, 1977), p. 417.

11 Wolfram Siemann, *The German Revolution of 1848–49*, trans. by Christiane Banerji (London, 1998), provides an excellent survey, especially table on p. 124; it will be supplemented by subsequent observations.

12 Botzenhart, *Deutscher Parlamentarismus*, p. 416.

13 Valentin, *Erste deutsche Nationalversammlung*, p. 28.

14 Ernst Rudolf Huber, *Deutsche Verfassungsgeschichte seit 1789*, 3rd edn, vol. 2 (Stuttgart, 1988), pp. 619–21.

15 Botzenhart, *Deutscher Parlamentarismus*, p. 425. For a survey of the programmes of other political parties cf. Walter Grab ed., *Die Revolution von 1848/49. Eine Documentation* (Stuttgart, 1998), pp. 96–104.

16 Cf. Siemann, *German Revolution*, pp. 125f.

17 Frank Eyck, *The Frankfurt Parliament 1848–1849* (London, 1968), pp. 93f.

18 Siemann, *German Revolution*, p. 124.

19 Grab ed., *Die Revolution*, p. 96.

20 Documented in Wigard ed., *Stenographischer Bericht*, vol. 1, pp. 28ff, 39, 44, 121, 155, 158, 198.

21 Wigard ed., *Stenographischer Bericht*, vol. 1, p. 37.

22 Huber, *Verfassungsgeschichte*, vol. 2, p. 622.

23 For a discussion of the various suggestions by different parties see Eyck, *Frankfurt Parliament*, pp. 164–205.

24 Formulated by Vice-President von Soiron, in Wigard ed., *Stenographischer Bericht*, vol. 1, p. 155.

25 Wichmann, *Denkwürdigkeiten*, pp. 149–52.

26 Wigard ed., *Stenographischer Bericht*, vol. 1, pp. 321f.

27 Cf. the King's letter to Radowitz of 13 June 1848, in Hans Fenske ed., *Quellen zur deutschen Revolution 1848–1849* (Darmstadt, 1996), pp. 107–9.

28 Berthold Auerbach, *Tagebuch aus Wien. Von Latour bis auf Windischgrätz* (Breslau, 1849), p. 40.

29 Beschluß der Nationalversammlung, 28 June 1848: 'The National Assembly decides, subject to the agreement of the individual German governments, that . . . until the definitive establishment of a government for Germany, a provisional central power shall be appointed for all common matters of the German nation.' Wigard ed., *Stenographischer Bericht*, vol. 1, p. 576.

30 Huber, *Verfassungsgeschichte*, vol. 2, p. 632.

31 Decree by the Regent to the German governments (16 July 1848), in Huber, *Verfassungsgeschichte*, vol. 2, p. 343.

32 Eyck, *Frankfurt Parliament*, p. 204.

33 Wigard ed., *Stenographischer Bericht*, vol. 2 (24 July 1848), p. 1098.

34 Letter by Heinrich Abeken to Droysen, 16 July 1848, in Fenske, *Quellen*, p. 131.

35 For example J. G. Droysen, 'Die Spitze des Reiches', in *Politische Schriften*, F. Gilbert ed. (Berlin, 1933), p. 184.

36 Rudolf Stadelmann, *Social and Political History of the German 1848 Revolution*, trans. by J. G. Chastain (Athens, OH, Ohio University Press, 1975), p. 124.

37 Valentin, *Die erste deutsche Nationalversammlung*, in part. pp. 80 and 140.

38 David Blackbourn, *Germany 1780–1918. The Long Nineteenth Century* (London, 1997), p. 149.

39 For easy access, see Grab ed., *Die Revolution*, pp. 180–92.

40 Jacob Grimm, *Kleinere Schriften*, E. Ippel ed., vol. 7 (Berlin, 1864), p.11.
41 Quoted from Hagen Schulze, *Staat und Nation in der europäischen Geschichte* (Munich, 1995), pp. 171f.
42 Daniel Defoe, *The True-born Englishman*, in G. Grigson ed., *The Oxford Book of Satirical Verse* (Oxford University Press, 1980), pp. 108f.
43 To this day, Germany's nationality law is based on the *jus sanguinis*, declaring nationality to be an indigenous right.
44 Cf. U. Muhlack, 'Johann Gustav Droysen: Das Recht der Geschichte', in Sabine Freitag ed., *Die Achtundvierziger, Lebensbilder aus der deutschen Revolution 1848/49* (Munich, 1998), pp. 263–77.
45 Cf. the list of donations in Wigard ed., *Stenographischer Bericht*, vol. 2, pp. 947f.
46 Eyck, *Frankfurt Parliament*, p. 289; Stadelmann, *Social and Political History*, p. 111.
47 Cf. Frederick William IV's letter to his sister, in Fenske, *Quellen*, p. 110.
48 Jacob Grimm, *Reden und Aufsätze*, W. Schoof ed. (Munich, 1966), p. 71.
49 Wigard ed., *Stenographischer Bericht*, vol. 3, p. 1862 (4 September 1848).
50 Ibid., p. 2116 (18. September 1848).
51 Ludwig Simon's speech of 17 September 1848, in Grab ed., *Die Revolution*, pp. 119–21.
52 Heinrich Simon, quoted from Eyck, *Frankfurt Parliament*, p. 298.
53 Wigard ed., *Stenographischer Bericht*, vol. 3, p. 2184.
54 For the official report see Grab ed., *Die Revolution*, pp. 123–5.
55 'Kundmachung der Vereinigten Linken', 22 September 1848, in Grab ed., *Die Revolution*, p. 127.
56 Siemann, *German Revolutions*, p. 151.
57 J. Breuilly, 'Nationalbewegung und Revolution', in Dipper and Speck eds, *1848 Revolution*, p. 322 refutes such attitudes convincingly.
58 Breuilly, 'Nationalbewegung', pp. 322f.
59 The vote had been 331–101 in favour of Posen. Cf. Protest declaration by *Donnersberg* faction on 27 July 1848, in Grab ed., *Die Revolution*, p. 109.
60 Arndt, 'Polenlärm und Polenbegeisterung', *Deutsche Zeitung*, 99 (Beilage) and 111 (Beilage), 8 and 20 April 1848.
61 L. B. Namier, *1848: The Revolution of the Intellectuals* (London, 1944), p. 67. Cf. also G. Wollstein, *Das 'Großdeutschland' der Paulskirche. Nationale Ziele in der bürgerlichen Revolution 1848/49* (Düsseldorf, 1977), pp. 146–9.
62 Wigard ed., *Stenographischer Bericht*, vol. 2, pp. 1143–54.
63 Ibid., p. 1146.
64 Ibid., p. 1143.
65 Ibid., p. 1184.
66 A. Ruge *et al.* eds, *Die Reform*, 31 (2 May 1848).
67 Wigard ed., *Stenographischer Bericht*, vol. 2, pp. 1184–7 (27 July 1848).
68 'Kundmachung der Vereinigten Linken', p. 107.
69 Thomas Nipperdey, *Deutsche Geschichte 1800–1866: Bürgerwelt und starker Staat*, 6th edn. (Munich, 1987), p. 628.
70 For a detailed account see Leo Haupts, 'Die Kölner Dombaufeste 1842–1880 zwischen kirchlicher, bürgerlich-nationaler und dynastisch-höfischer Selbstdarstellung', in Leo Haupts, *Öffentliche Festkultur. Politische Feste in Deutschland von der Aufklärung bis zum Ersten Weltkrieg* (Reinbeck, 1988), pp. 191–211.
71 Heinrich Heine, *Deutschland, ein Wintermärchen*, Kaput 4.
72 Huber, *Verfassungsgeschichte*, vol. 1, p. 375.

73 So Droysen in his speech before the Constitutional Committee, 26 September 1848, in Fenske ed., *Quellen*, p. 170.

74 *Verfassung des Deutschen Reiches*, Section 1, article 3, in Grab ed., *Die Revolution*, pp. 180f.

75 Heinrich Laube, *Das erste deutsche Parlament*, vol. 3 (Leipzig, 1849), pp. 47–9.

76 Ibid., p. 50.

77 Cf. the proposition by Julius A. Ambrosch, in Jessen ed., *Die deutsche Revolution*, p. 290.

78 Otto Dann, *Nation und Nationalismus in Deutschland, 1770–1990* (Munich, 1993), p. 126.

79 James J. Sheehan, *German History 1770–1866* (Oxford, 1989), pp. 371–88.

80 Franz Grillparzer, *Sämtliche Werke*, historisch kritische Gesamtausgabe, A. Sauer and R. Bachmann eds, 'Gedichte', 3. Teil, Sprüche und Epigramme Nr. 1182 (Vienna, 1937), p. 213.

81 Grillparzer, *Sämtliche Werke*, Prosaschriften, vol. 4, pp. 38f.

82 Ibid., p. 55.

Chapter 7

The revolution in crisis

The rejection of the imperial crown by Frederick William IV

It has become customary to refer to 'the' 1848 Revolution and to pronounce its demise with the Prussian king's refusal of the imperial crown. More recent interpretations have seen Frederick William's rejection of the crown as little more than a caesura in a chain of events which were to lead to the 'de-legitimization' and defeat of the revolution[1] while other commentators refer to the events from April to July 1849 as a 'Second' revolution,[2] To speak in terms of a first and second revolution can, however, lead to a serious distortion of the subject matter and should be avoided for the following reasons:

1. The assumption of a second revolution fails to take fully into account the many continuities, not only with the events of the spring and summer of 1848, but also with the Pre-March period. In particular, such an interpretation underestimates the persistent republican fervour in Baden and the Palatinate, attributing too much weight to the National Assembly which had in fact interrupted revolutionary activities and had sought to channel these activities into constitutional reform.

2. A separation of the revolutions into two parts tends to neglect the current of national and international developments. Hungary's struggle against Austria in the spring and summer of 1849 was a fight for national independence, which arose out of the Viennese revolution and had its antecedents in a Europe-wide struggle for democracy and national sovereignty, the two most important modernizing features of the age. Similar campaigns during the Italian *risorgimento*, under its intellectual leader Guiseppe Mazzini, led to a revolutionary uprising in Sardinia (March 1849) and to the declaration of a Roman Republic. Events in Germany must be seen as an integral part of this wider European movement whose momentum had left the aims of the Paris February Revolution behind, to focus instead on national self-determination.

3. The concept of a second revolution would detach the 1849 campaign from the counter-revolutions, which had already begun in September 1848 and reached their high point with the Prussian king's rejection of

157

the imperial crown and the constitution in April 1849. With the fruits of their labours destroyed and forsaken by their liberal colleagues, the democrats took up the revolutionary cudgel once more, in an attempt to preserve some hard-won rights.

In contrast to the earlier phase, the new insurrections, with no support from Vienna or Berlin, were largely limited to the 'Third Germany' and her provincial capitals. Apart from some diplomatic activities behind the scenes, Austria was not involved in this stage of the German revolutionary process. Satisfied with their gains from the 1848 campaigns, the peasants, too, fought shy of further revolutionary activities. The position of catholics had also changed: throughout 1848, the catholic Pius Associations had supported the struggle for constitutional reform but seemed to reverse their position in the spring of 1849, notably in the Prussian Rhine province.[4] Once the Prussian king had declined the imperial crown, catholics, wary of becoming a minority group within a 'lesser Germany', supported his policy of closer ties with Austria, rather than the National Assembly's agenda. This attitude was particularly strong within clerical circles but did not apply to catholic working-class movements in the more industrialized areas. The interests of the peasants and the catholic clergy were narrowly defined; in the case of the former by economic and in the case of the latter by confessional criteria. The Pius Association of Trier could not have made its position clearer: 'In written and spoken form they [catholic associations] must everywhere instruct the people and say to them that the question of the constitution is really about whether Germany shall be protestant or predominantly catholic.'[5] Rank and file catholics did not always agree with this change of policy. Catholics in Rastatt protested when their Frankfurt delegate Joseph Buß, leader of the Pius Associations of Baden, advised his flock to reject the constitution on the grounds that a protestant should not be head of Germany.[6] This political shift by official catholicism, foreshadowing the later dispute with Bismarck, revealed how the catholic church acted 'political' only in the narrow sense of wishing to strengthen its own position, with little concern for democratic, constitutional or national issues.

The military intervention during the September uprisings in Frankfurt had severely undermined the authority of the National Assembly, exposing its reliance on neighbouring garrisons and their Prussian troop contingents. As a result of this situation, and to oppose counter-revolutionary successes elsewhere, the struggle to preserve the gains of March 1848 spread to the German provinces. Motivated by nationwide revulsion over the execution of Robert Blum and in response to the defeat of the revolutions in Vienna and Berlin, delegates from *Donnersberg*, *Deutscher Hof* and *Westendhall* joined forces to form the Central March Association, a left-of-centre organization dedicated to the defence of the 'March achievements'. Its proclamation warned that 'freedom and the rights of the people are in danger of erosion and destruction'.[7] While they remained disunited on such important political considerations as the exact form of national government, members agreed in their defence of the basic democratic rights: 'We demand for the whole nation as for the people of individual states the right to determine their own form of government and to improve and transform it as they see fit, since every government exists solely for and through the will of the people.'[8]

The defence of the Imperial Constitution became the Central March Association's major task. By this time, half a million members in 950 branches nationwide had joined the Association.[9] Its committee included individuals who became prominent revolutionary leaders, such as Adolf von Trütschler who, after commanding the defence of Mannheim, would face execution by a Prussian military court in August.[10] Franz Raveaux took part in the revolution in the Palatinate, Johann G. Eisenmann in the protest movement in Franconia and Hugo M. Wesendonck was active in the Prussian province of the Rhine. In May, at the height of the campaign, Julius Fröbel became its leader, advocating revolutionary struggle to save the constitution. He implored soldiers to be loyal to the new constitution and to serve as the new guardians of law and order against counter-revolutionary princes. Fröbel also favoured the formation of a citizens' militia in defence of the constitution.[11]

The Association's main support was found in central and southern Germany, where the fiercest defence of the constitution was mounted. The Association's weaknesses accurately reflected the inherent defects of the revolutions: with a leadership drawn from the professions, including a large proportion of lawyers, elementary school teachers and journalists, the rank and file consisted of small businessmen, journeymen and master craftsmen.[12] Workers were conspicuously under-represented and the Association neglected to incorporate social and economic issues in its agenda, failures which were a source of contention with Karl Marx and various communist associations; they serve to explain why later interpreters of the revolutions categorized them as 'bourgeois'.[13]

With the Imperial Constitution finally approved, the new Germany was to remain a federation of states, excluding Austria, but maintaining a special relationship with her. Foreign policy, military matters and the economy were to be delegated to the central power. The Prussian king, Frederick William IV, was elected emperor of the Germans, with 290 votes in favour and 248 abstentions, a result which reflected the unease with which delegates reached their decision. Uhland contemptuously dismissed the Assembly's vote: 'a revolution with an hereditary monarch is a youth with grey hair'.[14] A delegation of thirty-two royalists, including Arndt, Dahlmann and Raumer, and led by the newly elected president, Eduard Simson, travelled to Berlin to offer the Imperial Crown to the king.[15] Frederick William's response to the delegates amounted to a carefully phrased rejection: deeply moved and honoured, he thanked them for their generous offer, assuring them of his devotion, love and loyalty to the German fatherland. However, he disputed that the Assembly had any right to bestow the crown, suggesting that he could only accept such an offer with the full consent of all the crowned heads of Germany.[16] The king's decision came as no surprise. Frederick William's belief in the divine right of kings was well known and he had not concealed his attitude in letters to the Assembly's president von Gagern, nor to the delegates Dahlmann and Arndt.[17] Nevertheless, the lower house of the Prussian parliament, supporting the National Assembly, tried to persuade the king to accept the crown. Individuals from within the Prussian army and from among his civil service also urged him to accept, or at the very least to enter into some serious negotiations.

A memorandum of 3 April from the Prussian ministry of state proposed that Frederick William might take over from Archduke John as imperial regent and a personal letter from the king to the Austrian minister president von Schwarzenberg went even further in pursuit of this objective, re-assuring himself of Austrian support in these uncertain times.[18] The king feared a new rivalry with Austria which was likely to succeed in forging a coalition with Russia and France. Added to this came von Schmerling's resignation as president of the Frankfurt Assembly, followed by a period of intense negotiations and communication between Vienna, Frankfurt and Berlin, in a concerted effort to prevent the 'lesser Germany' solution and to preserve Austria's position within the Confederation. An Austrian ministerial protocol recognized Prussia's interest in concluding an 'entente cordiale' with Austria, but at the same time expressed fears of Prussian aspirations towards hegemony in Germany.[19] Von Schmerling, now head of the Austrian delegation in Frankfurt, acted on these fears, proposing an enlargement of the Austrian delegation in Frankfurt and the formation of alliances with other German states. He warned the Vienna government against von Gagern's plans for a Germany that would confer the leadership on Prussia and relegate Austria to the position of special ally. Instead, Austria should remain an integral member at Frankfurt, with her delegates opting for a directorate rather than an hereditary monarch. The key sentence reiterates von Schmerling's chief anxiety 'that we do not break the governmental bonds with Germany, since we would otherwise play into the hands of the Prussians'.[20] The deep impact of von Schmerling's warning to Schwarzenberg is revealed in his confidential letter to the Austrian minister von Buol, where he re-assured his colleague that the Prussian king would not wish to accept the imperial crown from the Frankfurt parliament. Schwarzenberg, however, apparently aware of Prussian plans to extend the Customs Union across the rest of Germany, had severe misgivings about the Prussian government, warning that 'the proposal of a German federal state, in close alliance with Austria but obviously under Prussian hegemony, [was] completely unacceptable'.[21] The Austrian government accepted this unequivocal position:

> Austria is not prepared to surrender its thousand year old right as the premier German power, nor to give up its position in Germany which has developed over this course of time. These two guiding principles have led the cabinet to arrive at its position on the future shape of Germany.[22]

Other documents confirm that the question as to whether the Prussian king should accept or reject the Imperial Crown had become an issue of utmost importance for the future shape of Germany and the decision was increasingly wrenched out of the king's hands and left to government officials. Recognizing this, the 'lesser Germany' party around von Gagern attempted to gain support from southern German states, still hoping to win over some of the catholic clergy to its cause. Even after the king had declined the crown, which he had privately compared to a 'dog collar, binding [him] to the revolution of '48',[23] the power struggle between Austria and Prussia continued. The king stated that he would be prepared to take over from Archduke John, if 'unanimously elected by Germany's princes'.[24] He would, however, rule from Berlin and, in co-operation with the Austrian emperor, hoped to change 'the rules of the game' by imposing their monarchical constraints on Frankfurt's constitutional policy.[25] When all these machinations collapsed, the king's final note of rejection, issued on 28 April, did not even recognize the Imperial Constitution. Prussia's break with the National Assembly and with the revolution itself was now complete. On 14 May Prussia ordered its delegates to leave Frankfurt, Austria already having done so on 5 April. Despite these major setbacks, the National Assembly began preparations in May for the election of a *Volkshaus* by 15 July and for a properly constituted *Reichstag* on 22 August.[26] The struggle for the Constitution had commenced.

The campaign for the Imperial Constitution

On 14 April twenty-eight of the smaller German states accepted the Imperial Constitution. Their collective response, directed to the head of the Prussian delegation rather than to the Assembly, referred specifically to the Prussian government's memorandum, which stated that Frederick William was prepared to head a federation of German states.[27] The wording of their response brings into question the very nature of their support for the constitution. National priorities rather than liberal or constitutional sympathies seem to have motivated them, along with political opportunism.

However, apart from some minor reservations, they explicitly accepted the constitution. Their communication expressed the conviction that all German states that were not prevented by special circumstances – a clear reference to Austria – would accept the constitution and join a federation under Prussian leadership. On 5 May, in response to the final rejection of the crown by Frederick William, the National Assembly voted, by a majority of only two votes, that individual governments, local communities, together with the whole of the German people, should be asked to support the constitution. A heavy loss of liberal delegates had left the Assembly far more radical than ever before, yet its appeal to the country struck a very dry and legalistic note and did little to inspire public support. One reason for this low-key approach might lie with the Assembly's attempt to gain the support of the provisional central government and, in particular, Archduke John. The latter seemed little concerned about finding himself in opposition to the Assembly to which, admittedly, he was not constitutionally responsible but which he was expected to protect.[28] He reported to Prince Schwarzenberg that he had signed the Declaration of Empowerment only under duress, describing his action as an overstepping of his competence.

The campaign's failure can be attributed to four reasons.

1. The historical opportunity for a revolution had passed and counter-revolutionaries had already regained control, not only in the two most powerful German states, but also in France and Italy.
2. The revolutionary leaders were inhibited by their distrust of extremist policies, particularly anarchism and communism, their chief concern being the pursuit of the constitutional goal at the expense of everything else. This moderate stance on the part of the leadership, though certainly a weakness of the revolution, should be weighed against the fact that there existed no significant working-class potential in Baden and the Palatinate, the revolution's two centres.
3. Even more important, though of a somewhat instrumentalist nature, was a general failure of organization. With Struve discredited, Hecker in America and many of the foreign military commanders unable to understand German, any meaningful deployment of forces proved virtually impossible.
4. The absence of a political centre was perhaps the greatest impediment. The National Assembly had all but collapsed and the Central March Associations were not strong enough to take over its role. The view prevailed that 'the reason for the south German revolution, the German parliament, was the cause of its demise'.[29]

Several members of the Assembly, recognizing the impasse which confronted them, published a separate pamphlet, condemning the arbitrary disregard of the princes for the new constitution and invoking open revolt against them, citing revolutionary activity in the Palatinate as a model.[30] The general public's response to this passionate appeal was astonishingly sympathetic, the Imperial Constitution now assuming a symbolic significance in the minds of many people. It represented the culmination and only tangible achievement of the 'March events', indicating a successful compromise between liberals and democrats which could bring about the desired nation state. Furthermore, the public was by now politically mature enough to recognize that, although the constitution could do little to improve their economic and social ills, it nevertheless empowered them with fundamental rights which could in time alleviate their most basic problems. These sentiments are reflected in the key passage of the pamphlet:

> Germans! Once more, you are called upon to protect your freedom for the last time against the assaults of your princes. Take your inspiration from the men and women of the Palatinate, they are determined to act. Do not hesitate, take up arms, organize and make use of your organisations, elect chairmen for your defence committees, prepare manfully for the moment when you have to face the violent deeds of your arbitrary masters![31]

Within the National Assembly itself, the situation had become desperate. The establishment of a liberal and democratic constitution for all German states, once the chief objective, had been rejected: the Assembly was moribund. One last stand was attempted on 9 May when von Gagern issued a government statement, warning that the provisional central government would oppose 'any intervention by one or several states with the purpose of suppressing possible moves towards the recognition of the Imperial Constitution in other states'.[32] When Archduke John condemned this proclamation as an illegal incitement to civil war, von Gagern tendered his resignation in terms which indicated clearly that, in his opinion, the Archduke acted as an Austrian aristocrat, not as the upholder of the law and of democracy.[33] Initiated by Austria, Prussia and some medium-sized states, a number of measures followed which in fact amounted to 'a *coup d'état* against the constitution by which these states dissociated themselves from Frankfurt'.[34] In response, sixty-five delegates, mostly from the *Casino* club and including von Gagern, Dahlmann and Arndt, resigned their seats on 20 May. Others followed a week later, leaving behind a 'rump parliament' of 103 left-of-centre delegates. Fearful of Prussian military intervention and encouraged by the popular mood in Württemberg, where King William had been forced to accept the Imperial Constitution on 21 April, the rump parliament decided to move to Stuttgart.[35] The Assembly's arrival in Stuttgart caused some apprehension; many of those under the patronage of the royal household now feared for their livelihoods, while sympathizers were afraid to manifest their support for the delegates. Whether through desperate self-deception or in blatant defiance, the rump parliament elected a counter-government to the one appointed by Archduke John and claimed supreme command of all the armed forces in Germany. Württemberg troops were to be despatched to support the Baden revolutionary government in its stand against Prussian intervention and a law was passed for the formation of a citizens' militia, calling on all able-bodied men between eighteen and fifty to take up arms in defence of the constitution. The Württemberg government, though not wholly unsympathetic to the rump parliament, could not tolerate such activities within its territory. As Prussia threatened military action, Minister President Römer, a liberal and technically still a member of the National Assembly, employed troops to disperse the rump parliament. On 18 June, a group of thirty parliamentarians were threatened by Württemberg troops on their way to a parliamentary session, and subsequently arrested, expelled or otherwise silenced.

It would be easy to dramatize this inglorious demise of the Assembly and to criticize the Württemberg government for its use of force. Römer's memorandum to the last president of the Assembly all too clearly expresses the futility of its position. The Assembly barely counted a hundred delegates and could no longer claim to represent the various German states or the whole gamut of political opinions: 'Believe me, Mr President, you have been deceived. There are, indeed, strong sympathies for the Imperial Constitution and for the National Assembly amongst the people, but the great majority is not enthusiastic enough to be prepared to charge into battle, should such an improbable situation arise.'[36] Römer's message concluded with an appeal to reason and common sense which, nevertheless, was ignored.

Revolutionary patterns in the summer of 1849

Although the 1849 campaign was inspired by the threat to the National Assembly and the dispute over the recognition of the Imperial Constitution, both powerful symbols of national unity in the face of counter-revolutionary successes in Austria and Prussia, its centre was neither Frankfurt nor Stuttgart. The majority of states in the Third Germany and the Prussian province of the Rhine provided the setting for most revolutionary activities. While events in these regions differed markedly, dependent on revolutionary potential, distance from Prussia and historical tradition, certain common patterns can be discerned.

In the past, too much emphasis has been devoted to 'the working-class element' and to criticism of the *petit bourgeoisie* during the revolutions' final stages. Contemporary reports by utopian socialists such as Bruno Bauer and Frederick Engels[37] may explain this, with recent interpretations by some GDR historians contributing to the imbalance. Today it is generally recognized that the potential for any large-scale deployment of industrial workers simply did not exist and that a clear division between 'workers' and 'artisans' was yet to emerge. The provincial revolutionary centres were characterized on the whole by a socio-economic mixture of craftsmen and other workers, with a minority of participants from the farming community frequently themselves involved in crafts or trade. In Saxony, just over half the population was employed in industry and crafts, with such activity often centred in the villages of the Erzgebirge and the Vogtland mountains, far from major cities.[38] Only the Prussian province of the Rhine had a work force of similar density, while in Baden craftsmen were a mere 6.45 per cent of the population. More important to an understanding of the dynamics of the revolution was not the social constitution, but the political affiliation of activists. Saxony, for example, was characterized by rivalry between the republican *Vaterlandsverein* and the liberal *Deutscher Verein*. In general, divisions between liberal constitutionalists and democratic republicans were always evident, with the former concerned exclusively with defending the Imperial Constitution whereas the latter pursued more far-reaching radical objectives.

The political leadership and their agenda

This revolutionary phase had a leadership broadly similar to that of the previous year, with the same individuals frequently involved, but, in line with what was essentially a defence of the constitution, academics with a legal training were even more prominent. Many of these leaders were members of the National Assembly or of one of the liberal state parliaments. Of the ten members of the Palatinate Committee for the Defence of the State, all were academics and a majority were advocates.[39] The provisional government of Baden followed a similar pattern, headed by Lorenz Brentano, the Mannheim lawyer who had gained fame through his skilful defence of Hecker. No workers and only two craftsmen were included in this group, with one observer remarking that 'law courts had become centres for revolutionary agitation'.[40] Persuasive legal arguments were an integral part of the constitutional campaign: if the National Assembly was Germany's highest authority and the Imperial Constitution its noblest achievement, then those rejecting it, the counter-revolutionary princes and their high-ranking officers, were the true villains in violation of the law which the revolutionaries resolutely upheld. Such arguments were used not only to encourage regular troops and civil guards to change sides and join the revolution, but were also employed to justify military aid for neighbouring states. The Offenburg programme (14 May) stated:

The German peoples are obliged to guarantee each other's freedom, so as to observe completely the principle of popular sovereignty. They will therefore always support each other, wherever they are attacked. The people of Baden will therefore support the popular movement in the Palatinate with all the means at their disposal.[41]

Radical clubs and associations gained strong support from among elementary school teachers, a constituency traditionally involved in the community life of villages and small towns. Their General Association of Teachers (*Allgemeiner deutscher Lehrerverein*), founded in 1848, had the aim of furthering comprehensive elementary education throughout Germany.[42] They were soon singled out as the chief enemies of the counter-revolution.[43] Since these teachers tended to be recruited from among the lower social ranks, they approached their task with enormous enthusiasm, eager to emancipate their pupils and local communities. In the aftermath of the Dresden revolution, schoolteachers comprised the second largest group, after advocates, to face criminal prosecution.[44] In the Palatinate, elementary school teachers were singled out as the most active party of subversion.[45]

In the past, German historians saw the defence of the Imperial Constitution often as little more than a pretext for the promotion of anarchy or republican agitation,[46] a viewpoint which demands some qualification. Several regions involved in the 1849 revolutions already had a history of unrest, especially Baden and the Rhineland. These, together with certain other regions opposed to a Prussian hereditary monarch, therefore did not support that aspect of the constitution. Furthermore, provinces such as the Rhineland, the Palatinate, Franconia and Swabia had, within living memory, lost their independence and suffered annexation, a factor likely to overshadow the constitutional issue. Lastly, as in most revolutions, control mechanisms tended to disintegrate once the movement had gathered a certain momentum, with radicals coming to the fore. This was certainly the case in Baden and Saxony, possibly also in the Palatinate, all traditional strongholds of republicanism. And yet, an analysis of the speeches and programmes of the largest public meetings reveals a considerable degree of co-ordination, with the defence of the Constitution as the crux of the argument.

The first important meeting occurred in Dresden on 22 April, organized by the radical *Vaterlandsverein* in support of the Dresden parliament's acceptance of the Imperial Constitution. With a disunited leadership and an extremist majority demanding action rather than words, this first meeting ended in disarray. By the beginning of May, it had been agreed that the constitution was to be defended, if necessary by all available means.[47] The Central March Association organized meetings throughout Germany. Its next large gathering was held in Munich on 27 April; it declared its opposition to an hereditary emperor but urged its members to support the constitution unreservedly, with a subsequent petition gaining 12,000 signatures. On 2 May a gathering of 13,000 met in Kaiserslautern, centre of the Bavarian Palatinate, to elect a Committee for the Defence of the Country, empowered to oversee the introduction of the constitution.[48] Meetings in Nuremberg and Offenburg followed on 13 May, attracting crowds of 30,000 and 40,000 respectively.[49] The resolution taken at Nuremberg stated unambiguously: 'We act entirely within the law, for the Imperial Constitution, passed by the German parliament, is law in Germany; our government has followed the path of rebellion, for it has rejected this same law.'[50] The last of the major assemblies, at Reutlingen in Württemberg on 27 May, was addressed by the Baden delegates Fickler and Hoff, in the hope of gaining support for the Baden revolution. As Württemberg had accepted the constitution just a few weeks earlier, the major issue here was military support for Baden. A Baden Legion was promised, but following Fickler's arrest by Württemberg troops, support for this cause fell away.

The most important and best-documented gathering took place at Offenburg. Eye-witness accounts from Franz Raveaux, representing the National Assembly, from the popular poet Victor Scheffel, and from Amand Goegg, the chief organizer, as well as various newspaper reports, give a vivid description of events.[51] In view of the intransigent attitude exhibited by the Baden government, the assembly assumed a militant stance. Raveaux captured the general mood:

> a huge gathering of people was assembled. The crowd surged to and fro: the people from the Black Forest in traditional costume with their marten-skin caps, red waistcoats and black frocks, amongst them gymnasts, soldiers, burghers, women and girls. . . . However, no trace of the proletariat that you would find at public gatherings in northern Germany. The city itself was festively decked with German flags and green foliage. From the station to the meeting place I saw only the German tricolour; but some of the young folk, mainly gymnasts and young farmers, had attached red feathers and ribbons to their hats and one could hear them shout 'long live Hecker!' Yet nowhere among the thousands of flags did I see a single red one. . . . It became obvious to me that the majority of the [Offenburg] executive committee were confirmed republicans who, for the present, would unite with the rest of Germany to bring about the realisation of the Basic Rights and of the Imperial Constitution.[52]

A number of conclusions can be drawn from Raveaux's comments. The Offenburg Assembly had more in common with a German *Fest* than with a bloody revolution in the making. Despite a certain republican flavour there was little evidence of the imminent outbreak of an armed struggle; the public speakers, notwithstanding their republican inclinations, were concentrating their efforts in defence of the constitution. Their 'Sixteen Points' confirm such an analysis, they can be summarized under five headings:

1. defence of the Imperial Constitution and support for other, like-minded German states;
2. replacement of the existing government by a republican administration with a single-chamber, democratically elected parliament;
3. the establishment of a citizens' militia with free election of officers;
4. the release of all political prisoners, the right to jury trial and a free and publicly accountable local administration;
5. a national bank for the support of trade and agriculture and a progressive income tax.[53]

These priorities indicate the Assembly's desire to preserve their earlier March demands; the only radical aspect was the proposal of a republican government which their leader, Lorenz Brentano, successfully suppressed in order not to alienate other states.

The foreign involvement

An accusation frequently levied against the revolutionaries concerned the involvement of foreign anarchists, where the term 'foreign' deserves a closer definition. Reactionary forces used it in 1849 to describe both non-Germans and Germans entering other German states, a definition clearly at variance with the wording of the Imperial Constitution. The activities of the Russian anarchist Michael Bakunin in Dresden are perhaps best known. Although describing himself as a disciple of Hegel, he was neither a young Hegelian nor a disciple of Marx. He 'happened' to find himself in Dresden in May[54] and had himself elected to the Committee of Public Safety. Alongside the extremist Saxon lawyer Adolf Tzschirner and the physician Carl Ludwig d'Esther from Cologne and supported by the young composer Richard Wagner and the court architect Gottfried Semper, Bakunin organized the building of barricades. A professional revolutionary, who had already fought in Poland, Prague and elsewhere, Bakunin was certainly not fighting for the Imperial Constitution, but hoped to export the Dresden insurrection to Poland and Bohemia, to form a Pan-Slavonic confederation with the ultimate aim of overthrowing imperial Austria and tsarist Russia. Bakunin, however, was arrested during the final phase of the Dresden revolution and spent eight years in various prisons in Dresden, Prague, Ölmütz and St Petersburg, from where he was exiled to Siberia. Polish officers made up a significant element in the Dresden revolution. Once defeated, they moved on to Baden and the Palatinate to continue the fight against reactionary forces who sympathized with those elements who had once belonged to the Holy Alliance and who were responsible for the suppression of the national cause in Poland. Other Dresden revolutionaries, including Tzschirner and d'Esther, also managed to escape to Baden, or to the Palatinate where these 'outsiders' played a decisive role, particularly in their appeal to the more extreme elements. The strongest foreign presence was felt in Baden, its common borders to Switzerland and France and its revolutionary tradition facilitating influx from elsewhere. Most important among them was the Polish General Louis Mieroslawski, a veteran of the Polish liberation struggle of 1831 and of the Sicilian uprising of 1848. He was appointed supreme commander of the Baden troops and suffered the somewhat dubious support of the elderly Polish General Sznyde who commanded the army of the Palatinate. The former Prussian officer August Willich, expelled from France to Switzerland because of his anarchist tendencies, set up his own free corps in Baden. Johann Philipp Becker, a 'veteran' of the Hecker campaigns, returned from Switzerland to lead the militia and command the legion of foreigners. Among the disaffected Prussian officers in the Baden camp were Fritz Anneke and his redoubtable wife Mathilde. Several revolutionaries from France, Switzerland, Poland and Hungary joined the campaign, with Hungarians and Poles forming their own units. Exiled Germans in Geneva and Paris founded revolutionary committees and published the 'Manifesto of German Democrats Abroad'.[55] Some money and arms were dispatched from Paris and the Alsace, but official negotiations with France were never undertaken.

Such outside intervention on behalf of the revolutions in Saxony, the Palatinate and Baden will have indicated how 'foreign' influence was generally limited to military action and only occasionally led to genuine political involvement. Their common agenda was the defence of democracy and the establishment of a republican regime, and to this end their policies were extremist. In general, however, they failed to change the course of the revolutions in any profound manner and wherever their influence was felt to be significant, this was more to do with military prowess than with political skill.

The role of the military

There can be no doubt about the key role played by civil guards and regular troops, in deciding the fate of the revolutions in the spring and summer of 1849.[56] Just as the defence of the Imperial Constitution had become the focal point around which liberals and democrats could once more unite, so the various military units operated as a state within a state, to re-impose the old semi-feudal order and implement the counter-revolution. An important outcome of this clash of ideologies was seen in the rapid strengthening of the Prussian military tradition of unquestioning disciplinary loyalties, the concept of duty and faithfulness to king and state as ultimate values, and the supremacy of military discipline over democratic emancipation. Anxiety over the situation in March 1848 had already prompted Albrecht von Roon, future minister of war, to define the Prussian army as the sole embodiment of the Prussian state, as his only 'fatherland, for there alone have the unclean and violent elements who put everything into turmoil failed to penetrate'.[57] Similar pronouncements were made by Radetzky in Austria.

If seen within this context, all Prussian military operations gain in significance: Prussia assumed an hegemony, based on the 'virtues' of discipline and unquestioning obedience as against the liberalism of southern Germany and the Rhineland. Prussia, in the person of Crown Prince William, achieved within Germany what Windischgrätz' armies achieved in Prague and Vienna and what Russian troops managed in Hungary. The similar strategies employed by these three forces were symbolic of a return to the Holy Alliance and its anti-democratic despotism. The supreme role assumed by Prince William, the 'shrapnel-prince', cannot be underestimated. His appointment as supreme commander of all troops dispatched to the Palatinate, Hesse and Baden was interpreted as Prussian resolve not to enter into any form of negotiation with the revolutionaries.[58] The temporary defeat of the military in March 1848, symbolized by the crown prince's ignominious flight and exile, was now to be avenged. Prince William's return, to lead an invading army, served notice that the counter-revolution was bringing its might to bear on the Third Germany, in a cynical fulfilment of his brother's earlier promise that Germany could rely on the Prussian shield and sword against the enemy within and without. The king himself put the message powerfully, 'only soldiers can help fight democrats'.[59] Such attitudes justify the earlier warning of Gustav Julius, editor of the *Berliner Zeitungshalle*, that the military institution in its entirety should be abolished: 'any reconciliation with the class of profession of soldiers, as hitherto and still exists, is inconceivable. . . . It has to be eradicated, until there is no distinction between citizens and soldiers, until the soldier is no longer a tool of tyranny against the will of the citizen . . .'.[60]

In May 1849 the Central March Association appealed to 'German soldiers' to disregard the commands of their princes: 'Soldiers . . . You are being misused to fight against law and order, fatherland and family, freedom and equality; you are being turned into police lackeys who trample over human dignity. . . . Such black treason will sully your fame-endowed weapons in the service of Russian despotism.'[61] The provisional government of Saxony employed similar appeals, inviting soldiers to make common cause with the people in defence of the constitution: 'Follow the example of other brave soldiers, remember that you have sworn an oath as citizens and that you must protect the rights and liberties of the people.'[62] Unfortunately, these appeals fell on deaf ears. On 3 May the regular Saxon army opened fire on a crowd who were storming the armoury. The civil guard chose to remain 'neutral', in fact remaining loyal to the monarch. Fear of Prussian intervention may have played a significant part in the strategy of the Saxon military and could explain why regular Saxon troops intervened in the Dresden uprising, even before the arrival of Prussian forces. By this means Saxony hoped to keep the initiative. With the exception of Baden and possibly the Palatinate, this same pattern of events could be observed wherever a conflict arose between the princes and their people. In Breslau and in the Prussian Rhine province, particularly in the towns of Iserlohn, Hagen, Solingen, Elberfeld, Düsseldorf, Gräfrath, Siegburg and Prüm, there was public unrest over the mobilization of the militia.[63] Insurrections tended to be led by democratic clubs and workers' associations, while Communists either refused to support them or at best gave minimal assistance. A march from Elberfeld to Düsseldorf, organized by the German Militiamen's Association, gained the support of men from the lower Rhine region. At such events, the black-red-gold colours would be prominently to the fore, with the occasional red flag, and an open display of support for the Frankfurt constitution. Regular Prussian troop contingents, billeted in various fortresses with a strength of barely one hundred men, generally remained in their garrisons, fearful of an open confrontation with significantly larger, but lightly armed, militia units. Where local garrisons were in action, as in Elberfeld, their response was often half-hearted with some fear on the part of officers that their men would refuse to obey orders.[64] Larger Prussian troop contingents, who were experienced in defeating similar insurrections elsewhere, consisted of units who had no contact with the local community and displayed little apprehension at facing opposition. In general, attacks by regular troops were fierce and brutal, mobile artillery being employed to destroy the barricades. Iserlohn, a minor provincial town, suffered more than one hundred casualties, mostly factory workers and craftsmen, during such a confrontation.

Events in Württemberg clearly indicated the dilemma facing liberal regimes as the counter-revolution gained the upper hand. Prussian intervention would put in jeopardy the future of the Römer cabinet which had successfully forced King William to accept the constitution. The local militia was wholeheartedly behind the constitution and demanded the resignation of its royalist commander.[65] While assuring the king of his personal safety, militiamen warned that they would accept orders only from a minister of the elected government, not from the king or his officers. When Württemberg was 'offered' Prussian military assistance to suppress the revolution, Römer was forced to take prior action in order to maintain his country's independence. Even at this juncture Römer did not have the support of the various civil guards, who remained loyal to the National Assembly until faced by the threat of a confrontation with regular troops in Heilbronn and Löwenstein.[66]

In Bavaria, too, the outcome of the revolution depended on the loyalty of the militia and, particularly, on the role of regular army units. Franconian workers and craftsmen supported the constitution, though their ultimate aim was far-reaching social and economic reform. Troops in Nuremberg sympathized with the revolutionaries, but the potential for an armed insurrection was undermined by the indecision of a Frankfurt delegate. A more explosive situation developed in the 'Bavarian' Palatinate, where the Kaiserslautern Assembly convened a committee for the defence of the province. Various civil guard units declared their total support and more than 3,000 regular soldiers changed sides in defence of the newly founded regime. Public support began to weaken when the Kaiserslautern committee openly expressed republican sympathies, coming increasingly under the influence of radicals from outside the Palatinate, such as Carl Ludwig d'Esther, the Cologne physician and delegate to the Prussian parliament, and the Mainz democrat Ludwig Bamberger. In the last resort, only some 13,000 men were prepared to offer armed resistance to a Prussian expeditionary force.[67]

The revolutionary forces obviously suffered a major disadvantage when faced with the superior military equipment of the regular troops, especially that of the Prussian army. Many revolutionaries in the Palatinate and in Baden were armed only with antiquated rifles or improvized weapons, such as scythes. Arms procurement from Belgium, France and Britain largely failed, such was the success of Prussian troops or diplomats in preventing these weapons from reaching their destinations.

The revolutionaries' last stand in Baden

The revolution in Baden went further than in any other German state and can be used to illustrate certain features already discussed in this chapter. Baden had twice been the scene of revolutionary unrest; the effects of Hecker's insurrection in March 1848 and Struve's short-lived rebellion of September were still evident. The aims of the various revolutionary clubs and associations went far beyond a recognition of the Frankfurt constitution, they desired the process of democratization to become an everyday reality in their own state. The Offenburg Assembly was Baden's response to the revolutions in Dresden, in Prussia's Rhine province and in the neighbouring Palatinate. The liberal government in Karlsruhe was preparing to introduce an electoral law which seemed in conflict with the Basic Rights and was, furthermore, opposed to the general call to arms in defence of the constitution, as demanded by Mannheim democrats on 1 May.[68] The single most critical factor for the success of the Baden Revolution was the volatile state of the military, not only in the imperial fortress at Rastatt, but also in the garrisons of Bruchsal, Freiburg, Lörrach and even Karlsruhe itself. Discontent within the army had a number of causes. The officer corps and particularly the non-commissioned officers, whose conduct was described as 'collective brutality',[69] had lost the confidence of the rank and file. The Baden army, still enforcing corporal punishment, had not benefited from the military reforms applied in Prussia half a century earlier. Furthermore, with the army's strength increased to 2 per cent of the population, military conscription was rigorously imposed. The common practice of *Einsteher*, whereby young men with no social prospects were paid to 'stand in' for more prosperous and educated young men, was no longer condoned. The resulting change in the army's social structure therefore caused rifts between new conscripts, generally well educated and aware of the political situation at home and in the rest of Germany, and the old *Einsteher*, with the low rank of sergeant or corporal, feeling their status and career prospects threatened. Severe overcrowding in the garrisons led to extended leave periods for soldiers, which afforded them the opportunity to attend liberal and democratic clubs in their home towns. Military pay was ludicrously low, equivalent to one-third of the rate of a day labourer. Political leaflets and other propaganda, advocating improved remuneration, free elections of officers and the abolition of the hated puttees, circulated amongst soldiers. These soldiers' radical desire for freedom found expression in parodies such as this:

[freedom] ascended into the hearts of suppressed Germans, from whence it will return to claim its rights from tyrants and their fellow-citizens. I believe in the community of all freedom loving Germans, in the abolition of all oppressive dues, the resurrection of human rights and one common freedom and equality, Amen.[70]

Reports of fraternization between soldiers and the townspeople of Rastatt on 9 May indicated that military discipline was crumbling. Outright mutiny occurred when a soldier was imprisoned because of his radical political affinities and on 11 May political prisoners held in two of the local garrisons were released by rioting troops. In Freiburg the radical democrat Fickler and young Wilhelm Liebknecht were set free, the distinguished lawyer Carl von Rotteck persuading the garrison to take an oath not to fight against civilians. The following day the Baden minister of war travelled to Rastatt in an effort to restore order. Soldiers demanded an amalgamation with the civil guard, a new constitution for Baden, the release of political prisoners and participation at the Offenburg Assembly.[71] Unable to fulfil his mission, the minister fled the country. In several other garrisons officers were attacked by ordinary soldiers and forced to resign their commands. Even the Grand Duke's own Life Guards were in open revolt and used violence against their commanding officers.

The role of the Offenburg Assembly, as previously noted, cannot be under-estimated. Together with the military revolt, it contributed to the downfall of the Grand Duke's government and his flight into political exile to the Prussian Rhineland. With the release of the prisoners Struve, Blind and Eichfeld, a Committee of Public Safety (*Landesausschuß*) was formed and a new provisional government established under Lorenz Brentano. A procla-mation 'To the German people' swore death to the old confederation of tyrants and hailed a greater, free, united Germany.[72] This proclamation bore the signatures of the Baden Committee of Public Safety as well as those of the provisional government and of the three National Assembly delegates, Raveaux, Trütschler and Erbe. Nevertheless, the new provisional government under Brentano pursued a responsible, moderate policy, intent on averting military confrontation with other German states and prepared to carry out social and economic measures which would ensure the support of liberals and democrats alike. Amand Goegg in particular, chief organizer of the Offenburg Assembly and now in charge of state finance, was prudent in his economic policies.[73] The new government's attempt to buy arms in Switzerland, France and Belgium failed, notwithstanding essential financial guarantees, a sign that the 'international' money markets had little con-fidence in the revolutionary government.[74] Tensions between republicans and moderate pragmatists within the Safety Committee soon affected the operation of the provisional government. On the republican wing, Struve, in particular, advocated revolutionary armed intervention in neighbouring states. A defensive military union with the Palatinate was formed, but had little more than a symbolic effect. Attempts to gain military and political support from France, Württemberg and Hesse failed. With the formation of a one-chamber parliament, by equal, direct and secret ballot for all men over the age of twenty-one, a majority of democrats were elected, including Fickler and Hecker, with the latter still on his way back from American exile.[75] The new parliament, consisting mainly of lawyers, artisans and teachers,[76] supported Brentano's policies, in particular his adherence to the Imperial Constitution. It was, however, short lived; within three weeks of the election, it was forced to leave Karlsruhe, holding its fourteenth and final session in Freiburg. Despite this brief life span, it was to remain the most democratic parliament on German soil until well into the twentieth century. Republican radicals, mostly professional revolutionaries from out-side Baden, opposed Brentano's policies and rallied around Struve. They hoped to use Baden as the base for a Europe-wide revolution, already an anachronism by the summer of 1849, when preservation of the *status quo* was the best that could be hoped for. These radicals formed a free corps, with the intention of implementing a *coup d'état*, but Brentano avoided conflict by mobilizing the civil guard against them.

In the meantime, Prussian troops had massed at the borders of the Palatinate and Baden, threatening the survival of their revolutionary governments and endangering the balance of power between Prussia and Austria. The provisional government in Frankfurt, together with the governments of Württemberg, Bavaria and Austria, sought a political solution to the revolution and attempted to neutralize Prussia, or, at the very least, to integrate Prussian troops into an army under the authority of the provisional government.[77] Prussia circumvented these efforts, using Grand Duke Leopold's plea for military intervention as a pretext to send her troops into Baden, effectively reducing this state to a satellite under Prussian domination. Prussian foreign secretary von Arnim played the hard-liner, ordering immediate military intervention and advocating the harshest punishment for all revolutionaries. At the onset of the Prussian invasion, Prince William commanded nearly 100,000 men, whereas the revolutionary armies mustered just 45,000, many of whom were ill equipped and poorly trained.

By the middle of June the Baden revolution had reached its end phase. The Palatinate had already fallen, the republican movement in France had suffered its final defeat and the rump parliament in Stuttgart had just been dissolved. The revolutionary army was demoralized, short of weapons, ammunition and general provisions. On 21 June the battle at Waghäusel, a small village near Speyer, inflicted a decisive defeat on the revolutionaries, though General Mieroslawski managed an organized retreat to the Murg valley, only to suffer another defeat. Some 6,000 men withdrew to the fortress of Rastatt, which managed to hold out against superior Prussian forces until 23 July, when hunger and the utter hopelessness of the situation forced their surrender to Prussian troops who manifested inhuman brutality. The revolutionaries were imprisoned in the casemates of Rastatt, many dying from typhoid, others executed on the orders of Prussian military tribunals, among them soldiers from twenty-nine German states and many European countries. Special courts, staffed by Prussian judges, carried out sentences in accordance with Baden law. Protests against the death sentences and the general disregard of the basic rights remained unheeded:

> The public protests against the incessant continuation of blood trials in Baden are not only the expression of a natural feeling for justice. . . . This is not solely a matter for Baden. Should the Empire disintegrate, should our fatherland become more fragmented than ever, it, nevertheless, remains a German concern that the concepts of right and wrong do not also perish, that the system of justice, and with it German culture and national honour, do not become downtrodden.[78]

A closer study of this protest note would indicate the deep, post-romantic concern with German law, which was central to German culture and was considered to be the nucleus of German regeneration. These concerns turned into reality: the concepts of democracy, of self-determination and of liberalism were subverted. The counter-revolution ignored the achievements of the German Enlightenment in the same way as it ignored political developments in Western Europe and North America. The oppressive political climate affected all aspects of public life. Prussian tribunals remained in session until late October, dealing with nearly 250 cases. Denunciations were the order of the day and many freely elected city mayors were removed. Nearly one thousand people faced imprisonment; mere sympathizers and minor offenders faced responsibility for the cost of the revolutions, forced to pay punitive fines in reparation. All clubs and associations were declared illegal, with only a gradual return to pre-revolutionary activity. In face of such repression, thousands of citizens chose emigration, either to Switzerland or to the United States. A Prussian army of occupation of nearly 18,000 troops controlled every aspect of public life and Baden remained under military rule until 1852. Her regiments were transferred to Pomerania and Brandenburg, where Prussian military discipline was instilled into them. Despite draconian press censorship, the whole country was seized by virulent anti-Prussian sentiment. The Baden Lullaby, an adaptation of a song from the Thirty Years War, made the rounds:

> Sleep, child, a gentle sleep,
> A Prussian your guard will keep.
> He, who has murdered your father
> And impoverished your mother.
> Whoever won't sleep in quiet rest
> Will feel his eyes in their sockets pressed,
> Sleep, child, a gentle sleep.[79]

The next chapter will examine the political and social consequences of the defeat of the German revolutions. It will explore how the change of political culture, towards a *Realpolitik* based on the principle that might is right, channelled all nobler sentiments into unrestrained nationalism, at the expense of those humanist values which remain the touchstones of a civil society.

Notes

1 Wolfram Siemann, *The German Revolution of 1848–49*, trans. by C. Banerji (London, 1998), p. 202.

2 In particular Golo Mann, *The History of Germany since 1789* (London, 1968); Jonathan Sperber, *Rhineland Radicals. The Democratic Movement and the Revolution of 1848–1849* (Princeton, NJ, 1991) and D. Blackbourn, *The Fontana History of Germany 1780–1918. The Long Nineteenth Century* (London, 1997).

3 Veit Valentin, *Geschichte der deutschen Revolution 1848–49*, vol. 2 (Berlin, 1930/1), p. 545, refers to a 'second outbreak' of the revolution, placing the events squarely within a broader context of revolutionary activity.

4 Sperber, *Rhineland Radicals*, pp. 384f.

5 Ibid., p. 357: *Der katholische Volksbote*, 9–10 May 1849.

6 'Adresse des vaterländischen Vereins', Rastatt, 29 March. Similar addresses from Weinheim and Lahr are mentioned in Valentin, *Geschichte*, vol. 2, p. 509.

7 'Kundmachung des demokratischen Zentralmärzvereins an das deutsche Volk' (November 1848), in Walter Grab ed., *Die Revolution von 1848/49. Eine Dokumentation* (Stuttgart, 1998), p. 150.

8 Ibid., p. 151.

9 Manfred Botzenhart, *Deutscher Parlamentarismus in der Revolutionszeit 1848–1850* (Düsseldorf, 1977), pp. 402f.

10 Wolfgang Duffner, *Der Traum der Helden. 12 Nachrufe auf im Sommer und Herbst 1849 hingerichtete Kämpfer der badischen Revolution* (Schauenburg, 1997), pp. 105–17.

11 Cf. Rainer Koch, 'Julius Fröbel: Demokratie und Staat', in Sabine Freitag ed., *Die Achtundvierziger. Lebensbilder aus der deutschen Revolution 1848/49* (Munich, 1998), p. 155; cf. also 'Aufruf des Zentralmärzvereins an die deutschen Soldaten', 6 May 1849, in Grab ed., *Die Revolution*, pp. 200–2.

12 Cf. Siemann, *German Revolution*, p. 98.

13 In a series of articles published in the *Neue Rheinische Zeitung*, Marx asserted that the middle classes in Frankfurt and the counter-revolution itself were inextricably allied against the interests of the working classes. Cf. *Neue Rheinische Zeitung*, 10 December 1848 and following issues. Cf. also P. H. Noyes, *Organisation and Revolution. Working Class Associations in the German Revolutions of 1848–1849* (Princeton, NJ, 1966), pp. 281–4. Noyes seems to overstate the case for a social revolution; evidence exists to demonstrate that many working-class leaders were involved in defending the constitution.

14 Ludwig Uhland, *Werke*, H. Fröschle and W. Scheffler eds, vol. 4 (Munich, 1984), p. 716.

15 Hans Jessen ed., *Die deutsche Revolution 1848/49 in Augenzeugenberichten*, 2nd edn (Düsseldorf, 1968), p. 309.

16 Jessen ed., *Die deutsche Revolution*, p. 309.

17 For a fuller account cf. Frank Eyck, *The Frankfurt Parliament 1848–1849* (London, 1968), pp. 341f.

18 Letter from King Frederick William IV to Schwarzenberg, in Hans Fenske ed., *Quellen zur deutschen Revolution 1848–1849* (Darmstadt, 1996), pp. 312ff.

19 Protocol by the Austrian Council of Ministers, 25 December 1848, in Fenske ed., *Quellen*, p. 243.

20 Protocol by the Austrian Council of Ministers, 26 December 1848, in Fenske ed., *Quellen*, p. 247.

21 Schwarzenberg's letter to Count Buol, in Fenske ed., 31 December 1848, *Quellen*, p. 249.

22 Ibid., p. 250.

23 King Frederick William IV to Ernst August of Hanover, in Jessen ed., *Die deutsche Revolution*, p. 311.

24 Letter from King Frederick William IV to Schwarzenberg, in Jessen ed., *Die deutsche Revolution*, p. 313.

25 Ibid., p. 314.

26 Siemann, *German Revolution*, p. 201.

27 'Die Akzeptierung der Reichsverfassung der Paulskirche durch 28 kleine Teilstaaten Deutschlands', 14 April 1849, quoted from E. R. Huber, *Deutsche Verfassungsgeschichte seit 1789*, 3rd edn, vol. 1 (Stuttgart, 1988), pp. 410f.

28 Ibid., pp. 340f (Article 7).
29 J. Ph. Becker and Ch. Esselen, *Geschichte der süddeutschen Mai-Revolution des Jahres 1849* (Geneva, 1849), p. 11, quoted from Christoph Klessmann, 'Zur Sozialgeschichte der Reichsverfassungskampagne von 1849', in *Historische Zeitschrift*, 218, 2 (1974), pp. 336f.
30 Pamphlet of the National Assembly's left-wing parties, 5 May, in Jessen ed., *Die deutsche Revolution*, p. 318.
31 Ibid.
32 Demands by the Offenburg, *Landesversammlung*, 13 May, in Fenske ed., *Quellen*, p. 325.
33 Cf. also letter from Archduke John to Schwarzenberg, in Fenske ed., 10 May, *Quellen*, pp. 320ff.
34 Huber, *Deutsche Verfassungsgeschichte*, vol. 2, p. 860.
35 Some delegates opposed this action, aware that the Assembly, in surrendering its politically and geographically central position, might lose its representative character. Cf. Michael Kienzle and Dirk Mende, '*Wollt Ihr den alten Uhland niederreiten?' Wie die 48er Revolution in Stuttgart ausging* (Stuttgart, 1998), p. 2.
36 Letter from the Württemberg Minister for the Interior to the President of the National Assembly, 17 June, in Fenske ed., *Quellen*, p. 350.
37 Bruno Bauer, *Der Untergang des Frankfurter Parlaments* (Berlin, 1849), pp. 279ff, quoted from Klessmann, 'Zur Sozialgeschichte', pp. 284/4. Cf. also Frederic Engels in Marx and Engels, *Collected Works*, vol. 11 (London, 1977), pp. 91–6.
38 Klessmann, 'Zur Sozialgeschichte', p. 291.
39 Ibid., p. 306.
40 Becker and Esselen, *Geschichte der süddeutschen Mai-Revolution*, pp. 53ff.
41 *Offenburger Wochenblatt*, 14 May, quoted from Franz X. Vollmer, *Offenburg 1848/ 49. Ereignisse und Lebensbilder aus einem Zentrum der badischen Revolution* (Karlsruhe, 1997), p. 176.
42 'Wanders Aufruf zur Gründung des Allgemeinen Deutschen Lehrervereins', in C. L. A. Pretzel, *Geschichte des deutschen Lehrervereins in den ersten 50 Jahren seines Bestehens* (Leipzig, 1921), p. 44.
43 King Frederick William's accusation that elementary school teachers were responsible for 'irreligious mass-wisdom', in M. Michael and H. H. Schepp eds, *Politik und Schule von der Französischen Revolution bis zur Gegenwart*, vol. 1 (Frankfurt/M., 1973), pp. 313f.
44 Cf. Valentin, *Geschichte*, vol. 2, p. 489.
45 Klessmann, 'Zur Sozialgeschichte', p. 309.
46 For evidence cf. Klessmann, 'Zur Sozialgeschichte', pp. 286f and Alfred G. Frei and Kurt Hochstuhl, *Wegbereiter der Deomokratie. Die badische Revolution 1848/49. Der Traum von der Freiheit* (Karlsruhe, 1997), pp. 95ff.
47 Valentin, *Geschichte*, vol. 2, p. 480.
48 Klessmann, 'Zur Sozialgeschichte', p. 306.
49 Ibid., p. 315, and Vollmer, *Offenburg*, p. 173.
50 Protocol of *Volksversammlung* in Nuremberg, quoted from Valentin, *Geschichte*, vol. 2, p. 492.
51 Cf. Vollmer, *Offenburg*, pp. 173–9.
52 Ibid., p. 174.
53 Ibid., pp. 176f.
54 Edmund Wilson, *To the Finland Station* (London, 1966), p. 272.

55 Cf. Valentin, *Geschichte*, vol. 2, p. 517.
56 Ibid., p. 509.
57 Gordon A. Craig, *The Politics of the Prussian Army, 1640–1945* (New York and Oxford, 1956), p. 107.
58 Cf. report by Oberstleutnant Staroste of 12 June, in Jessen ed., *Die deutsche Revolution*, p. 328.
59 King Frederick William IV to Bunsen (3 April), quoted from Botzenhart, *Deutscher Parlamentarismus*, p. 695. Cf. also Ranke's report in Leopold von Ranke, *Preußische Geschichte, vol. 4, 1815–1871* (Munich, 1966), p. 86.
60 Quoted from R. Hachtmann, *Berlin 1848. Eine Politik- und Gesellschaftsgeschichte der Revolution* (Bonn, 1997), p. 231. Julius' prophetic words finally became reality after the Second World War, when the new German *Bundeswehr* was created specifically as an army of 'citizens in uniform'.
61 Proclamation of the *Zentralmärzverein* to German soldiers in Grab ed., 6 May, *Die Revolution*, p. 200.
62 Quoted from Valentin, *Geschichte*, vol. 2, p. 484.
63 Events in these areas have been fully discussed in Sperber, *Rhineland Radicals*, Valentin, *Geschichte*, vol. 2, pp. 448–545 and Klessmann, 'Zur Sozialgeschichte'; here only a summary which will focus on the military situation.
64 Cf. Sperber, *Rhineland Radicals*, p. 368.
65 Valentin, *Geschichte*, vol. p. 497.
66 Ibid., p. 505.
67 Klessmann, 'Zur Sozialgeschichte', p. 309.
68 Cf. Frei and Hochstuhl, *Wegbereiter*, p. 99.
69 Ibid., p. 101.
70 Ibid., pp.102f.
71 For a detailed account cf. the report by the Imperial Commissioner Friedrich Joseph Zell, in Fenske ed., *Quellen*, pp. 332f.
72 Proclamation of 19 May, in Grab ed., *Die Revolution*, p. 209.
73 Valentin, *Geschichte*, vol. 2, p. 513.
74 Frei and Hochstuhl, *Wegbereiter*, p. 117.
75 Ibid., p. 125.
76 Ibid., p. 126.
77 Cf. Valentin, *Geschichte*, vol. 2, p. 523.
78 Uhland, *Werke*, vol. 4, pp. 725f.
79 Cf. reprint of original version in Frei and Hochstuhl, *Wegbereiter*, p. 176.

Chapter 8

Forces of reaction, the counter-revolution and the decline of political life

Introduction

Most accounts of the 1848/9 revolutions conclude with either the collapse of the National Parliament in Stuttgart or with the surrender of the fortress in Rastatt. The decade between 1849 and 1859 has usually been neglected within this context and until recently has been the least well researched decade in nineteenth-century German history.[1] However, the impact of the revolutions' 'defeat' cannot be fully appreciated without an assessment of the major developments of this post-revolutionary decade, involving the reconstitution of the German Confederation and its imposition of repressive measures in public life.

The common denominator of this decade was one of reaction, a concept which has been employed to epitomize that whole period.[2] It denotes an attempt to return to the *status quo ante* and acquired symbolic popularity in 1849 through the image of the crab and the pigtail, defined in political and economic terms as a return to the feudal order of pre-revolutionary days.[3] An analysis of political life in the 1850s will illustrate how the situation had not gone completely into reverse but had, nevertheless, rolled back significantly. While democratic and emancipatory concerns had once again been relegated to the lowest level, Germany, however, avoided a return to the repressive position of the Pre-March period. Although the forces of reaction were once more in control, the industrial revolution, powered by the continuing advance of the railways, was under way. Furthermore, the nationality issue and renewed competition between Austria and Prussia for national leadership ensured that there could be no return to a pre-industrial, anti-modern position. This chapter will concentrate on developments in Austria and Prussia, but will also touch on political positions within the 'Third Germany', as an illustration of how the balance of power between the two major German players was affected by changing alliances elsewhere.

Reactionary policies in Austria and Prussia, a comparison

Austria's position in 1849 differed from that of Prussia in at least three respects.

1. Despite defeating the revolution in her capital by armed force, peace had not yet been secured. The new Austrian government had to turn its attention to Hungary, relying on Russian military help to reverse the losses which she had suffered. With Russia's reputation as Europe's most reactionary state, such an alliance could not fail to leave its mark on the Austrian government.
2. Austria's 'German policy' was fraught with problems. Opposed to the creation of a German nation state, it could neither support the 'larger Germany' solution recommended by von Schmerling, whose position as Minister President in Frankfurt it had undermined,[4] nor could it approve of the 'smaller Germany' solution, necessitating the surrender of its position as premier German power to Prussia.
3. In view of the crucial role played by the Austrian generals and their armies in quashing the revolutions, the Austrian military was able to assume an even more influential position than was the case in Prussia.

While paying lip service to the constitution devised in Kremsier in the immediate aftermath of the revolution, the newly crowned emperor prepared for a neo-absolutist rule. Baron Karl Friedrich von Kübeck, a former associate of Metternich, became president of the newly established *Reichsrat*, an imperial council designed to strengthen the emperor's position in relation to parliament and the Council of Ministers. Throughout 1851 the *Reichsrat* gained in importance, leaving more liberal ministers such as von Schmerling little option but to resign. Ministerial responsibility was virtually at an end and their political influence was transferred to a circle of reactionary advisors who had the ear of the emperor. The *Sylvester Patent* of 1851, inspired by Napoleon's *coup d'état* in Paris,[5] led to the revocation of the liberal constitution of March 1849, to the abolition of most of the Basic Rights and to an inevitable severing of the last bonds with German national democratic aspirations. Only the emancipation of serfs and the guarantee of equal rights for all citizens remained in force, both more in line with the enlightened reforms of Joseph II than with the aims of the German revolutions. The new political system operated on strictly bureaucratic lines, based on 'a standing army of soldiers, a sitting army of officials, a kneeling army of priests and a creeping army of denunciators'[6] and laid the foundation of the 'K and K' monarchical regime.[7] One critic of the new regime described it as 'a second edition of the Metternichian system, on cheaper paper and with worse type'.[8] The climate for political turncoats had arrived. Kübeck abandoned his liberal democratic outlook to revert to his original conservatism, while Alexander Bach, the reformer of spring 1848 and justice minister in the Wessenberg government, now became Kübeck's closest confidant and took over the new government on his death in 1855. The 'Bach system' was based on the 'omnipotence of the bureaucracy and the police, the influence of generals and aristocrats on the Emperor, government by the cabinet and, above all, on the church, the Jesuits and clericalism'.[9]

This new reactionary absolutism was modernist to the extent that it deployed the latest advances in science and technology and pursued a modernist economics policy. A treaty with the German Customs Union was agreed in 1853, further enhanced by a currency agreement; a free-market policy was applied to trade and industry from 1859. Following Schwarzenberg's death in 1852, Francis Joseph effectively took over the running of the army and, the next year, the regulation of military affairs was transferred from civilian control to the authority of the army. The church continued as a pillar of imperial power. Bishops were more closely bound by imperial edict than by papal influence, with virtually no direct access to Rome and requiring the emperor's seal of approval prior to their investiture.[10] When ecclesiastical pressure sought to remedy this absolutist situation,[11] a compromise was reached in 1855, when Frances Joseph signed a concordat with Rome, securing an important measure of independence for the Austrian clergy and affirming its links with the Habsburg throne. Through its own network of officials and bureaucratic institutions, the administration, preserving a degree of independence even from imperial influence, managed to erect a system that was virtually unaccountable to politicians. Representing not only a state within a state, it actually took over the body politic, with expenditure on the administration increasing eight-fold.[12] The command structure was both centralized and 'Germanized'. German became the official language throughout the Austrian Empire, its influence surviving well beyond 1918 and accounting for the widespread knowledge of German throughout the Balkan countries today. The *Gendarmerie* became a 'chief instrument of the new regime',[13] its significance to be discussed later. A measure of the administration's success was the ending of martial law, previously imposed over Vienna and Prague,[14] as the new methods of police surveillance and a major increase in police strength rendered the old emergency laws superfluous.

In contrast to Austria, Prussia emerged from the revolutionary upheavals in a less stable, but essentially more modern shape. Although Frederick William's rejection of the imperial crown had effectively ended the revolution in Prussia, it failed to extinguish all opposition to the new reactionary policies, especially in Prussia's western territories. The rejection of the crown must be seen in the context of the king's own plans for a united Germany. He still sought to adhere to his self-imposed role as national leader, hoping to assume the position of regent by seeking the consent of all the crowned heads of Germany and thus bypassing the 'populist democratic' National Assembly.[15] To this end, a special role was assigned to Joseph Maria von Radowitz who had gained the king's confidence during the Berlin revolution of March 1848. Radowitz had recognized, at an early stage of the revolutions, that liberal constitutionalists were in opposition to the social policies of democrats, leaving these political forces divided. Elected to the National Assembly, he had joined the *Café Milani* faction, the most extreme right-wing group at Frankfurt. After the spring of 1849 many prominent liberals joined him, in an effort to salvage what remained of the nationality issue. A Prussian memorandum of 9 May mapped out a revised plan,[16] with the objective of forming a German Federation based on the existing dynastic order, but envisaging a 'smaller Germany' with special links to Austria. When Schwarzenberg rejected this proposal, a new conflict between Austria and Prussia seemed probable. In an attempt to avoid war, Radowitz organized the Berlin Conference, where the governments of Prussia, Hanover, Saxony, Württemberg and Bavaria met to consider the establishment of a German Federation. The southern German states, traditionally closer to Austria than to Prussia, soon withdrew from this venture, leaving the three remaining kingdoms to form the *Dreikönigsbündnis* (26 May 1849).

Although its new constitution contained several liberal elements, adopted from the Frankfurt Imperial Constitution, the major democratic input was omitted. The principle of 'agreement' between the various princes and their parliaments was intended to loosen basic constitutional constraints and an absolute veto guaranteed the new chief authority, effectively the Prussian king, virtual independence from parliament.[17] The king's absolutist position was further strengthened by the nature of the new parliament, which was no longer elected by universal suffrage, but by an indirect, class-based system. At this stage, Saxony and Hanover already expressed some reservations, obviously fearful of Austria's likely reaction. The majority of former liberal delegates to the National Assembly met at Gotha and signed a declaration in support of the Prussian plan. Despite this gesture of liberal backing for the new national federation, all the major states of the Third Germany withheld their support and by the end of the year only twenty-six minor states endorsed the union. The newly constituted *Reichstag*, which met in Erfurt in March 1850, consisted predominantly of liberal delegates, while – for different reasons – factions of both the right and the left in Germany failed to support this experiment.

Austrian–Prussian rivalry

Austria's political and military position had by now recovered and Schwarzenberg managed to form a powerful alliance against the Prussian plans for a 'lesser Germany'. Reactionary Russia and the formerly liberal southern German states found themselves alongside Austria in opposition to the German Union. When old constitutional conflicts erupted again in Holstein as well as in Hesse, the traditional rivalry between Prussia and Austria could no longer be contained. On both occasions, Austria supported the established, reactionary forces, manoeuvring Prussia into siding with the new nationalists. In both instances Prussia was defeated, in the case of Holstein, having to concede ultimate control over Schleswig and Holstein to Denmark. Prussia's case was thwarted, especially after the re-establishment of the German Confederation, which a majority of German states had re-joined, and by the settlement agreed at the London Conference of 1852. The Holstein conflict had strengthened Radowitz' position, leading to his appointment as Prussian Foreign Secretary,[18] but the problems in Hesse brought about his downfall. In February 1850, Grand Duke Frederick William sacked his liberal-reformist cabinet, in an effort to gain absolute government control. The Hesse parliament refused to sanction either this move, or the new government's change of political direction, away from Prussia and towards Austria and the revival of the German Confederation. In the wake of its refusal to sanction the new government's budget, the Grand Duke dissolved parliament (12 June 1850), invoking a constitutional crisis. Hesse's civil servants, army officers and judges refused to renounce their oath to the constitution, tenaciously upholding the old liberal order. In September a state of emergency was declared. At the height of the conflict the Grand Duke and his prime minister fled, requesting military assistance from Austria and the German Confederation. The Confederation's decision to intervene in Hesse also threatened Prussia's established rights of passage through the Grand Duchy, the essential link between the two parts of her territory. By November, Prussian army units confronted the Confederation troops, primarily Bavarian, Württemberg and Austrian contingents. Radowitz was prepared to risk a war, but a majority of the Prussian government advised a more conciliatory policy. With the signing of the Olmütz Proclamation (November 1850), Prussia effectively conceded defeat, abandoning the Erfurt Union together with its national aspirations,[19] while Austria's superiority was re-established in Germany. Her position as leader of the Confederation was confirmed in August 1851, allowing for a return to the reactionary legislation passed in 1819 and 1834. Following the defeat of the liberal cause in the spring and summer of 1849, Austria's re-entry into German politics meant that the national cause was also lost.

Radowitz was forced to resign his position; his downfall caused not primarily by the political defeat imposed on Prussia, but by the Prussian *camarilla*, where the Gerlach brothers opposed him from a narrowly Protestant and 'Borussian' base. Ludwig von Gerlach, in particular, a prominent member of the *Treubund mit Gott für König und Vaterland*, condemned Prussia's new German policies and worked towards a revival of traditional Prussian monarchical principles. Backed by the *Treubund*, which recruited mostly from among the lower middle classes and the civil service, he pursued a neo-absolutist policy and tried to retain the old corporate order.[20] His brother Leopold opposed Radowitz on the grounds that his 'sharp logical reasoning' would influence the king into adopting a policy of modernizing Prussia by furthering the German national cause.[21]

These divisions inside Prussian court circles must be seen as part of the counter-revolutionary re-alignment. As Radowitz' fall signified victory for the reactionary *camarilla*, the Olmütz Proclamation was not universally denounced. The agreement was viewed as a humiliating defeat for Prussia, both by the 'Gotha liberals' and national-conservative politicians, who had supported a federative principle, based on a constitution along the lines of the British system.[22] However, this was not the view of Prussia's neo-absolutist faction, associated with the *Treubund*, who had a majority of its support within the army and among the *Junkers* east of the Elbe. Totally opposed to any form of 'Vereinbarung' (agreement), which to them was a move towards popular sovereignty and ultimately democracy, they resisted any means of allowing parliamentary influence over the setting of the budget, fearful that such a step would damage a future German emperor's suspensive veto.[23] To counter such 'democratic' tendencies they advocated discipline, total loyalty to the crown and a further extension of military control over public life.[24] In similar vein they opposed the liberal national colours, which were no longer displayed at the Frankfurt Confederation after 1852, and they vetoed the establishment of a German navy, recalling the Prussian contingents to the home fleet.[25] Otto von Manteuffel, succeeding Brandenburg as prime minister after his sudden death in 1850, saw the Olmütz Proclamation as an opportunity to promote his own reactionary policies and Otto von Bismarck, conservative member of the Erfurt parliament and opposed to Radowitz, declared that there was nothing shameful in the agreement. Bismarck's own memoirs vividly relate the tensions at the Berlin court. He condemned Radowitz as a 'catholicizing opponent of Prussia',[26] dismissed Gagern as an arrogant demagogue and, in his speech to the *Landtag*, days after the Olmütz Proclamation, criticized liberals and supporters of a German nation state:

In my opinion Prussia's honour is not upheld by assuming the role of Don Quixote throughout Germany, on behalf of resentful municipal office holders, fearing for their local constitutions. I would rather seek to uphold the honour of Prussia by keeping her distance, in particular, from all shameful associations with democracy, by denying that in this as well as in all other issues anything may happen in Germany without Prussia's consent, so that whatever Prussia and Austria, jointly and independently, consider to be reasonable and politically right, will be carried out together by these two protecting powers of Germany.[27]

The historian Leopold von Ranke, an early admirer of Bismarck, considered Olmütz a 'defeat' for Prussia,[28] but one which could be exploited to accelerate Prussian regeneration. While accepting the need for constitutional government as a means of overcoming internal divisions, he supported a strengthening and reorganization of the army and, in the short term, an accommodation with Austria within the German Confederation, despite his own conviction that such a federative order was outdated.

The position of the 'Third Germany'

The two supreme powers were not alone in undoing the political achievements of the Frankfurt National Assembly. Virtually all the 'March Ministries' in the 'third' Germany were replaced by reactionary politicians, usually opposed to any constitutional reforms. In Württemberg, where the Römer government had forced the king to accept the Imperial Constitution and a one-chamber parliament promoted liberal and democratic issues, this episode ended with Römer's dismissal and the dissolution of parliament (28 October 1849).[29] When new elections in December returned the radical-democratic party with a decisive majority, the king proceeded to dissolve parliament three times, finally abolishing the constitution in favour of a pre-revolutionary system, based on corporate principles. By 1851 the democrats faced defeat; the new constitution and the royal *coup d'état* were approved by a new parliament. The new government under Freiherr von Linden revived the pre-revolutionary political order, prohibiting almost all clubs and associations, severely restricting press freedom, purging the civil service of liberal elements and exercising strict control over the universities.[30]

In Baden and Saxony military rule was sanctioned in order to revoke the liberal legislation, defy the parliamentary majorities and crush popular dissent. Only Bavaria managed to pursue her liberal course for some time, under the government of Ludwig Freiherr von der Pfordten. He forged a coalition of the patriarchal nobility with the popular catholic clergy and local notables, but on the basis of Pre-March principles of constitutionalism. Pfordten's chief policy was to retain Bavaria's independence, avoiding too close an association with Austria while supporting her anti-Prussian policy, in particular her opposition to the Erfurt Union. With the support of the centrist parties, he steered a middle course between the ultra-conservative aristocracy and the party of democratic liberalism. New press and assembly restrictions indicated a reactionary trend, but adhered to the country's constitution. From 1852 the powers of the police increased markedly and in 1859 a constitutional crisis, brought about by Pfordten's break with the democratic liberals, led to the abolition of parliament and new electoral laws.[31] Bavaria had become the last state to succumb to the reactionary order, just at a time when new policies in Prussia heralded the end of this reactionary decade.

With the exception of Austria and Mecklenburg, every German state had retained at least some semblance of constitutional government, retaining a fragile consensus between liberal and conservative forces. It is difficult to know whether this consensus was a sign of weakness on the part of the liberals[32] or whether it reveals a traditional liberal tendency of ultimately rejecting radical and revolutionary forces.[33]

The nature of internal Prussian strife will have indicated that the long-standing rivalry between Austria and Prussia was in fact largely the result of factional conflict between reactionary and modernist forces and could soon be overcome in the pursuit of mutual interests. Both countries were paralysed by anxiety over new revolutions and international threats, leading Alexis de Tocqueville to comment that the revolutionary disease in Germany 'may be temporarily arrested but . . . cannot be cured'.[34] The efforts of the German states in establishing a defence against potential revolutionary turmoil resulted in the creation of an efficient, all-pervasive bureaucracy, intent on regulating the public sphere. In the case of Austria this involved a closer rapprochement with the German Confederation, in Prussia's case it meant moving away from the national objectives of Frankfurt and Erfurt and a return to the pre-revolutionary political order.[35] The new system of surveillance and control, though outwardly less oppressive than under Metternich, proved significantly more efficient. Improved methods of control could by now take advantage of new technical advances and of a bureaucratic system which was virtually unanswerable to parliamentary or government authority and had an unprecedented degree of independence.

Several historians have attempted to weigh the 'negative' reactionary policies of the 1850s against the 'positive' achievements in economic and technical terms.[36] Such a favourable interpretation seems, on the whole, too concerned with the purely instrumentalist functions of modernism, with industrial advances and market forces, overlooking the decline in political awareness and a reversal in the emancipation process, which were ultimately responsible for the anti-democratic and a-political outlook of the Austrian and German public after 1870. The term 'reactionary modernism' comes to mind, employed by Jeffrey Herff in a different context[37] to describe the typically German bifurcation between industrial progress and the rejection of those major political tenets which are associated with the Enlightenment and the adoption of a democratic political culture.[38]

This simultaneity was itself the hallmark of a period of reactionary policies in Germany. The division occurred following a time when moral values and idealistic concepts in philosophy were being undermined, encouraging a purely functional, predominantly materialistic approach to all aspects of the human domain. In order to demonstrate the dangers inherent in such a bifurcation, three issues, significant for the post-revolutionary decade, will be examined: 1. An all pervasive bureaucratization with its 'nationwide' control of public life, 2. the emergence of *Realpolitik* and 3. the failure of liberalism during the 1850s.

The bureaucratization of public life

In the aftermath of the 1848/9 revolutions, the systems of bureaucracy developed in Austria and Prussia extended state control into virtually all walks of life, replacing pre-revolutionary absolutism with a system of control which consolidated and refined the German tradition of political *étatism*[39] to a hitherto unimaginable degree. It is customary to seek the roots of this *étatism* in absolutism and in Hegel's philosophy of state, but its fullest flowering can be found in the post-revolutionary decade, when state control was employed specifically to implement reactionary policies.[40] Prussian education was to face the full force of this agenda through the 'school regulative' of 1854. This regulative, responsible for elementary schools and teacher-training colleges, used its authority to eradicate all enlightened forms of pedagogy and to suppress teachers' associations. Through a number of reactionary edicts, general education was transformed into a system that would produce citizens, unquestioning in their loyalty to the royal family and to state religion, and destined for a life of submission and servitude. These secondary virtues of obedience, discipline and the mechanical repetition of the catechism became the mainstay of school routine. Student teachers were no longer instructed in psychology, pedagogy or other academic disciplines normally associated with the teaching profession and were even denied the pleasure of reading modern literature – including Goethe and Schiller. In the spirit of Friedrich Julius Stahl's anti-emancipatory, anti-enlightened doctrine of the Christian state,[41] the 'regulative' was a 'first attempt by the state to consistently abuse the public education system as a means for ideological indoctrination and discipline'.[42] This process was deliberately designed to subdue elementary school teachers, who – in the opinion of the king – had been chiefly responsible for the kind of 'irreligious wisdom of the masses', designed to alienate ordinary people from the monarchy and to incite them to revolutionary anarchy.[43]

State bureaucracy was also involved in refining a police and surveillance system that could be deployed throughout the German Confederation. The *Polizeiverein* (Police Association), a secret police force, initially operating in the seven largest states inside the Confederation became the chief instrument through which reactionary bureaucrats could monitor political parties, associations, newspapers and liberal parliamentarians. Originally envisaged as a unified police force covering the whole Confederation and unaccountable, even to individual state governments, it proved unsuccessful against states such as Bavaria which were anxious to preserve their independence.[44] However, such was the power of state bureaucracy that it was possible to establish an improved system of clandestine police operations, based on the cooperation of chief of police Hinkeldey in Berlin and his colleagues in Vienna, Munich and Stuttgart. The necessity for such an initiative was confirmed at a top-level secret police conference in Dresden between Manteuffel and Schwarzenberg in April 1851. Permission for such co-operation was usually granted by royal consent, without any parliamentary consultation or official documentation. The objectives of this new force were 'the shared surveillance of all of Germany' and speedy communication between individual forces.[45] Special attention was paid to 'suspect' cities such as Hamburg, Bremen and Frankfurt and to exiled organizations in London and Paris. Individual police forces went beyond exchanging suspects' details; they were also prepared to circulate confiscated and secretly intercepted communications, providing information on prominent figures and literary material. Through agents in New York, Paris, Brussels, Zurich and London, the police investigated not only German exiles, but all 'heads of revolutionary parties',[46] and activists including Giuseppe Mazzini, Victor Hugo, Louis Blanc and Karl Marx. The names of the various organizations under surveillance are too numerous to mention, they included workers' associations, gymnasts' clubs, student fraternities, artists' groups and masonic lodges. At local level, social structures became strained under the weight of such police scrutiny and even party politics was criminalized, with the terms 'political police' or even 'state police' being used in police documents.[47]

The use of censorship was also refined, with some states persecuting newspapers and journals in an attempt to destroy the last bastion of a democratic public. The Prussian press laws of March 1850 were outwardly perhaps no worse than the laws of the Metternich era. In substance, however, the new control mechanisms were far more restrictive: censorship, now transferred from the police to the administration, became more remote and even less transparent than during the Pre-March period. Responsibility for the printed word was no longer solely the author's, but extended to the publisher, the printer and even the bookseller. Shopkeepers were particularly vulnerable, since they could hardly be expected to have an intimate knowledge of every book in stock. While the number of confiscated publications was not particularly high, authorities staged special operations to intimidate booksellers who were naturally reluctant to risk severe fines or confiscation. The Prussian press law is only one example of what was commonplace in other states. Newspapers and magazines had to be submitted to specially appointed censors prior to distribution, and sales could be delayed by weeks. The *Nürnberger Kurier*, for instance, was confiscated fifty-three times within a three-month period. Most seizures were arbitrary, amounting to mindless harassment: the Munich *Volksbote* was seized for allegedly undermining the authority of the Bavarian minister president, by reporting that he had slipped on an icy road.[48] Print media from abroad or from other German states fared little better. Their prohibition could be effected by the ministry of the interior without any prior approach to a court of law.

Despite the strictures of the Prussian school regulative, academic freedom was formally guaranteed. Nevertheless, persecution and surveillance was widespread and a number of university professors lost their position or faced prosecution. The most spectacular case was that of Professor Gervinus who was accused of high treason on the grounds that he expressed the view that the age of monarchies was over. In references to France and the United States, he welcomed the prospect of a democratic system in Germany, a controversial opinion that cost him his post as professor and a prison sentence of four months, later suspended.[49]

> If a democratic order can be formed in Germany, emanating out of her aristocratic order, in the same manner in which the aristocratic emanated from the imperial [the Holy Roman Empire], with the same clear succession and structure and without major and debilitating disruption, then Germany will have a successful historical continuity of enviable security and in a similar vein of modest grandeur.[50]

Although there are no precise details of university life available for this period, it is known that at least fourteen other professors lost their positions.[51] By the end of the 1850s pressure on the universities receded, but the damage had been done. The liberal climate had vanished from the universities to be replaced by a fiercely nationalistic outlook, strengthened by the fact that science and technology were expanding at the expense of the humanities.[52]

Bureaucratic neo-absolutism was also instrumental in hardening governmental attitudes to constitutional checks and balances. The German Confederation became the vehicle for reviving pre-revolutionary laws in this area. The *Bundesreaktionsbeschluß* of August 1851 was established as a means of examining all reformist laws, especially those introduced in the more liberal states of the Third Germany. In addition to press freedom and the surveillance of suspect activities, three further issues were rigorously scrutinized.

1. **Military allegiance to the constitution.** Members of the regular armies no longer swore their loyalty to the constitution, but bore allegiance to their respective crowned heads of state. As already discussed in the case of Hesse, the Confederation supported the actions of the Grand Duke and his government, contrary to the laws of the existing constitution.[53]

2. **A class-based franchise.** Here the Confederation exercised its influence mainly against smaller states, especially those which still supported the Basic Rights. It sought to promote Prussia's three-tier electoral system, based on an individual's tax obligations, whereby the vote of a wealthy man with high taxation obligations would be worth three times more than that of a low-paid worker or modest craftsman. Furthermore, an open voting system left anyone who depended on the wealthier classes no choice but to vote for their influential patrons. The resulting changes in the Prussian parliament and in the Berlin city council were grotesque: of the Berlin electorate, only 3.1 per cent belonged to the first class, 9.4 per cent belonged to the second class and 87.5 per cent belonged to the third. The July elections demonstrated the impact of the new franchise. While previously Berlin, with its high proportion of working-class citizens had sent only democratic delegates to the Prussian parliament, now only conservative members were returned.[54] In many other cities the lower classes boycotted the July ballot. In Wetzlar, democrats did not vote and also abstained from elections to the Erfurt parliament,[55] while in other German towns and districts fierce battles waged between those liberals who supported the new suffrage system and a democratic majority who favoured an election boycott.[56]

3. **Fiscal control** One of the major achievements of the March governments was the right of parliament to determine their government's budget. With the return of the old political process, parliaments all over Germany lost this budgetary control, giving rise to constitutional conflicts such as occurred in Prussia in 1861, where Bismarck was successful in effectively removing parliament's last chance to retain any constitutional power.[57]

The emergence of *Realpolitik*

The counter-revolutionary victory meant, above all else, the defeat of constitutional reform with disastrous consequences for parliamentary democracy in general.[58] The new authoritarianism led to a re-alignment of the whole state apparatus, affecting in particular the attitudes of the predominantly liberal middle and lower ranks of the civil service, who now became increasingly more attached to the monarchic system. Such changes would not have been possible without a fundamental change of values, comparable perhaps to the changes which affected public life in the Western world in the post 1968 era. Any discussion of such changes must take into account the wider ideological implications of the philosophical positions that were prevalent during the first six decades of the nineteenth century. The Pre-March period had already experienced a move away from the idealistic philosophies of the 'spirit', usually associated with Hegel and Fichte, towards more 'realistic' positions, favouring the superiority of matter over spirit. It was precisely in this context that Marx could claim that he had turned Hegel from his head back on to his feet, in order 'to discover the rational kernel within the mystical shell':

> My dialectical method is not only different from the Hegelian, but is its direct opposite. To Hegel, the life process of the human brain, i.e., the process of thinking, which, under the name of 'the Idea', he even transforms into an independent subject, is the demiurgos of the real world, and the real world is only the external, phenomenal form of 'the Idea'. With me, on the contrary, the ideal is nothing else than the material world reflected by the human mind, and translated into forms of thought.[59]

Although the actual changes in philosophy cannot be mapped out here, it is important to recognize that the 1848/9 revolutions were themselves part of a wide change of parameter. More than mere proclamations of intent, they, too, had looked towards real political power and measurable social and economic change. Once this slow, but continuous change has been recognized, it will become clear that the counter-revolutions were themselves part of the revolutionary process and that both tendencies constituted elements within a wider shift of philosophical outlook.

The emergence of the term *Realpolitik* must be viewed in this broader context. Though normally associated with Bismarck's policies, which placed the interests of the new German nation state above moral or philosophical considerations, the term was actually coined by August Ludwig von Rochau, a writer broadly sympathetic to the ideas of 1848 who, in his younger years, had been associated with radical democratic policies. A member of the *Burschenschaften* at Göttingen University, he had joined in storming the guardhouse in 1833; he also had contacts with the writers Jakob Venedy, a democratic republican and August Werth, the principal organizer of the *Hambach* festival. In the aftermath of the revolutions Rochau anonymously published his *Grundsätze der Realpolitik, angewandt auf die Zustände Deutschlands* in 1853.[60] Rochau summarized his experiences during the 1830s and 1840s with the conclusion that 'the law of power exercises a similar dominance on matters of state as the law of gravity does over bodies'.[61] The critical issue for Rochau was no longer the theoretical problem of the nature of right, virtue, wisdom, but the practical problem of how to exercise power most effectively: 'To rule means to exercise power and this can only be done by those in possession of power. This immediate connection between power and domination forms the basic truth of all politics and the key to all history.'[62] With reference to Germany, Rochau believed that 'the fragmented German powers will not be united by a principle, an idea, or a treaty, but only by an overwhelming power that will subdue the rest', for 'power is the precondition for a nation's fortune'.[63] In contrast to Bismarck's later *Realpolitik*, Rochau does not attribute this power to the army, the government or any other state authority, but to the educated and property-owning middle classes. In this, he approaches the liberal position of Dahlmann who had suggested in 1845 that politics must be 'reduced to the base and the extent of existing [political and social] conditions'.[64]

Rochau's concept anticipated historical developments by more than a generation. For the time being, actual political power remained with the state and, in particular, with state bureaucracy and the army. Power became wedded to *Staatsräson* (reasons of state). This concept adhered to the principle that the political process should enhance the power of the state, regardless as to whether this power is used internally against specific groups or externally for imperialist aims. Rochau came to embrace the formula of 'might is right', believing that the successful outcome of an enterprise justified its political means. In the second volume of his *Grundsätze*, Rochau invested Prussia with the task of developing the new Germany, describing this as 'a necessary natural law that cannot be judged by private morality'.[65] For him, success became the final judgement of history, and it is in such statements that the naked imperialism and the nationalist search for *Lebensraum* (living space), which were to curse the twentieth century, can be anticipated.[66]

There seems to be some valid connection between Rochau's political formula and Gustav Freytag's best-selling novel *Soll und Haben*, published in 1855. This work depicts a change from the old corporate order of aristocrats, artisans and peasants to the newly emerging middle classes whose fortunes were founded on trade, commodities and manufacturing. A sound balance of 'credit and debit', the title of the book, is rated more highly than sentimental feelings[67] or an impressive aristocratic lineage. At the height of the love scene between the two main characters, the young lady discloses her accounts to the conscientious, reliable, but slightly timid young man. Accepting him as a husband, she also sees him as her business partner, suggesting that he 'come and have a look at my credit and debit,' leaving her brother to comment that, 'Property and prosperity are of no value for the individual or for the state, without the wholesome energy which grasps the inert metal in a life-giving momentum'.[68] The book rejects revolution, associating it with disorder, ugly excess and false romanticism.[69] With no mention of the German revolutions, the Polish revolution is shown in a very negative light. The 'Polish economy' appears not to be based on discipline, industriousness and firm government, but subject to the effects of insurrection, anarchy, lascivious drunkenness and a very superficial *joie de vivre*.[70] Germans are inevitably seen as the superior race, with a mission to colonize Eastern Europe:

> We and the Slavs, it is an old struggle. And we acknowledge with pride that on our side is education and culture, a delight in work, profit. Whatever Polish country squires may have become in this region – and there are many intelligent and rich men amongst them – every *thaler*, which they can afford to spend, they have acquired in one way or the other, through German efficiency. . . . Not the policies of intrigue, but our peaceful methods, our labour, has given us rightful authority over this land.[71]

This passage and the other quotations serve to illustrate how the least salient aspects of the German revolutions, national pride and faith in a new national destiny, were honed into a fierce nationalism, while the democratic aspects have been discarded in favour of secondary values. Freytag's novel suggests that the political will of the people can best be displayed in conflict situations beyond their borders or, in dealing with Jews, seen as an undesirable minority within their own society.[72]

Within this development of *Realpolitik*, Rochau and Freytag both recognized a definitive split between the industrial working class and the broader spectrum of middle-class craftsmen.[73] This new post-revolutionary working class was seen to recruit from among farm labourers, small-scale craftsmen and journeymen who accepted the term 'proletarian', attributed to them both by the political left and by reactionary forces. The term 'Lumpenproletariat', frequently used by Marx and Engels[74] is echoed in the *Lumpensammlerlied* of 1849,[75] where the term is accepted in anticipation of the development of an emancipated proletariat, of a future society where 'silk and velvet', 'splendour and folly' will be rejected. This new self-esteem on the part of the proletariat was one of the more important aspects which emerged during the revolutions and which survived beyond the period of reaction. While the new bourgeoisie sought to establish itself by association with the aristocracy, imitating their life styles and adopting their social values, the new working class had grown in confidence and found expression in a separate identity, eventually leading to the wider network of trade unionism.[76]

The 'failure' of liberalism

The established view among historians and political scientists interpreted the defeat of the revolutions as the failure of German liberalism,[77] but, since the 1980s, such assumptions have been questioned.[78] There is no doubt that most liberals assumed an anti-revolutionary position almost as soon as the revolutions were under way, seeing their own achievements in danger of being overturned by more radical, democratic and republican policies. They attempted to focus on constitutional reform and the establishment of a comprehensive set of basic laws, as preconditions for a liberal rule of law (*Rechtsstaat*). Following the demise of the National Assembly in Frankfurt and Stuttgart, most liberal politicians pursued an increasingly opportunistic course, prepared to accept even the most deleterious compromise in exchange for political recognition.

While virtually no liberals supported Austria's claim to German leadership, since she had established herself as 'the wicked principle of Germany', associated with the dark forces of Jesuitism and an autocratic police system,[79] they generally believed that Prussia could bring about the desired unification of Germany. To this end, they followed Gagern, Dahlmann and Droysen along the more 'realistic' path of post-revolutionary politics, abandoning the constitutional positions of the 'old' liberals of the southwest, associated with Rotteck and Welcker.[80] Whereas Rotteck had preferred liberty, even at the expense of national unity,[81] Dahlmann stipulated a different concept of freedom, based on political power which was unsustainable without national unification. Most liberals accepted Dahlmann's interpretation of *Realpolitik*: 'the drive to power is the only route which can satisfy the seething urge for freedom. For it is not only freedom which we Germans demand; it is, to an even greater extent, power which we crave.'[82]

However, the motives for such a political shift cannot be exclusively explained as the result of a new 'materialistic' ideological approach, but are deeply embedded in a romantic historicism. Jacob Grimm, the founder of *Germanistik*, is one such individual who was willing to give preference to everything German or Germanic, be this the Lutheran interpretation of the Christian faith[83] or German domination in Italy and Poland. Ernst Moritz Arndt took a similarly nationalistic stance. Written while a delegate at Frankfurt, his political poems envisaged a new dawn for 'Germania',[84] a revival of Barbarossa's glorious empire, now transposed on to the Hohenzollern dynasty, while attacking cosmopolitan French, English and Polish influences. These nationalist demands were by no means the exception: during the summer of 1848, Dahlmann had come to advocate a united Germany under Prussian domination, no longer based on Rousseau's principle of the sovereignty of the people, but on love for the fatherland, fused into a nation state, representing a 'divine order which would unite the king and his people'.[85] Together with his political allies, including his friends Gagern, Bassermann, Beseler, Duncker, Grimm, Haym and Mathy who had been associated with the centrist Casino party in Frankfurt, Dahlmann was now prepared to sacrifice essential liberal positions in order to achieve Germany's future unity and greatness.[86] With this aim they entered into coalition with their former political opponent Radowitz, prepared even to abandon basic tenets of the Imperial Constitution, which they had supported only a year earlier.

Only very few liberals remained faithful to their original principles, accepting that their political aspirations could never be realized in a Germany under Prussian hegemony. Georg Gottfried Gervinus and Ludwig Bamberger remained steadfast in their liberal convictions, although this led to political isolation and contempt from former associates. As editor of the *Deutsche Zeitung*, Gervinus had once been the unofficial spokesman of the Casino party and had supported the political concept of a constitutional monarchy, but by the autumn of 1848 he gradually shifted his position in favour of a republic.[87] During the campaign for the Imperial Constitution he sympathized with delegates from Hanover, who ignored their government's instructions to leave the National Assembly and even accused British politicians of supporting anti-constitutional policies in various German capitals.[88] In his famous *Introduction to the History of the Nineteenth Century*, Gervinus finally broke with his liberal friends. He rejected British constitutionalism, even expressing some scepticism about the idea of the nation state and pronounced himself in favour of the American Declaration of Independence, where governments derived their powers from the consent of the governed:

> And by introducing the general franchise for all citizens as equal participants within the state, the great democratic principle was pronounced: the rule of the will of the people was expressed in the form of a law.[89]

For Gervinus America had become 'the state of the future' reaching beyond 'self contained nationality' towards 'a universal, all-embracing society . . . and with the nature of world citizenship'.[90] Bearing in mind the German situation, Gervinus perceived the United States 'not as a unitary state, but as a federation, in which the individual states aspire to impose their sovereignty over and above that of the whole, just as the individual aspires to the highest degree of independence within the state'.[91] With such ideas Gervinus found himself in collision with his fellow liberals at Gotha and Erfurt, who had moved in the opposite direction, seeking to integrate the individual into the nation state at the expense of basic individual rights.

Ludwig Bamberger was the other liberal to break ranks with the Gotha party in pursuit of a modernist solution to the German question. Coming from an established banking family and having developed a passionate interest in printing and journalism, Bamberger developed a natural interest in the emancipatory potential of modern technology and commerce. He spoke up for universal progress, a secular society, open to individual enterprise and independent of oppressive state control. During his time as a journalist with the *Mainzer Zeitung* (March–May 1848) he expressed his commitment to a German nation state, based on a democratic constitution, advocating general tolerance and closer links with revolutionary France. While a reporter at the National Assembly he joined the left-of-centre democratic circle of Ruge, Fröbel, Zitz and Jacoby, but also forged contacts with democratic liberals. He supervised the organization of self-help banking facilities for craftsmen and traders and was temporarily involved in the campaign to defend the Imperial Constitution. In exile in Switzerland, he sought to clarify his political position. He was opposed to the Gotha party and a German nation state under Prussian hegemony but supported a united Germany, which was to remain receptive to the influence of Western democracies and devoid of 'völkisch' concepts of nationalism. For similar reasons he also opposed various Eastern European nationalist movements and Prussia's intervention in the Schleswig–Holstein conflict. 'Steam and electricity' were for him the natural exponents of the ideas of 1789,[92] and he advocated a system of free-market capitalism which would give individuals maximum freedom from state interference and guarantee the kind of personal liberty affirmed in the American Declaration of Independence.

Neither Gervinus nor Bamberger were successful in promoting views which could withstand a rising tide of nationalism and a concept of *Realpolitik* which was in strident opposition to the democratic, cosmopolitan and modernist ideas of Western Europe. However, their names remain associated with the more progressive traditions of the German revolutions of 1848/9, with the principles of universal self-determination, of political equality and of a modernism that was prepared to utilize technological advances in the service of an emancipated, progressive society.

One tragic postscript to the history of this formative decade in German history was the loss of thousands of citizens who emigrated to France and Switzerland, but mainly to North America. Exact figures are difficult to obtain, numbers varying considerably, depending on whether they apply only to the United States or include all those who left Germany in the wake of the revolutions.[93] While the number of emigrants before 1848 hardly ever exceeded 100,000 per annum and fell markedly during the years of the revolutions, it rose well above the 100,000 average during the 1850s, reaching a record of approximately 300,000 emigrants in 1854. With their energies, talents and aspirations, many of these men and women made a significant contribution to the development of their new homelands, especially in the USA where they made their mark in journalism, education and the army, taking a major role during the Civil War.[94]

Notes

1 Wolfram Siemann, *Gesellschaft im Aufbruch. Deutschland 1848–1871* (Frankfurt/M., 1990), p. 12.
2 Cf. Gerd-Klaus Kaltenbrunner ed., *Was ist reaktionär?: Zur Dialektik von Fortschritt und Rückschritt* (Munich, Freiburg, Basel and Vienna, 1976).
3 Siemann, *Gesellschaft*, pp. 38f.
4 Cf. von Schmerling's report to the Austrian government (26 December 1848) and Schwarzenberg's memorandum to the Austrian minister von Buol, in Hans Fenske ed., *Quellen zur deutschen Revolution 1848–1849* (Darmstadt, 1996), pp. 244–8 and 248–52.
5 James J. Sheehan, *German History 1770–1866* (Oxford, 1989), p. 723.
6 Ibid., p. 723.
7 This abbreviation refers to the *kaiserlich-königliche* dual monarchy, the union of the Austrian empire with the Hungarian Kingdom.
8 Sheehan, *German History*, p. 723.
9 Frederick Hertz, *The German Public Mind in the Nineteenth Century. A Social History of German Political Sentiments, Aspirations and Ideas* (London, 1975), p. 282.
10 Ernst Rudolf Huber, *Deutsche Verfassungsgeschichte seit 1789*, 3rd edn, vol. 3, (Stuttgart, 1988), p. 155.
11 The minister for education, Count Thun, sided with the Clerical Party, and the minister of police, Freiherr von Keupen, in cahoots with the reactionary old Josephine party, attempted to prevent any rapprochement with the Vatican.
12 Sheehan, *German History*, p. 725.
13 Ibid.
14 Sept. 1853, cf. Huber, *Deutsche Verfassungsgeschichte*, vol. 3, p. 153.
15 Letter by Frederick William IV to Schwarzenberg, 6 April, 1849, in Fenske, *Quellen*, p. 314.
16 Huber, *Deutsche Verfassungsgeschichte*, vol. 2, p. 886.
17 Ibid., p. 887.
18 Ibid., pp. 907f.
19 Ibid., pp. 908–22.
20 Sheehan, *German History*, p. 726.
21 L. v. Gerlach, *Denkwürdigkeiten*, vol. 1 (Berlin, 1850), p. 514, quoted from O. Fürst von Bismarck, *Gedanken und Erinnerungen*, vol. 1 (Stuttgart and Berlin, 1905), pp. 83f.
22 Huber, *Deutsche Verfassungsgeschichte*, vol. 2, pp. 342f.
23 Manfred Botzenhart, *Deutscher Parlamentarismus in der Revolutionszeit 1848–1850* (Düsseldorf, 1977), p. 623.
24 Veit Valentin, *Geschichte der deutschen Revolution 1848–49*, vol. 2 (Berlin, 1931), p. 559.
25 Ibid., p. 567.
26 Bismarck, *Gedanken und*, vol. 1, pp. 83 and 86.
27 Ibid., pp. 92f
28 Leopold von Ranke, *Preußische Geschichte vol. 4, 1815–1871* (Munich, 1966), pp. 94f.
29 Huber, *Deutsche Verfassungsgeschichte*, vol. 3, p. 186.
30 Ibid., pp. 189–91.

31 Ibid., pp. 183–6.
32 Sheehan, *German History*, p. 717 seems to suggest this.
33 Cf. end of this chapter.
34 Alexis de Tocqueville, *Recollections* (New York, 1970), pp. 279f.
35 Huber, *Deutsche Verfassungsgeschichte*, vol. 3, p. 131.
36 In particular Sheehan, *German History*, pp. 710ff and David Blackbourn, *The Fontana History of Germany 1780–1918. The Long Nineteenth Century* (London, 1997), pp. 225ff. Siemann, *Gesellschaft*, p. 20 speaks of a society on the move.
37 Jeffrey Herf, *Reactionary Modernism. Technology, Culture and Politics in Weimar and the Third Reich* (Cambridge University Press, 1984).
38 While today's historians often dispute the theory of a German *Sonderweg*, a case can be made for such a special development, typified by the simultaneity of technological and economic progress and regression in participatory politics.
39 Cf. Kurt Sontheimer, *Grundzüge des politischen Systems der Bundesrepublik Deutschland*, 5th edn (Munich, 1976), p. 86.
40 Cf. Siemann, *Gesellschaft*, p. 19.
41 Cf. Rüdiger Hachtmann, *Berlin 1848, Eine Politik- und Gesellschaftsgeschichte der Revolution* (Bonn, 1997), p. 840.
42 Herwig Blankertz, *Die Geschichte der Pädagogik, von der Aufklärung bis zur Gegenwart* (Wetzlar, 1982), p. 165.
43 Frederick William IV, in B. Michel and H. H. Schepp eds, *Politik und Schule von der Französischen Revolution bis zur Gegenwart*, vol. 1 (Frankfurt/M., 1973), pp. 313f.
44 Cf. Siemann, *Gesellschaft*, p. 43.
45 Ibid., p. 45.
46 Ibid., p. 47.
47 Ibid., p. 50.
48 Ibid., p. 70.
49 Cf. Walter Boehlich, *Der Hochverratsprozeß gegen Gervinus* (Frankfurt/M., 1967).
50 G. G. Gervinus, *Einleitung in die Geschichte des neunzehnten Jahrhunderts* (Leipzig, 1853), pp. 180f.
51 Cf. Siemann, *Gesellschaft*, p. 153.
52 For a more detailed study cf. F. K. Ringer, *The Decline of the German Mandarins* (Harvard University Press, 1969), chapter 1.
53 Huber, *Deutsche Verfassungsgeschichte*, vol. 2, pp. 908ff.
54 Hachtmann, *Berlin 1848*, p. 806.
55 Irene Jung, Hans-Werner Hahn and Rüdiger Störkel, *Die Revolution von 1848 an Lahn und Dill* (Wetzlar, 1998), p. 116.
56 Ibid., pp. 225ff.
57 Thomas Nipperdey, *Deutsche Geschichte 1800–1866. Bürgerwelt und starker Staat*, 6th edn (Munich, 1987), p. 755.
58 Valentin, *Geschichte*, vol. 2, p. 548.
59 Karl Marx and Frederick Engels, *Collected Works, Capital*, vol. 35 (London, 1996), p. 19.
60 August Ludwig von Rochau, *Grundsätze der Realpolitik, angewandt auf die Zustände Deutschlands*, 2 vols. New edn. by H.-U. Wehler (Frankfurt, Berlin and Vienna, 1972).
61 Rochau, *Grundsätze*, vol 1, p. 1.
62 Ibid., p. 2.
63 Ibid., pp. 191 and 59.

64 Friedrich Christoph Dahlmann, 'Die Politik auf den Grund und das Maß der gegebenen *Zustände* zurückgeführt' (1845), quoted from Huber, *Deutsche Verfassungsgeschichte*, vol. 2, p. 387.

65 Rochau, *Grundsätze*, vol. 2 (Heidelberg, 1869), quoted from Karl-Georg Faber, 'Realpolitik als Ideologie. Die Bedeutung des Jahres 1866 für das politische Denken in Deutschland', *Historische Zeitschrift* 203/2 (1966), p. 21.

66 Cf. Sheehan, *German History*, pp. 853f, who sees Rochau as someone who combines 'the heritage of the *Vormärz* with the insistent demands of the new, post-revolutionary age'. Sheehan apparently fails to see the inherent dangers of Rochau's *pleonexia*, unrestrained egoism, a concept pilloried since Plato for its lack of moral justice.

67 Gustav Freytag, *Soll und Haben*, 140th edn, vol. 2 (Leipzig, 1920), p. 311.

68 Ibid., vol. 2, pp. 402 and 404.

69 Ibid., vol. 1, p. 402.

70 Ibid., vol. 2, pp. 17 and 215.

71 Ibid., vol. 2, pp. 155f.

72 The novel is not explicitly anti-Semitic, but it clearly associates Jews with an inferior eastern culture, with corruption and a misappropriation of money. (Cf. also G. Bücher-Hauschild, *Erzählte Arbeit. Gustav Freytag und die soziale Prosa des Vor- und Nachmärz* (Paderborn, 1987), p. 89.

73 Hans-Ulrich Wehler, *Deutsche Gesellschaftsgeschichte*, vol. 2 (Munich, 1987), p. 767.

74 Cf. for instance *Neue Rheinische Zeitung*, 1 and 29 June and 6 November 1848. The term seems derived from Italian *lazzaroni* and suggests an early form of the proletariat, not yet organized and emancipated to strive for political recognition.

75 Quoted from Valentin, *Geschichte*, vol. 2, p. 553.

76 Cf. K. Schönhoven, *Die deutschen Gewerkschaften* (Frankfurt/M., 1987), pp. 24–9.

77 Ralf Dahrendorf, *Society and Democracy in Germany* (New York, 1969), in particular chapter 1.

78 Cf. Christian Jansen, *Einheit, Macht und Freiheit. Die Paulskirchenlinke und die deutsche Politik in der nachrevolutionären Epoche 1849–1867* (Düsseldorf, 2000).

79 Ludwig Bamberger, 'Juche nach Italia', quoted from Christian Jansen, 'Ludwig Bamberger: Mit Dampf und Elektrizität für ein modernes Deutschland', in Sabine Freitag ed., *Die Achtundvierziger. Lebensbilder aus der deutschen Revolution 1848/49* (Munich, 1998), p. 211.

80 Lothar Gall, 'Liberalismus und "bürgerliche Gesellschaft". Zu Charakter und Entwicklung der liberalen Bewegung in Deutschland', in Luthar Gall ed., *Liberalismus*, 2nd edn (Königsstein, 1980), p. 174.

81 Huber, *Deutsche Verfassungsgeschichte*, vol. 2, p. 381.

82 Dahlmann, quoted from Friedrich Meinecke, *Die Idee der Staatsräson in der neueren Geschichte* (Munich and Berlin, 1924), p. 493.

83 Jacob Grimm, quoted from Jürgen Habermas, *Die postnationale Konstellation. Politische Essays* (Frankfurt/M., 1998), p. 21.

84 Ernst Moritz Arndt, *Blätter der Erinnerung, meistens um und aus der Paulskirche in Frankfurt* (Leipzig, 1849), pp. 50f.

85 Friedrich Christoph Dahlmann, 'Zur Verständigung', in *Kleinere Schriften und Reden* (Stuttgart, 1886), p. 260.

86 Cf. Lothar Gall, 'Friedrich Daniel Bassermann: Sei dein eigner Herr und Knecht, das ist des Mittelstandes Recht', in Freitag ed., *Die 48er*, p. 110.

87 Gervinus in *Deutsche Zeitung*, Nr. 149 (1 June 1849, p. 1) He comes to view the monarchic principle as an anachronism. Cf. also Beilage, 'Reaktion oder Revolution'.

88 Ibid., p. 2.
89 Gervinus, *Einleitung*, p. 94.
90 Ibid., p. 95.
91 Ibid.
92 Jansen, 'Ludwig Bamberger', p. 213.
93 Cf. Valentin, *Revolution*, vol. 2, p. 552 and Wehler, *Deutsche Gesellschaftsgeschichte*, p. 775.
94 Valentin, *Revolution*, vol. 2, p. 553.

Chapter 9

The receptions of the 1848/9 revolutions in the German-speaking countries

The first hundred years

This final chapter was originally conceived as a research survey. However, while working on this book, it became apparent that the memory of the revolutions remained so alive in Germany that it was more pertinent to discuss their actual receptions within the context of political and social changes and to conclude with some comments on research in the USA and in Britain.[1]

Divergent views on the outcome of the revolutions and on the legacy that they bestowed were already evident in the immediate aftermath of the upheavals. These interpretations emerged in the personal and official versions of events and through the various developments which have shaped Germany's history. The extent to which academics as a group were involved in the various national parliaments in Vienna, Berlin and Frankfurt has been covered in earlier chapters. Their close association with liberal issues and their efforts to preserve some of the revolutionary gains, by opting for a 'smaller Germany' solution under Prussian hegemony, were a major aspect of such studies. Historians, constitutionalists and scholars of German literature, in particular, felt that their academic interests would best be served by the formation of a German nation state, a combination of academic and political interests which lay at the root of the concept of the German mandarin. The term 'mandarin' was adopted by F. K. Ringer, to describe the typical features of those German academics who saw themselves as the 'bearers of culture',[2] thus linking them to a predominantly German interpretation of national sovereignty, based on the concept of *Volk* and its cultural aspects. The Pre-March period already demonstrated how constitutional issues came to dominate the revolutionary debate and the National Assembly deliberated over a shift in political power from semi-feudal monarchies to the authority of 'an abstract and rational state'.[3]

In view of the over-representation of academics in the Assembly and subsequently in the various German parliaments, it is not surprising that historical accounts of the revolutions diverged into two directions. A large group of historians, mostly university professors, could justify their democratic role in the National Assembly, while feeling some necessity to distance themselves from the violent street disturbances of the 'mad year'. What now came to be seen as a period of aberration had to be discarded so that, in pursuit of the 'national question', some form of reconciliation with the various governments in office could be initiated. Although no longer openly supporting the revolution, a smaller, more radical group of academics felt the need to record the events of 1848/9 for posterity. Documents of the constitutional proposals were collected and edited, appearing in the *Deutsche Chronik* or in the encyclopedic series *Die Gegenwart*[4] and such works presented the earliest interpretation of key events. Karl Biedermann, for instance, attempted to justify the offer of the imperial crown to Frederick William IV, on the grounds that it was an integral feature of the Imperial Constitution.[5] On another occasion he maintained that 'a reaction [had] swept through the whole of Germany, assaulting the nation's finest feelings in a methodical, merciless manner, the like of which had never been encountered before'.[6] Biedermann and other committed liberals who persisted in questioning the new officially sanctioned chorus of revisionism, suffered for their recalcitrance and lost their university positions. During Gervinus' trial, a fellow historian commented that 'this trial is about whether it will continue to be possible to write history in Germany, a country famous for its scholarship'.[7] The majority of historians joined the revisionists and blamed the liberal and democratic minorities in parliament for the revolutions' failure.[8] Rudolf Haym's comprehensive history of the Frankfurt National Assembly was soon to become the official version for the political establishment. The 'mad year' was declared a failure; public unrest was denounced as rebellion on the barricades, a demonstration of anarchist violence. The work of the Assembly was ignored as the nationality issue came to outweigh all the constitutional achievements. In similar vein, Bismarck's nation building success was celebrated at the expense of the work of the Frankfurt parliament: the events of 1848/9 and 1870/1 were played out against each other by politicians and historians alike, finding their symbolic expression in the quarrels over Germany's prime national emblem. The black, red and gold of Frankfurt became a symbol of democratic republicanism, while the black, red and white of Berlin represented the triumph of national power and *Realpolitik*.[9]

Another conflict arose over the commemoration of the Berlin victims of 18 March 1848.[10] The Prussian government erected a monument in honour of her soldiers killed during this crucial event; civilian victims were officially ignored. Public celebrations at *Friedrichshain* were banned until the late 1860s, and by then only Social Democrats attended. During the 1870s, the victims were jointly honoured with those of the Paris Commune and after 1890, when the Social Democrats were declared illegal, the commemoration gained a new momentum.[11] In time, international May Day celebrations overshadowed those of March 1848, which were all but forgotten. Most academic historians supported conservative and nationalist parties, citing the events of 1848 at best as a precursor of 1871. Liberal historians associated 1848 with the potential for constitutional monarchism, but remained opposed to all forms of popular unrest. The reception in Austria was substantially the same. In the immediate aftermath of the revolutions, respected liberal politicians such as Pillersdorf lost all official standing. Despite several documentary accounts, mostly published abroad,[12] the revolution itself was seen in terms of a threat to the Habsburg dynasty.

Apart from some early literary accounts by Karl Gutzkow and Adolph Streckfuß, novelists failed to exploit the dramatic potential of 1848/9. Theodor Fontane, who had played a marginal role on the barricades on 18 March, remained typically ambivalent, an attitude reinforced after joining the staff of the *Kreuzzeitung* in 1851. Still describing himself as a National Liberal, his outlook became one of resignation.[13] The brothers Thomas and Heinrich Mann adopted characteristically different attitudes to the revolutions in their novels. Thomas Mann's *Buddenbrooks* strikes an ironical note, indicating the alienation and rejection felt by senators and the propertied classes, while the riotous crowds seem strangely unaware of their own power, retreating into submission on being addressed by their patron. Nevertheless, revolutionary events are portrayed as the end of an era, symbolically expressed in the sudden death of the old senator, a stalwart of the old order. Heinrich Mann's *Untertan* (*Man of Straw*) assumes a radically different perspective. Critical of both Wilhelminian nationalism and militarism, as seen through the subaltern character of the young upstart Hessling, the author portrays 'the old Buck' as the hero of the revolution and guarantor of democratic and humanist values. Although overwhelmed by the new Wilhelminian spirit, he represents the voice of Germany's conscience, particularly when, towards the end of the novel, he and his son anticipate a new beginning, based on 'the spirit of mankind'. He states with great conviction: 'You must believe in it, my son. When the catastrophe, which they hope to avoid, is over, rest assured, mankind will not describe what followed the first revolution as less shameful and irrational than the conditions we endured.'[14] *Buddenbrooks* was completed in 1901, *Der Untertan* in 1914, though not published until 1918.

Throughout the Wilhelminian period German historians kept their distance from the events of 1848/9 or treated them with some scepticism. Veit Valentin, a liberal democrat, was critical of the reactionary attitudes of his contemporaries. His major work on the revolutions, completed in 1918, was entirely ignored by the history establishment and failed to get published until 1930. His criticism of Admiral von Tirpitz involved him in a libel suit and ruined his prospects for a professorship.[15] According to Valentin, German historians after 1918 continued with 'their particular taste for the spirit of tradition and order'.[16] During the Weimar Republic, he sought to revive the revolutionary spirit of 1848/9[17] and became the target of reactionary historians such as Heinrich von Srbik.[18] After Hitler's rise to power, Valentin lost his status as civil servant and emigrated, first to London and later to New York.

However, it would be misleading to suggest that the Weimar Republic completely failed to reassess the revolutions. Theodor Heuß, later to become the first President of the Federal Republic, suggested that the Imperial Constitution should become the basis for the Weimar model. A new episode in the debate about Germany's national colours reflected the serious conflict between her different political factions. Whereas Social Democrats and Liberals again opted for the black, red and gold of 1848, reactionary and conservative parties wanted to retain the imperial black, white and red, in allegiance to Bismarck's Prussia and the 'smaller Germany' solution. This conflict haunted the Republic throughout its life, with various bizarre compromise solutions attempted.[19] While Valentin's comprehensive history of the revolutions remained unsurpassed, other liberal historians also attempted to counter prevailing anti-democratic and reactionary trends.[20] Friedrich Meinecke's *Die Idee der Staatsräson in der neuern Geschichte* is a good example. For Meinecke, the revolutions symbolized the permanent conflict between freedom and power. The revolutions' failure led to Rochau's *Realpolitik*, finding in Bismarck the ultimate 'successful synthesis' between national greed for power and democratic and constitutional reasons of state. Meinecke blamed Treitschke and Nietzsche for the irresistible advance of a Machiavellian lust for power, which critically weakened the traditions of humanism and its associated public ethics, so that the advance of technological rationality, supported by a new utilitarianism, destroyed the very basis of *Staatsräson*. In the age-old conflict between freedom and necessity, freedom was the loser. Elementary passions were destroying those liberal, democratic, national and social elements which had once enhanced the state, but were now being transformed into a destructive force.[21]

Meinecke's warnings, echoing those of the old Buck in Heinrich Mann's novel, went unheeded and, as the Third Reich tightened its grip, the revolutions were exploited by an ideological necessity to justify Nazi policies. Once again 1848 was denigrated as a 'mad year'. In *Mein Kampf* Hitler had acknowledged the revolutionary character of the age, but rejected it as inherently suspect, since it helped 'to awaken the spirit of Western democracy'.[22] By 1938 Hitler's views had become more 'positive', no doubt coloured by the annexation of Austria which he viewed as having some legitimacy within the context of Frankfurt.[23] Historians now interpreted the revolutions in the service of National-Socialism. Srbik blamed socialists and communists for driving the liberal bourgeoisie into the arms of conservative forces and the reactionary establishment. By 1938 the revolutions were seen as the first national uprising to pursue the aim of establishing a Greater Germany and during the war itself, foreign powers, together with Western concepts of constitutionalism and democracy, were blamed for the failure of the revolutions.[24]

The end of the war and the centenary celebrations of 1948 presented an opportunity for yet another re-evaluation of the German revolutions. The bomb-damaged Paul's Church was hastily repaired in time for the centenary celebrations, though Frankfurt failed to be chosen as the seat of the new West German parliament. The emerging Cold War began to make an impact. The Soviet Occupied Zone used the centenary as a means of identifying with other socialist revolutions and with the workers' fight for emancipation; Western zones focused on the legacy of the National Assembly's Basic Rights of 1848. The origins of the 'Battle for the Legacy' (*Erbschaftsstreit*) were laid in 1948 and continued until the demise of the GDR. East German statements during this early phase, amounting to little more than propaganda, can be largely ignored. In West Germany, the old 'Weimar' historians, such as Meinecke, Otto Vossler, Hans Rothfels and Rudolf Stadelmann, presented a more complex interpretation, but only Stadelmann saw the revolutions in their social and economic context. Meinecke's centennial retrospective may serve as an example for an understanding of the revolutions a hundred years on. He remembered joining in the *Friedrichshain* processions of 1871, when the memorial was seen as 'an eerie remnant of a bygone, bad and evil world',[25] and he saw Germany's national situation after the defeat of Nazism in similar terms. Meinecke interpreted the revolutions as part of a greater tradition, beginning in 1819 and including 1866,[26] a tradition which had failed to introduce liberal democracy and had instead opted for national unity and power politics. The 'obsessive obedience' of the German people is considered responsible for the German catastrophe and a social regeneration of her people, in the spirit of 1848, is seen as a solution to Germany's problems.[27]

The revolutions of 1848/9 within the ideological concepts of the GDR

It hardly needs to be spelt out that a society which justifies its existence by its own socialist revolutionary origins will choose to integrate 1848/9 into its own heritage. Much has been written on the political and historical reception of the revolutions in the GDR and this account can at best summarize and briefly evaluate the result of half a century of historiography.[28] The various interpretations reflect fairly accurately the different stages of ideological change within the country, which can be divided into three: 1. The period of the actual inception of the GDR, marked by crude Marxist ideology and centred on the role of the working classes. The revolutions are understood within a wider parameter of revolutionary strife, including both the sixteenth century Peasants' War and the *Spartakus* uprising of 1919. Added to this 'fixation on Marx',[29] a concept from which later generations of GDR historians distanced themselves,[30] was the dominant reputation of Lenin and his influential views on the German revolutions. 2. A second stage of GDR research seems to coincide with the workers' uprising in June 1953 and a subsequent political thaw on the part of the SED. Although still sourced almost exclusively from accounts in the *Neue Rheinische Zeitung*, the historical perspective now broadened to include Pre-March social and political developments, as well as working-class traditions in the first half of the nineteenth century. Regional studies gained in importance, though largely based within GDR territory, they included the cities of Cologne and Stuttgart. The 'bourgeois-liberal tradition' was interpreted from a narrowly Marxist angle and the concept of the 'treason of liberalism' became established. 3. A third phase of development took place in the late 1960s and early 1970s, broadly shadowing the change of political leadership from Ulbricht to Honecker and marked by a growing international recognition of the GDR. While the revolution was still interpreted as part of the wider socialist development, along scientifically determinable laws, a certain refinement of earlier, populist and narrowly Marxist presentations can be detected. The hagiographic fixation on Marx and Engels gave way to a more open study of the events of 1848/9. The role of the bourgeoisie in the early stages of its development became a topic for research, especially where it was seen to impact on the course of the revolutions. Non-Marxist and non-communist workers' associations, particularly those associated with Stephan Born, Andreas Gottschalk, Wilhelm Weitling and François Babeuf began to attract attention. While the complete works of Marx and Engels were edited in 1975, following an earlier popular but incomplete edition of 1956, other important works of literature, often in editions accessible to a wider public, now appeared, including revolutionary songs and the works of Herwegh, Freiligrath and Weerth. As a new interest in the intellectual leaders of the revolutions emerged, their contribution was no longer dismissed as political failure. The roles of the bourgeoisie and of the various national parliaments gained greater prominence, with biographical studies undertaken on liberals such as Dahlmann, Rotteck and Gagern.

A crude evaluation of the strengths and weaknesses of GDR historiography would suggest that it gained an early lead in the somewhat neglected research area of the 1848/9 revolutions, supported by the establishment of specific research centres in Berlin, Leipzig and Jena.[31] From 1960, regular reports on the various research projects were published every ten years. Much of this work concentrated on specific themes and was carried out under the guidance of eminent historians such as Karl Obermann, Rolf Weber and Günther Hildebrandt. Their publications gradually gained international recognition, first within COMECON countries, but later also in Western Europe and the United States. Their democracy studies, for instance, diverged from the typically Western preoccupation with institutional and constitutional details, to consider democracy as the expression of the universal will of the people, workers, peasants and petit bourgeoisie. Divisions between a liberal political culture and a more spontaneous grass-roots movement were discussed and the first comparative studies of the revolutions emerged. Dealing in the main with France and the German-speaking countries, even these indicate a certain ideological bias, with an emphasis on the participation of peasants and workers at the expense of craftsmen. By the 1980s a more pragmatic approach signalled a further convergence towards the output of West German research.

Research in the Federal Republic

This short summary cannot possibly do justice to the wealth of research that has emerged over the last fifty years. Prevalent themes and perspectives will be outlined, with an attempt to relate them to prominent social and political developments, albeit at the expense of maintaining a strictly chronological survey. Some excellent surveys give a detailed and specialist account of trends and directions among West German historiographers.[32]

Although there is little evidence of external pressure on West German historians, particularly in comparison to the situation in East Germany, there were, nevertheless, certain discernible influences, with the 'battle for the legacy' also engaging the West, especially during the Cold War period. During the 1950s West German historians tended to concentrate on constitutional issues, such as comparing the Frankfurt Basic Rights with those established by the Bonn Republic. In addition to paying tribute to the adoption of individual rights and to the democratic institutions promoted by the National Assembly, the role of liberalism was also high on the agenda. While 1848 was now regarded as the *annus spectabilis*, the 'second revolution', to preserve the Imperial Constitution, was all but ignored. Against the background of a newly divided country, the revolution's failure to achieve national unification was emphasized. A 'Commission for the History of Parliamentarianism and Political Parties' was set up in Bonn in 1951, but until the early 1970s its impact was limited.[33] With the reception of

American research in the social sciences in the early 1960s, a first change of emphasis was apparent, reflected in Werner Conze's work on the Pre-March period. Such innovations still met with some suspicion, since the mainstream tended to regard 1871 as the benchmark for the emergence of a German nation state.

The student unrest of 1968 and its aftermath marked yet another change of direction. While social history had by now come into its own, a neo-conservative backlash became apparent, usually seen as part of the *Tendenzwende* of 1974. Largely unaffected by these ideological shifts were two monumental works whose origins lay in the 1950s; Ernst Rudolf Huber's constitutional history, first published in 1960, and Manfred Botzenhart's study on parliamentarianism during the revolutions. Of some significance at the time was the speech delivered by President Gustav Heinemann on the occasion of the unveiling of the Rastatt memorial.[34] Heinemann's speech came to be dismissed as yet another episode in the Cold War battle for the legacy, but it went far beyond that. Heinemann, whose own ancestor had been killed at Rastatt, had initiated the idea of the memorial, seeking the advice of the historians Conze and Jäckel. He himself had frequently been criticized for countering West German hysteria in the face of Red Army Faction terrorism. This latter phenomenon may explain the strong negative reaction by an older generation of mostly conservative historians[35] to a speech which sought to correct the prevailing tradition in German history of hailing Bismarck as the guardian of a strong, united Germany. Heinemann speculated on the role of both winners and losers in history and advocated a new approach to research, affording more weight to the campaign for the Imperial Constitution, to a more interdisciplinary approach, involving the social sciences, empirical culture studies as well as literary criticism.

West German historians increasingly turned their attention to the examination of working-class cultures, to regional differences, Pre-March initiatives and the formation of political parties. Of particular importance in this context are publications by Hans-Ulrich Wehler, studies on liberalism by Lothar Gall and Dieter Langewiesche and Werner Conze's research into the working classes. The last thirty years has seen interest in the German revolutions growing steadily. While this survey cannot refer to all the important works published during this period, the most notable publications will be covered under nine headings; reprints and re-editions will normally not be mentioned.

1. **General surveys**. Thomas Nipperdey's *Deutsche Geschichte* devotes a prominent chapter to the German revolutions, ranging over a variety of aspects, from extra-parliamentary action to nationality conflicts, regional differences and economic issues. He interprets these often contrasting themes

within a general framework of the 'failed revolution', but emphasizes, nevertheless, that they constituted a turning point in nineteenth-century German history. On the whole, his book is less innovative and less inter-disciplinary than Wolfram Siemann's important study which focuses on the outbreak and defeat of the revolutions, on popular protest and the emer-gence of a political culture in clubs and associations, rather than presenting a more narrative account of the course of the revolutions. Siemann inter-prets 1848/9 as part of a pan-European crisis of modernization, involving various attempts at nation building and experiencing co-ordination problems which affected the dynamics of the revolutions. Drawing on his earlier study, he includes important features of the post-revolutionary decade. The East-German historian Günther Wollstein concentrates on the nationality issue, which has been somewhat neglected in recent years, but here is allowed to dominate most other aspects of the revolutions. Rassow's newly revised *Deutsche Geschichte* contains a chapter on the revolutions, written by Michael Behnen. As part of a one-volume study, it is very accessible, but cannot contribute many new insights. Wehler's social history covers the period 1815–49 and offers perhaps the most optimistic interpretation, recog-nizing that, despite the revolutions' ultimate failure, they did, however, transform German society, laying the foundation for a new political cul-ture. Wehler interprets the failure of 1848/9 as an unsuccessful attempt to resolve too many varied and often complex aspects of modernization, when an inevitable coincidence of social, political and industrial change produced a general crisis of modernization which had to address a thousand years of German feudalism.

2. **National and international aspects.** The nationality issue has gained a new importance with Germany's reunification in 1990, with particular emphasis given to previous manifestations of the sovereignty of the people (*Völkerfrühling*) and to parliamentary debates on German attitudes to Poland and other Slavonic countries, as well as to the Schleswig–Holstein issue. Günther Wollstein and Hans-Georg Kraume examine the nationality issue as a party political question, underlining the dilemma of the liberals who accepted *Realpolitik* and a compromise with established conservatism, at the expense of the universal and in particular the West-European concept of the sovereignty of the people. In marked contrast to Wollstein, Kraume sides with Stadelmann and W. E. Mosse in defence of left-of-centre democrats, whose national concerns are seen as more 'modern' than those of the main parties at Frankfurt. Günther Heydemann compares the early phase of the German revolutions with the Italian *Risorgimento*, in relation to British foreign policy. His work comes within the scope of other inter-European comparative studies,[36] the national dimension emerging almost

by necessity within an international context. Reinhard Rürup's recent study also examines the German revolutions within the European context and compares 1848/9 with other pivotal dates in the continent's revolutionary calendar.[37]

3. **Biographies and documentary collections.** Hans Jessen's collection of eye witness accounts is still valuable as a first insight into the 1848 events, though its approach and general layout no longer meet today's requirements. Similar observations apply to Hans Fenske's *Quellen*: though more scholarly in its general presentation, it does not correspond to the more stringent demands of authenticity. Furthermore, in concentrating largely on the Frankfurt parliament and on national issues, Fenske's selection fails to cover the 'sentiments, intentions and actions of those in the centre of events'.[38] The latest edition of Walter Grab's miscellany is accessible in an affordable publication and includes pamphlets and documents from extra-parliamentary sources. Fenske and Grab seem to be on opposite sides of a clear ideological divide, with the latter more interested in those parties and associations which were in opposition both to the National Assembly and the existing monarchies. Grab's choice seems to have been influenced by Obermann and other GDR commentators, but he is also indebted to Huber. In comparison with the host of research on most aspects of the German revolutions, biographies are rare. Sabine Freitag's collection of twenty-five biographies of distinguished men and women is therefore particularly valuable; it ranges from David E. Barclay's portrait of King Frederick William IV to Rudolf Muhs's account of Karl Blind, who experienced most of the revolutions from his prison cell. Between these two extreme positions are the stories of activists of all political and social backgrounds, presenting a vivid picture of the various trends and ideological positions which competed with each other during these tempestuous years. Though not strictly biographical, Christian Jansen's important study of left-wing opposition to the National Assembly deserves to be mentioned here. His weighty *opus* follows the opposition movement from the end of the revolutions up to German unification under Bismarck. Brilliant biographical studies of men like Bamberger, Biedermann, Fröbel, Jacoby, Ruge and others illustrate how their various political careers continued beyond 1849, to throw a new light on the verdict of the 'failed revolutions'. Another important feature of Jansen's work concerns the academic elite, whose significant contribution to the political debate has, in the past, too often been dismissed in terms of the 'parliament of professors' or overshadowed by the activities of other social groups.

4. **Revolutionary centres.** In his research survey of 1981 Langewiesche remarks that the Vienna Revolution has received a good deal more attention than events in Berlin,[39] a state of affairs which has been more than rectified

by Rüdiger Hachtmann's recent study. The late 1970s saw Wolfgang Häusler and Herbert Steiner produce valuable new insights into the social and economic conditions of the working class and of craftsmen in the industrialized outskirts of Vienna, but little work of such an eminent standard has since appeared. An exception is Heinrich Lutz's comparative study of the rivalry between Austria and Prussia for German hegemony, which considers Austria's socio-economic backwardness as a critical dimension in the equation.[40] Research into revolutionary Berlin has been transformed by Hachtmann's book which traces developments from the Pre-March to Erfurt. His main concern lies with the actual revolution of 1848 but he includes valuable chapters on clubs and associations, on the civil guard and the military and on conservative trends. Numerous other aspects are covered and a most useful short bibliography and detailed index are provided. In assessing revolutionary centres, the Swiss *Sonderbund* struggle is a seriously neglected area. While there have been some recent publications in this field,[41] including a biography on Guilleaume-Henri Dufour, only the popular study by Heinz Rieder attributes some prominence to Switzerland which can be seen as a springboard for the German revolutions.

5. **Socio-cultural aspects**. A variety of topics come under this heading and many studies are the result of inter-disciplinary co-operation. The Tübingen *Ludwig Uhland Institut* has been of groundbreaking importance here, influencing numerous studies by Wolfgang Kaschuba, Carola Lipp and Martin Scharfe, whose regional analyses of southern German towns focused on town halls, public houses and the streets as centres of protest action. Studies on the role of women, on the participation of the Jewish community, on Gymnasts' associations and in particular on the press and political pamphlets also fall into this category.[42] Schools, universities and churches can also be included here, despite the fact that their roles transcend this somewhat simple categorization. K. E. Jeismann's work on the history of education deserves some special mention,[43] together with research by K. H. Jarausch and Albert Reble. Some studies, mainly on southern German universities, seem to suggest that they followed the general trend in society, towards a more corporate attitude, with liberal elements being pushed into the background.[44]

6. **Working classes**. In view of the tremendous interest in working-class research in the GDR and, since the late 1960s, also in the FRG, it is not surprising that more recent work has little to add to the previous output. Some new insights can, however, be gained through regional studies, such as Hartmut Zwahr's book on class-based organizations in Leipzig[45] or in Hachtmann's study on revolutionary Berlin. Some new impetus also comes from an analysis of the minutes and records of meetings held by

working-class or craftsmen's organizations.[46] New light has been shed on the allegedly conservative nature of craftsmen's organizations, concluding that their 'economic conservatism' should not be too readily confused with political conservatism. More recent investigations into journeymen's organizations seem to indicate that 'workers' should not be seen as isolated from craftsmen or from other groups on the fringes of society.[47]

7. **Economic history**. Although there has recently been some general interest in the economic and banking sphere, relatively few studies seem to have emerged. Of particular interest would be the fluctuating fortunes of the Rothschild and Oppenheim banking houses. Further information can be gleaned through regional studies of the Rhineland, Vienna and Berlin and from biographies of public figures such as Hansemann or Bassermann, but a further examination of this topic would be welcome.

8. **Parliaments and constitutions**. So much has been published on this topic that it is surprising that recent studies have managed to offer any new perspectives, especially where the Frankfurt Assembly is concerned. J. D. Kühne examined the constitution from the point of view of a legal expert, while also considering local government.[48] Günther Hildebrandt, still somewhat indebted to the Marxist approach, developed a complex analysis of the liberals and their policy compromise with individual governments. Heinrich Best argues that the ultimate failure of the Assembly was the result of severe fragmentation among its participating groups, for whom the dual aim of national unification and democratization proved too onerous a task. Jansen has taken up some of Best's arguments, but only in relation to left-of-centre liberals, tracking their progress through the following decades.

9. **Conservative and military aspects**. Research in this subject area has seen an acceleration during the last fifteen years, with important works by Hachtmann, Michael Wettengel, Eckhard Trox and Dieter Langewiesche. These studies indicate that, while catholic conservatism could establish itself even in the middle and smaller states, especially in Bavaria, the actual stronghold of conservatism was Prussia. Membership of the various conservative associations was no longer limited to the nobility and the landed gentry, but included many civil servants, industrialists and, in particular, master craftsmen.[49] The different military associations soon became an important coalition partner of the conservative forces, constituting the 'Borussian' element and usually to the right of even the Prussian monarch. While Prussia and the Third Germany developed a type of conservatism which was not hostile to modernist reform, Austrian conservatives depended far too heavily on the military, thus consolidating a new form of absolutism.

213

A brief survey of Anglo–American research

It scarcely needs stating that historiography in the United States and in Britain tended to be more progressive and modernist than in the German-speaking countries, whose outlook was too often inhibited by a reactionary or fascist past or by national divisions. German historians, on the whole, had failed to take advantage of new approaches elsewhere, something that has changed dramatically during the last two decades. Space will not permit more than the most superficial survey of American and British publications, limited to those works which have significantly influenced German research.[50] P. H. Noyes's important study on working-class associations was of crucial importance to German historians, stimulating a more broad-scale approach to research in this area. Though his more recent contributions concern the nationality issue, John Breuilly's studies on German workers' associations must also be mentioned, disproving previous Marxist inspired views which suggested that master craftsmen and journeymen were hostile towards the earlier associations. Frank Eyck's detailed work on the Frankfurt Parliament encouraged lively debate on a topic which had hitherto often been dealt with in too abstract and hypothetical a manner. William J. Orr's study of the *Kreuzzeitung* and J. R. Gillis's book on Prussian bureaucracy contributed towards a shift in the debate, giving prominence to reactionary and counter-revolutionary aspects.[51] Roger Price placed the German revolutions into their European context and Eda Sagarra's social history successfully exploited an interdisciplinary approach by linking literary and historical topics with socio-cultural issues.

Three names, above all, had a major impact on German historiography and have significantly promoted a broader understanding of the German revolutions. James J. Sheehan's book on German liberalism did much to widen our knowledge of liberalism during the Pre-March period and beyond; his detailed analysis of regional issues countered earlier attitudes which were too ready to associate liberalism with the purely economic sphere. Sheehan's *German History 1770–1866* has been indispensable for this book; his deep insights into the cultural, social and intellectual aspects of the time have been of immeasurable value. Jonathan Sperber's brilliant study of *Rhineland Radicals*, as well as his earlier work on popular catholicism, encouraged a whole generation of younger German historians to embrace regional studies and to examine the extra-parliamentary domain. The book by David Blackbourn and Geoff Eley on the 'peculiarities' of German history, first published in German, met with an overwhelming response among German historians and social scientists. The authors sought to dispel the notion of a German *Sonderweg* and – essentially – tried to prove that a successful bourgeois revolution is not the only means of achieving 'synchronization between economic, social and political spheres'.[52] The Historians' Dispute of the late 1980s reopened the debate about a special German development, though eventually a general consensus seemed to emerge that every nation has a unique special development and that no Western norm should be imposed world wide. Many other contributions by historians in Britain and the United States cannot be included here, but this brief survey will have indicated that the German revolutions of 1848/9 have become a topic for serious international research. The numerous works translated from English into German and *vice versa* bear witness to the genuine co-operation and partnership that has developed during the last few decades.

The reception of the 150th anniversary of the German revolutions

A satirical programme recently made the point that 1998 was the first time in 150 years that the Germans had managed to find time to celebrate this event. On the fiftieth anniversary the *Kaiser*'s war preparations preoccupied the nation, 1923 witnessed the crisis of uncontrollable inflation, in 1948 Germany was still struggling to emerge from the devastation of war and in 1973 the international oil crisis overshadowed the commemorative activities.[53]

As if to compensate for lost time, 1998 marked a period that seemed to crave anniversaries and lavished excessive attention on a host of events. The central German government, however, did little to commemorate the revolutions, leaving it to regional authorities and the media to celebrate this first attempt to establish a democratic German state. Berlin also largely abstained from the proceedings and Vienna's response was low key, concentrating mainly on economic and banking factors. The main centres for festivities were in Baden-Württemberg, the Palatinate, Hesse, North-Rhine Westphalia and Saxony. In Mannheim, the president of the Constitutional Court commemorated the formation of the Basic Rights, reminding his audience to be vigilant in the observation of human rights and tolerance towards others, while the minister presidents of Baden-Württemberg, the Palatinate and Hesse participated in local festivities. Valentin's pioneering work was reprinted and many publications were marketed to coincide with the anniversaries, ranging from academic studies to popular illustrated accounts.[54] Information on most of these publications can be gained via the VLB (*Verzeichnis lieferbarer Bücher*) list which contains some 120 titles, including catalogues of various exhibitions. A special Internet page was created, to provide details of publications, exhibitions, lectures and other events, though information was largely confined to the southwest.[55]

Baden-Württemberg seemed particularly active in promoting the anniversary; its *Haus der Geschichte* subsidized many events, most prominent among them the exhibition at Karlsruhe which was augmented by 350 special activities, including live performances, attracting the largest number of visitors to any exhibition in Germany in 1998. SPD members of the *Land* parliament celebrated the opening in authentic style, sporting the fashion of the time and singing revolutionary songs. The Offenburg 'freedom festival' attracted 130,000 visitors and Mannheim mounted a touring exhibition, sponsored by a building society and transported by train to more than 100 railway stations across the country. The Mannheim *Reiss* museum organized an exhibition of caricatures and the city of Rastatt provided guided tours to places of historic interest, including the casemates where revolutionaries had been imprisoned.

Centre stage was given to Frankfurt's Paul's Church, where on 19 May, the Federal President, accompanied by the leaders of the federal and regional parliaments, took part in a commemorative act to commission a new bell, replacing the original one which had been destroyed during a bell ringing festival the previous year. It may have been an act of historic irony that the new bell failed to hit precisely the right note! A major Frankfurt exhibition was organized by the German Historical Museum in Berlin, whose curator, the Frankfurt historian Lothar Gall, arranged an accompanying programme of lectures by leading German experts. The forty-second conference of German historians, dedicated to the revolutions, was also held in Frankfurt.

Prominent German papers published articles by eminent German historians[56] and most universities put on lectures to commemorate the revolutions; Freiburg, for instance, hosted Mommsen, Fenske, Langewiesche and Siemann, among others. Particularly welcome was an essay competition for school children, entitled 'Starting into freedom', sponsored by the federation of German newspaper editors and aimed at stimulating interest in local and regional history. A survey of radio and television reveals a similar picture. The majority of anniversary programmes were transmitted by *Südwest 3*, the regional broadcasting station in the south west. Apart from looking at political songs, poems and documentary sources, there were special features on leading figures such as Hecker, Struve and von Gagern and on the historic importance of Offenburg, Mannheim and Rastatt. Hecker's Baden Revolution was covered a number of times and one interesting programme focused on the revolutionaries Schurz and Stadelmann on their way into American exile.[57] The most spectacular and most stirring programme was a film version of Stefan Heym's novel *Lenz oder die Freiheit* which revolved around the 1849 revolution in Baden.[58] A specially commissioned opera by Detlef Heusinger, on the theme of the political apathy of the legendary *deutsche Michel*, had its inaugural performance in the Paul's Church, and Lortzing's opera *Regina* was televised. While Hecker, Herwegh, Struve and Sigl were particularly popular characters, Brentano was hardly mentioned and Marx and Engels were afforded only a marginal role. The satirical impact of Heinrich Hoffmann's *Struwwelpeter* was recognized by articles in several papers, though no specific political message was related to his work. In general, the early Baden revolution received more attention than the struggle to retain the Imperial Constitution. The latter was commemorated more particularly in the Tauber and Main regions and in Rastatt, but it is likely that by 1999 the major interest in the anniversary had begun to diminish.

Most exhibitions, broadcasts and reports were of a high standard and should have stimulated a new interest in local research, providing a further impetus to national and international research. Inevitably, however, some events involved the promotion of tourism, rather than academic research. The Lake of Constance region, in particular, commemorated revolutionary events with special boat and train excursions, walking tours and open-air festivals to attract visitors. Political correctness was always observed, attributing the special roles played by women and Jews, frequently irrespective of inner divisions within these groups or of their actual social status at the time. Some newspapers attempted to play down or ridicule the revolutions. The *Wertheimer Zeitung* for instance reproduced observations from 1948 which condemned the revolutions as chaotic and anarchic, peace being restored only after 'thousands of political cranks had been dispatched to America'.[59] The *Rheinische Merkur* described Franz Sigl as 'a failed homosexual lieutenant and law student', dismissed Herwegh's poems as of scant literary value and their author as the 'pioneer of an aggressive nationalism . . . in the vicinity of Bismarck's blood and iron rhetoric', while celebrating Archduke John as 'a patriot and liberal'.[60] Such examples illustrate that, despite much valuable work in enlightening today's citizens, future generations will still have plenty of opportunity to continue to revise the many images of the German revolutions.

Notes

1 For full book titles please refer also to the Select Bibliographical Essay and to previous chapters.
2 Fritz K. Ringer, *The Decline of the German Mandarins. The German Academic Community, 1890–1933* (Hanover and London, 1990), p. 3.
3 Ibid., p. 9.
4 For a detailed account cf. Veit Valentin, *Geschichte der deutschen Revolution 1848–49*, vol. 2 (Berlin, 1931), p. 595.
5 Karl Biedermann, *1840–1870, Dreißig Jahre deutscher Geschichte. Vom Thronwechsel in Preußen 1840 bis zur Aufrichtung des neuen deutschen Kaiserthums*, 3rd edn, vol. 1 (Breslau, no date), p. 401.
6 Quoted from Wolfram Siemann, *The German Revolution of 1848–49*, trans. by Christiane Banerji (London, 1998), p. 1.

7 Ibid., p. 3.

8 Cf. Siemann, *German Revolution*, p. 2; Valentin, *Geschichte*, vol. 2, p. 596.

9 Cf. Valentin, *Geschichte* vol. 2, p. 597.

10 Cf. chapter. 4.

11 M. Hettling, 'Nachmärz und Kaiserreich', in Christoph Dipper and Ulrich Speck eds, *1848. Revolution in Deutschland* (Frankfurt/M. and Leipzig, 1998), p. 16.

12 Cf. Valentin, *Geschichte*, vol. 2, p. 696.

13 Quoted from Georg Lukács, 'Der alte Fontane', in Wolfgang Preisendanz ed., *Theodor Fontane* (Darmstadt, 1973), p. 36.

14 Heinrich Mann, *Der Untertan* (Hamburg and Berlin, 1958), p. 475.

15 E. Fehrenbach, 'Veit Valentin', in Hans-Ulrich Wehler ed., *Deutsche Historiker*, vol. 1 (Göttingen, 1971), pp. 73f.

16 Valentin, *Geschichte*, vol. 2, p. 608.

17 Cf. Veit Valentin, *Die 48er Demokratie und der Völkerbundgedanke* (Berlin, 1919).

18 Fehrenbach, 'Veit Valentin', p. 76.

19 Friedrich Naumann played an important part in this, cf. M. Vogt, 'Weimar und die NS-Zeit', in Dipper and Speck eds, *1848 Revolution*, pp. 26f.

20 In particular Erich Marcks, Erich Brandenburg and Ludwig Bergsträßer, cf. Vogt, 'Weimar und', pp. 30f.

21 Friedrich Meinecke, *Die Idee der Staatsräson in der neuern Geschichte* (Munich and Berlin, 1924), pp. 493, 518, 521, 529 respectively.

22 Adolf Hitler, *Mein Kampf*, 743–47th edn (Munich, 1942), p. 80.

23 Cf. Vogt, 'Weimar und', p. 32.

24 Ibid., p. 33.

25 Friedrich Meinecke, *1848, eine Säkularbetrachtung* (Berlin, 1948), p. 7.

26 The Karlsbad Decrees and Prussia's defeat of Austria.

27 Meinecke, *1848*, p. 24.

28 In particular Dieter Langewiesche, 'Die deutsche Revolution von 1848/49 und die vorrevolutionäre Gesellschaft: Forschungsstand und Forschungsperspektiven', in *Archiv für Sozialgeschichte*, 21 (1981), pp. 458–98 and 'Die deutsche Revolution von 1848/49 und die vorrevolutionäre Gesellschaft: Forschungsstand und Forschungsperspektiven, Teil II', in *Archiv für Sozialgeschichte*, 31 (1991), pp. 331–443; W. Schmidt, 'Forschungen zur Revolution von 1848/49 in der DDR, Versch eines historischen Überblicks und einer kritischen Bilanz', in Walter Schmidt ed., *Demokratie, Liberalismus und Konterrevolution. Studien zur deutschen Revolution von 1848/49* (Berlin, 1998), pp. 11–80 and E. Wolfrum, 'Bundesrepublik Deutschland und DDR', in Dipper and Speck eds, *1848 Revolution*, pp. 35–52.

29 W. Schieder, 'Auf dem Wege zu einer neuen Marx Legende', *Neue politische Literatur*, 9 (1964), pp. 259ff.

30 Schmidt, 'Forschungen', p. 30.

31 Cf. Schmidt, 'Forschungen', pp. 20–3: Jena as a centre for the study of bourgeois parties and organisations; Leipzig as a centre for comparative revolution research.

32 For details cf. Langewiesche, 'Die deutsche Revolution' (1981) and (1991) and Wolfrum, 'Bundesrepublik Deutschland'.

33 Cf. Wolfrum, 'Bundesrepublik Deutschland', p. 39.

34 Gustav W. Heinemann, 'Die Freiheitsbewegung in der deutschen Geschichte', *Geschichte in Wissenschaft und Unterricht*, 10 (1974), pp. 601–6.

35 In particular Thomas Schieder, for details cf. Wolfrum, 'Bundesrepublik Deutschland', p. 46.

36 On the wider ranging works by Berding, Cocka and Langewiesche, cf. Günther Heydemann, *Konstitution gegen Revolution. Die britische Deutschland- und Italienpolitik 1815–1848* (Göttingen and Zurich, 1995), p. 11.

37 Reinhard Rürop ed., *The Problem of Revolution in Germany, 1789–1990* (Oxford and New York, 2000).

38 Hans Fenske ed., *Quellen zur deutschen Revolution 1848–1849* (Darmstadt, 1996), p. x.

39 Langewiesche, 'Die deutsche Revolution' (1981), p. 482.

40 Cf. Langewiesche, 'Die deutsche Revolution' (1991), pp. 335f.

41 Alfred Kölz, *Neuere Schweizerische Verfassungsgeschichte. Ihre Grundlinien vom Ende der alten Eidgenossenschaft bis 1848* (Berne, 1992).

42 Cf. T. Mergel and C. Jansen, 'Von "der Revolution" zu "den Revolutionen". Probleme einer Interpretation von 1848/49', in Christian Jansen und Thomas Mergel eds, *Die Revolutionen von 1848/49, Erfahrung, Verarbeitung, Deutung* (Göttingen, 1998), p. 9.

43 Cf. in particular Karl-Ernst Jeismann and Peter Lundgreen eds, *Handbuch der deutschen Bildungsgeschichte*, vol. 3 (Munich, 1987).

44 Cf. Langewiesche, 'Die deutsche Revolution' (1981), p. 488.

45 Hartmut Zwahr, *Zur Konstituierung des Proletariats als Klasse. Strukturuntersuchung über das Leipziger Proletariat während der industriellen Revolution* (Berlin, 1987).

46 For a detailed survey cf. Langewiesche, 'Die deutsche Revolution' (1991), p. 366.

47 In particular the studies by Kaschuba, Bergmann, Lipp; cf also Langewiesche, 'Die deutsche Revolution' (1991), pp. 368f.

48 Jörg-Detlef Kühne, *Die Reichsverfassung der Paulskirche. Vorbild und Verwirklichung im späteren deutschen Rechtsleben* (Frankfurt/M., 1985).

49 Langewiesche, 'Die deutsche Revolution' (1991), p. 376.

50 By contrast, the Cold War climate discouraged a serious debate on Eastern Europe.

51 William J. Orr, *The Foundation of the Kreuzzeitungs Party in Prussia 1848–1850* (Wisconsin, 1971) and J. R. Gillis, *The Prussian Bureaucracy in Crisis, 1840–1860* (Stanford, CA., 1971).

52 David Blackbourn and Geoff Eley, *The Peculiarities of German History. Bourgeois Society and Politics in Nineteenth-Century Germany* (Oxford University Press, 1984), pp. 6f.

53 'Bunter Abend für Revolutionäre', *Südwestfunk 3*, 1 May, 22.20.

54 For example: H. W. Hahn and W. Greiling eds, *Die Revolution von 1848/49 in Thüringen. Aktionsräume, Handlungsebenen, Wirkungen* (Rudolstadt, 1998); I. Jung, H. W. Hahn and Rüdiger Störzel, *Die Revolution von 1848 an Lahn und Dill* (Wetzlar, 1998); O. Dascher and E. Kleinertz' survey of the Rhineland, M. Schmittner, *Der Traum von der freien Republik* (1998), on the Main valley and Spessart.

55 The Internet home page is: http://www.revolution 1848–1849.de

56 For instance: G. Wollstein and K. O. von Aretin in *Rheinischer Merkur*, R. Hachtmann, W. Siemann, F. Vollmer and others in a special issue of *Zeitpunkte*. published by the *Zeit Verlag*.

57 *Südwestfunk 3* presented a series of programmes from September 1997 until May 1998. Some programmes gave a survey of the Revolution in Baden, others concentrated on individual figures such as Hecker, Herwegh's wife, Struve and Heinrich von Gagern, others again portrayed the Gymnasts' Societies involvement. The feature 'Traum von der Freiheit', presenting Schurz and Stadelmann was broadcast on 12 and 19 April, 1998 at 17.00.

58 Broadcast under the title 'Lenz oder die Freiheit' on 20, 21 and 28 April, 1998 at 21.20.
59 *Wertheimer Zeitung*, 4 June 1999.
60 *Merkur*, 18 December 1998, *Merkur plus*, 17 July 1998 and 10 September 1999 respectively.

Select bibliography

Adelshauser, W. and D. Petzina, *Deutsche Wirtschaftsgeschichte im Industriezeitalter: Konjunktur, Krise, Wachstum* (Düsseldorf, 1981)

Aretin, Karl Otmar von, *Das Reich, Friedensordnung und europäisches Gleichgewicht 1648–1806* (Stuttgart, 1992)

Arndt, Ernst Moritz, *Blätter der Erinnerung, meistens um und aus der Paulskirche in Frankfurt* (Leipzig, 1849)

Asche, Susanne *et al.*, *Für die Freiheit streiten! 150 Jahre Revolution im Südwesten 1848/49* (Stuttgart, 1998)

Auerbach, Berthold, *Tagebuch aus Wien. Von Latour bis auf Windischgrätz* (Breslau, 1849)

Bach, Maximilian, *Geschichte der Wiener Revolution im Jahre 1848* (Vienna, 1898)

Bamberger, Ludwig, *Erinnerungen*, P. Nathan ed. (Berlin, 1899)

Barclay, David E. and Eric D. Weitz eds, *Between Reform and Revolution. German Socialism and Communism from 1840 to 1990* (New York and Oxford, 1998)

Bauer, Bruno, *Die bürgerliche Revolution in Deutschland seit dem Anfange der deutschkatholischen Bewegung* (Berlin, 1849)

Bauernfeld, Eduard von, *Aus Alt- und Neu-Wien, Deutsche Hausbücherei 87* (Vienna, 1923)

Berding, Helmut and Hans-Peter Ullmann eds, *Deutschland zwischen Revolution und Restauration* (Düsseldorf, 1981)

Bergmann, Jürgen, *Wirtschaftskrise und Revolution. Handwerker und Arbeiter 1848/49* (Stuttgart, 1986)

Bergsträsser, Ludwig ed., *Das Frankfurter Parlament in Briefen und Tagebüchern* (Frankfurt/M., 1929)

Best, Heinrich, *Die Männer von Bildung und Besitz. Struktur und Handeln parlamentarischer Führungsgruppen in Deutschland und Frankreich 1848/49* (Düsseldorf, 1990)

Birker, K. *Die deutschen Arbeiterbildungsvereine 1840–1870* (Berlin, 1973)

Bismarck, Otto Fürst von, *Gedanken und Erinnerungen* (Stuttgart and Berlin, 1905) [English version: *Bismarck, The Man and the Statesman: Being the Reflections and Reminiscences of Otto, Prince von Bismarck* (New York and London, 1899)

Blackbourn, David, *The Fontana History of Germany 1780–1918. The Long Nineteenth Century* (London, 1997)

Blackbourn, David and Geoff Eley, *The Peculiarities of German History. Bourgeois Society and Politics in Nineteenth-Century Germany* (Oxford University Press, 1984)

Blos, Anna, *Frauen der deutschen Revolution 1848* (Dresden, 1928)

Blum, Robert, *Briefe und Dokumente*, S. Schmidt ed. (Leipzig, 1981)

Boehlich, Walter, *Der Hochverratsprozeß gegen Gervinus* (Frankfurt/M., 1967)

Born, Stephan, *Erinnerungen eines Achtundvierzigers*, 3rd edn (Leipzig, 1898)

Börne, Ludwig, *Gesammelte Schriften* (Hamburg and Frankfurt/M., 1862)

Borst, Otto ed., *Aufruhr und Entsagung, Vormärz 1815–1848 in Baden und Württemberg* (Stuttgart, 1992)

Botzenhart, Manfred, *Deutscher Parlamentarismus in der Revolutionszeit 1848–1850* (Düsseldorf, 1977)

Bovenschen, Sylvia, *Die imaginierte Weiblichkeit* (Frankfurt/M., 1979)

Breuilly, John ed., *The State of Germany. The National Idea in the Making, Unmaking and Remaking of a Modern Nation-State* (London and New York, 1992)

Breuilly, John, *Labour and Liberalism in 19th Century Europe* (Manchester, 1992)

Conze, Werner ed., *Staat und Gesellschaft im deutschen Vormärz 1815–1848* (Stuttgart, 1962)

Conze, Werner and Jürgen Kocka eds, *Bildungsbürgertum im 19. Jahrhundert, Teil 1: Bildungssystem und Professionalisierung im internationalen Vergleich* (Stuttgart, 1985)

Craig, Gordon A., *The Politics of the Prussian Army, 1640–1945* (New York and Oxford, 1956)

Dahlmann, Friedrich Christoph, *Kleinere Schriften und Reden* (Stuttgart, 1886)

Dahrendorf, Ralf, *Society and Democracy in Germany* (New York, 1969) [German original first published in 1965]

Dann, Otto ed., *Vereinswesen und bürgerliche Gesellschaft in Deutschland* (Munich, 1984)

Dann, Otto, *Nation und Nationalismus in Deutschland, 1770–1990* (Munich, 1993)

Dawson, W. H., *Treitschke's History of Germany in the Nineteenth Century*, trans. by E. and C. Paul (London, 1916)

Dipper, Christoph, *Die Bauernbefreiung in Deutschland 1790–1880* (Stuttgart, 1980)

Dipper, Christoph and Ulrich Speck eds, *1848. Revolution in Deutschland* (Frankfurt/M. and Leipzig, 1998)

Dowe, Dieter, *Aktion und Organisation. Arbeiterbewegung, sozialistische und kommunistische Bewegung in der preußischen Rheinprovinz 1820–1852* (Hannover, 1970)

Droysen, J. G. *Politische Schriften*, F. Gilbert ed. (Berlin, 1933)

Duffner, Wolfgang, *Der Traum der Helden. 12 Nachrufe auf im Sommer und Herbst 1849 hingerichtete Kämpfer der badischen Revolution* (Schauenburg, 1997)

Evans, Richard, G. and William R. Lee eds, *The German Peasantry* (London, 1986)

Eyck, Frank, *The Frankfurt Parliament 1848–1849* (London, 1968)

Fenske, Hans ed., *Quellen zur deutschen Revolution 1848–1849* (Darmstadt, 1996)

Fichte, J. G., *Briefwechsel, Kritische Gesamtausgabe*, Hans Schulz ed. (Leipzig, 1925)

Fisher, H. A. L., *A History of Europe* (London, 1960)

Flitner, Andreas and K. Giel eds, *Wilhelm von Humboldt, Werke*, vol. 4, *Schriften zur Politik und zum Bildungswesen* (Stuttgart, 1964)

Flüeler, N. *et al.* eds, *Die Schweiz vom Bau der Alpen bis zur Frage nach der Zukunft* (Zurich, 1975)

Fontane, Theodor, *Von zwanzig bis dreißig, Sämtliche Werke, Aufsätze, Kritiken, Erinnerungen* (Munich, 1973)

Ford, Guy Stanton, *Stein and the Era of Reform in Prussia, 1807–1815* (Gloucester, MA, 1965)

Frei, Alfred Georg and Kurt Hochstuhl, *Wegbereiter der Demokratie. Die badische Revolution 1848/49. Der Traum von der Freiheit* (Karlsruhe, 1997)

Freiligrath, Ferdinand, *Werke in einem Band*, W. Ilberg ed., 3rd edn (Berlin and Weimar, 1976)

Freitag, Sabine ed., *Die Achtundvierziger. Lebensbilder aus der deutschen Revolution 1848/49* (Munich, 1998)

Freytag, Gustav, *Soll und Haben*, 140th edn, vol. 2 (Leipzig, 1920)

Friedrich Wilhelm IV, König von Preußen, *Revolutionsbriefe 1848. Ungedrucktes aus dem Nachlaß König Friedrich Wilhelm IV. von Preußen*, K. Haenchen ed. (Leipzig, 1930)

Gagliardo, John G., *Reich and Nation: The Holy Roman Empire as Idea and Reality 1763–1806* (Bloomington, IN, 1980)

Gagliardo, John G., *From Paria to Patriot: The Changing Image of the German Peasant 1770–1840* (Lexington, Ky, 1969)

Gailus, Manfred, *Straße und Brot. Sozialer Protest in den deutschen Staaten unter besonderer Berücksichtigung Preußens, 1847–1849* (Göttingen, 1990)

Gall, Lothar ed., *Liberalismus*, 2nd edn (Königsstein, 1980)

Gall, Lothar, *Bürgertum in Deutschland* (Berlin, 1989)

Gerlach, Leopold von, *Denkwürdigkeiten aus dem Leben Leopold von Gerlachs, Generals der Infanterie und General-Adjudanten König Friedrich Wilhelms IV. Nach seinen Aufzeichnungen herausgegeben von seiner Tochter* (Berlin, 1891)

Gervinus, G. G., *Einleitung in die Geschichte des neunzehnten Jahrhunderts* (Leipzig, 1853)

Grab, Walter ed., *Die Revolution von 1848/49. Eine Dokumentation* (Stuttgart, 1998)

Grillparzer, Franz, *Sämtliche Werke*, A. Sauer ed. (Vienna, 1932)

Gutzkow, Karl, *Unter dem schwarzen Bären. Erlebtes 1811–1848* (Berlin, 1971)

Habermas, Jürgen, *Die postnationale Konstellation. Politische Essays* (Frankfurt/ M., 1998)

Habermas, Jürgen, *The Structural Transformation of the Public Sphere. An Inquiry into a Category of Bourgeois Society*, trans. by T. Burger (Cambridge, MA, 1989) [German original first published in 1962]

Hachtmann, Rüdiger, *Berlin 1848. Eine Politik- und Gesellschaftsgeschichte der Revolution* (Bonn, 1997)

Hahn, Hans Joachim, *Education and Society in Germany* (Oxford and New York, 1998)

Hahn, Hans-Werner and W. Greiling eds, *Die Revolution von 1848/49 in Thüringen. Aktionsräume, Handlungsebenen, Wirkungen* (Rudolstadt, 1998)

Haupts, Leo, *Öffentliche Festkultur. Politische Feste in Deutschland von der Aufklärung bis zum Ersten Weltkrieg* (Reinbeck, 1988)

Häusler, Wolfgang, *Von der Massenarmut zur Arbeiterbewegung. Demokratie und sozale Frage in der Wiener Revolution von 1848* (Vienna and Munich, 1979)

Hecker, Friedrich, *Die Erhebung des Volkes in Baden für die deutsche Republik im Frühjahr 1848* (Basel, 1848)

Helfert, J. A. Freiherr von, *Geschichte der Österreichischen Revolution* (Freiburg, 1907)

Henning, F.-W., *Die Industrialisierung in Deutschland 1840–1914* (Paderborn, 1973)

Hertz, Frederick, *The German Public Mind in the Nineteenth Century. A Social History of German Political Sentiments, Aspirations and Ideas* (London, 1975)

Herwegh, Georg, *Werke in einem Band*, H.-G. Werner ed., 3rd edn (Berlin and Weimar, 1977) [First published in 1956]

Heuss, Theodor, *Deutsche Gestalten. Studien zum neunzehnten Jahrhundert* (Stuttgart, 1949)

Heydemann, Günther, *Konstitution gegen Revolution. Die britische Deutschland- und Italienpolitik 1815–1848* (Göttingen and Zurich, 1995)

Hildebrand, Thomas and Albert Tanner eds, *Im Zeichen der Revolution. Der Weg zum Schweizerischen Bundesstaat 1798–1848* (Zurich, 1997)

Hildebrandt, Günther, *Parlamentsopposition auf Linkskurs. Die kleinbürgerlich-demokratische Fraktion Donnersberg in der Frankfurter Nationalversammlung 1848/49* (Berlin, 1975)

Huber, Ernst Rudolf, *Deutsche Verfassungsgeschichte seit 1789*, 3rd edn, 3 vols (Stuttgart, 1988)

Hundt, Martin, *Geschichte des Bundes der Kommunisten 1836–1852* (Frankfurt/ M., 1993)

Jansen, Christian, *Einheit, Macht und Freiheit. Die Paulskirchenlinke und die deutsche Politik in der nachrevolutionären Epoche 1849–1867* (Düsseldorf, 2000)

Jansen, Christian and Thomas Mergel eds, *Die Revolution von 1848/49. Erfahrung, Verarbeitung, Deutung* (Göttingen, 1998)

Jarausch, Konrad H., *Deutsche Studenten 1800–1970* (Frankfurt/M., 1984)

Jarausch, Konrad H. and L. E. Jones eds, *In Search of a Liberal Germany. Studies in the History of German Liberalism from 1789 to the Present* (New York, Oxford and Munich, 1990)

Jeismann, Karl-Ernst and Peter Lundgreen eds, *Handbuch der deutschen Bildungsgeschichte*, vol. 3 (Munich, 1987)

Jessen, Hans ed., *Die deutsche Revolution 1848/49 in Augenzeugenberichten*, 2nd edn (Düsseldorf, 1968)

Jung, Irene, Hans-Werner Hahn and Rüdiger Störkel, *Die Revolution von 1848 an Lahn und Dill* (Wetzlar, 1998)

Kaiser, F., *Ein Wiener Volksdichter erlebt die Revolution*, F. Hadamowsky ed. (Vienna, 1948)

Kaltenbrunner, Gerd-Klaus ed., *Was ist reaktionär?: Zur Dialektik von Fortschritt und Rückschritt* (Munich, Freiburg, Basel and Vienna, 1976)

Kaschuba, Wolfgang, *Lebenswelt und Kultur der unterbürgerlichen Schichten im 19. und 20. Jahrhundert* (Munich, 1990)

Kaschuba, Wolfgang and Carola Lipp, *1848 – Provinz und Revolution, Kultureller Wandel und soziale Bewegung im Königreich Württemberg* (Tübingen, 1979)

Kellenheinz, H. ed., *Agrarische Nebengewerbe und Formen der Reagrarisierung* (Stuttgart, 1975)

Kienzle, Michael and Dirk Mende, '*Wollt Ihr den alten Uhland niederreiten?*' *Wie die 48er Revolution in Stuttgart ausging* (Stuttgart, 1998)

Klötzer, W. *et al.* eds, *Ideen und Strukturen der deutschen Revolution 1848* (Frankfurt/M., 1974)

Kocka, Jürgen, *Weder Stand noch Klasse. Unterschichten um 1800* (Bonn, 1990)

Kölz, Alfred, *Neuere schweizerische Verfassungsgeschichte. Ihre Grundlinien vom Ende der Alten Eidgenossenschaft bis 1848* (Berne, 1992)

Kossock, Manfred and W. Loch eds, *Bauern und bürgerliche Revolution* (Vaduz, 1985)

Kraume, Hans-Georg, *Außenpolitik 1848. Die holländische Provinz Limburg in der deutschen Revolution* (Düsseldorf, 1979)

Kühne, Jörg-Detlef, *Die Reichsverfassung der Paulskirche. Vorbild und Verwirklichung im späteren deutschen Rechtsleben* (Frankfurt/M., 1985)

Langewiesche, Dieter, *Europa zwischen Restauration und Revolution 1815–1849* (Munich, 1985)

Langewiesche, Dieter, *Liberalism in Germany* (London, 2000) [German original first published in 1988]

Lewis, Hanna Ballin, *A Year of Revolutions, Fanny Lewald's Recollections of 1848* (Providence and Oxford, 1997)

Lipp, Carola ed., *Frauen im Vormärz und in der Revolution 1848/49* (Moos, 1986)

Lipp, Carola ed., *Schimpfende Weiber und patriotische Jungfrauen. Frauen im Vormärz und in der Revolution 1848/49* (reprint Baden-Baden, 1998)

Lutz, Heinrich, *Zwischen Habsburg und Preußen. Deutschland 1815 bis 1866* (Berlin, 1985)

Mann, Golo, *Deutsche Geschichte des 19. und 20. Jahrhunderts* (Frankfurt/M., 1969)

Marschalck, P., *Deutsche Überseewanderung im 19. Jahrhundert. Ein Beitrag zur soziologischen Theorie der Bevölkerung* (Stuttgart, 1973)

Marx, Karl, *Early Writings* (New York, 1975)

Marx, Karl and F. Engels, *Collected Works* (London, 1977)

Meinecke, Friedrich, *1848, eine Säkularbetrachtung* (Berlin, 1948)

Meinecke, Friedrich, *Die Idee der Staatsräson in der neuern Geschichte* (Munich and Berlin, 1924)

Michel, Berthold and H. H. Schepp eds, *Politik und Schule von der Französischen Revolution bis zur Gegenwart*, vol. 1 (Frankfurt/M., 1973)

Möhrmann, Renate ed., *Frauenemanzipation im deutschen Vormärz. Texte und Dokumente* (Stuttgart, 1978)

Motteck, H. *et al.*, *Wirtschaftsgeschichte Deutschlands*, vol. 2 (Berlin, 1973)

Namier, L. B., *1848: The Revolution of the Intellectuals* (London, 1944)

Nipperdey, Thomas, *Deutsche Geschichte 1800–1866. Bürgerwelt und starker Staat*, 6th edn (Munich, 1987)

Noyes, P. H., *Organisation and Revolution. Working Class Associations in the German Revolutions of 1848–1849* (Princeton, NJ, 1966)

Obermann, Karl, *Die deutschen Arbeiter in der ersten bürgerlichen Revolution* (Berlin, 1950)

Offermann, Toni, *Arbeiterbewegung und liberales Bürgertum in Deutschland 1850–1863* (Bonn, 1979)

Orr, William, J. *The Foundation of the Kreuzzeitungs Party in Prussia 1848–1850* (Wisconsin, 1971)

Otto, Louise, *Dem Reiche der Freiheit werb' ich Bürgerinnen. Die Frauenzeitung von Louise Otto*, Ute Gerhards *et al.* eds (Frankfurt/M., 1980)

Paletschek, Sylvia, *Frauen und Dissens. Frauen im Deutschkatholizismus und in den freien Gemeinden 1841–1852* (Göttingen, 1990)

Passant, E. J., *A Short History of Germany 1815–1945* (Cambridge University Press, 1962)

Prittwitz, Karl Ludwig von, *Berlin 1848: das Erinnerungswerk des Generalleutnants Karl Ludwig von Prittwitz und andere Quellen zur Berliner Märzrevolution und zur Geschichte Preußens um die Mitte des 19. Jahrhunderts*, G. Heinrich ed. (Berlin, 1985)

Ranke, Leopold von, *Preußische Geschichte 1815–1871* (Munich, 1966)

Rassow, *Deutsche Geschichte*, Martin Vogt ed. (Stuttgart, 1987)

Rath, R. John, *The Viennese Revolution of 1848* (New York, 1969)

Rieder, Heinz, ed., *Die Völker läuten Sturm. Die europäische Revolution 1848/49* (Gernsbach, 1997)

Ringer, Fritz K., *The Decline of the German Mandarins* (Harvard University Press, 1969)

Rochau, August Ludwig von, *Grundsätze der Realpolitik, angewandt auf die Zustände Deutschlands*. 2 vols. New edn. by H.-U. Wehler (Frankfurt, Berlin and Vienna, 1972)

Rosenberg, Hans, *Bureaucracy, Aristocracy and Autocracy, The Prussian Experience 1660–1815* (Cambridge, MA, 1958)

Rothfels, Hans, *1848 – Betrachtung im Abstand von hundert Jahren* (Darmstadt, 1974)

Rotteck, Carl von and Carl Welcker eds, *Das Staatslexikon. Encyklopädie der sämmtlichen Staatswissenschaften für alle Stände*, 2nd edn (Altona, 1845)

Rürup, Reinhard, *The Problem of Revolution in Germany, 1789–1990* (Oxford and New York, 2000)

Rürop, Reinhard *et al.* eds, *Revolution and Evolution, 1848 in German–Jewish History* (Tübingen, 1981)

Sabean, D. W., *Property, Production and Family in Neckarhausen, 1700–1870* (Cambridge, 1990)

Sagarra, Eda, *A Social History of Germany 1648–1914* (London, 1977)

Schmidt, Walter ed., *Demokratie, Liberalismus und Konterrevolution. Studien zur deutschen Revolution von 1848/49* (Berlin, 1998)

Schönhoven, K., *Die deutschen Gewerkschaften* (Frankfurt/M., 1987)

Schulze, Hagen, *Staat und Nation in der europäischen Geschichte* (Munich, 1995)

Sheehan, James J., *German Liberalism in the Nineteenth Century*, 2nd edn (Chicago, Co and London, 1995)

Sheehan, James J., *German History 1770–1866* (Oxford, 1989)

Siemann, Wolfram, *Gesellschaft im Aufbruch. Deutschland 1848–1871* (Frankfurt/M., 1990)

Siemann, Wolfram, *The German Revolution of 1848–49*, trans. by Christiane Banerji (London, 1998) [German original first published in 1985]

Sperber, Jonathan, *Popular Catholicism in Nineteenth-Century Germany* (Princeton, NJ, 1984)

Sperber, Jonathan, *Rhineland Radicals. The Democratic Movement and the Revolution of 1848–1849* (Princeton, NJ, 1991)

Springer, Anton, *Friedrich Christoph Dahlmann* (Leipzig, 1872)

Srbik, Heinrich Ritter von, *Deutsche Einheit: Idee und Wirklichkeit vom Heiligen Reich bis Könbigsgrätz* (Munich, 1942)

Stadelmann, Rudolph, *Social and Political History of the German 1848 Revolution*, trans. by James G. Chastain (Athens, OH, 1975) [German original first published in 1948]

Stiles, W. H., *Austria in 1848–49: A History of the Late Political Movements in Vienna, Milan, Venice and Prague, with a Full Account of the Revolution in Hungary* (New York, 1852)

Sydow, Anna von ed., *Wilhelm und Caroline von Humboldt in ihren Briefen* (Berlin, 1906)

Taylor Allen, Ann, *Feminism and Motherhood in Germany 1800–1914* (New Brunswick, NJ, 1991)

Tocqueville, Alexis de, *Recollections* (New York, 1970)

Träger, Claus ed., *Die Französische Revolution im Spiegel der deutschen Literatur* (Leipzig, 1975)

Trox, Eckhard, *Militärischer Konservatismus. Kriegsvereine und 'Militärpartei' in Preußen zwischen 1815 und 1848/49* (Stuttgart, 1990)

Uhland, Ludwig, *Werke*, H. Fröschle und W. Scheffler eds (Munich, 1980–4)

Valentin, Veit, *Die erste deutsche Nationalversammlung. Eine geschichtliche Studie über die Paulskirche* (Munich and Berlin, 1919)

Valentin, Veit, *Geschichte der deutschen Revolution 1848–49*, 2 vols. (Berlin, 1930/1)

Vitzhum von Eckstädt, Carl Friedrich Graf, *Berlin und Wien in den Jahren 1845–1852. Politische Privatbriefe*, 2nd edn (Stuttgart, 1886)

Vollmer, Franz X., *Offenburg 1848/49. Ereignisse und Lebensbilder aus einem Zentrum der badischen Revolution* (Karlsruhe, 1997)

Voss, Jürgen ed., *Deutschland und die Französische Revolution* (Munich, 1983)

Vossler, Otto, *Die Revolution von 1848 in Deutschland* (Frankfurt/M., 1948)

Walter, F., *Österreichische Verfassungs- und Verwaltungsgeschichte von 1500–1955* (Vienna and Graz, 1972)

Weber, Rolf, *Die Revolution in Sachsen 1848/49. Entwicklung und Analyse ihrer Triebkräfte* (Berlin, 1970)

Wegert, K. H., *German Radicals Confront the Common People. Revolutionary Politics and Popular Politics 1789–1849* (Mainz, 1992)

Wehler, Hans-Ulrich ed., *Sozialgeschichte heute. Festschrift für Hans Rosenberg zum 70. Geburtstag* (Göttingen, 1974)

Select bibliography

Wehler, Hans-Ulrich, *Deutsche Gesellschaftsgeschichte*, vol. 2 (Munich, 1987)

Wettengel, Michael, *Die Revolution von 1848/49 im Rhein-Main-Raum. Politische Vereine und Revolutionsalltag im Großherzogtum Hessen, Herzogtum Nassau und in der freien Stadt Frankfurt* (Wiesbaden, 1989)

Wigard, Franz ed., *Stenographischer Bericht über die Verhandlungen der deutschen constitutierenden Nationalversammlung zu Frankfurt am Main* (Frankfurt/M., 1848)

Wilson, Edmund, *To the Finland Station* (London, 1966)

Wollstein, Günther, *Das 'Großdeutschland' der Paulskirche. Nationale Ziele in der bürgerlichen Revolution 1848/49* (Düsseldorf, 1977)

Wollstein, Günther, *Deutsche Geschichte 1848/49. Gescheiterte Revolution in Mitteleuropa* (Stuttgart, 1986)

Zwahr, Hartmann ed., *Die Konstitutierung der deutschen Arbeiterklasse von den dreißiger bis zu den siebziger Jahren des 19. Jahrhunderts* (Berlin, 1981)

General index

General index

Index of names

Names in italics refer to researchers, figures in bold refer to major aspects.

233

Index of names

Printed in Great Britain
by Amazon.co.uk, Ltd.,
Marston Gate.